Talking a
GOOD GAME
Inquiries into the Principles of Sport

Talking a
GOOD GAME
Inquiries into the Principles of Sport

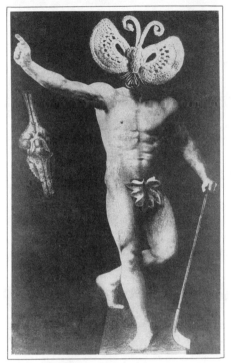

Spencer K·Wertz

Southern Methodist University Press
Dallas

First edition, 1991
Requests to reproduce material from this work should be sent to:

Permissions
Southern Methodist University Press
Box 415
Dallas, Texas 75275

Design by Whitehead & Whitehead

Cover art: *La Santé par le sport* by Max Ernst, ca. 1920, 39⅞″ × 23½″. Courtesy
of The Menil Collection, Houston, Texas. Photo by Hickey-Robertson.

Library of Congress Cataloging-in-Publication Data

Wertz, Spencer K.
    Talking a good game : inquiries into the principles of sport /
Spencer K. Wertz. — 1st ed.
        p.   cm.
    Includes bibliographical references (p.   ) and index.
    ISBN 0-87074-320-1 : — ISBN 0-87074-321-X (pbk.) :
    1. Sports—Philosophy.   2. Sports—Moral and ethical aspects.
3. Sports in art.   I. Title.
GV706.W44   1991
796′.01—dc20   90-53579

For Charlotte

CONTENTS

ACKNOWLEDGMENTS

I WISH TO EXPRESS my special indebtedness to the following people (and this is only the short list): Linda Loflin Wertz, my wife, who has served as a careful critic of my work. Without her guidance this book would not have been as readable as it is and probably would never have been written. Her encouragement kept me working. With untiring assistance, Maura Carmody Cuny typed and assisted in editing the final draft. My colleagues Ted Klein, Gregg Franzwa, Richard Galvin, David Vanderwerken, and others at Texas Christian University have critiqued several of the chapters in one form or another. Members of the Philosophic Society for the Study of Sport have all been very helpful with their comments and suggestions on the papers I have read at various annual meetings. In particular Klaus Meier, Scott Kretchmar, Drew Hyland, David Aspin, Hans Lenk, and Paul Weiss have aided me in refining the arguments present in this book. The anonymous readers for the Southern Methodist University Press, its staff, and especially Matthew Abbate, also assisted me in the final draft with their insightful reviews. Finally I wish to gratefully acknowledge my students, who have tolerated my exploratory discourse on the philosophy of sport and who have also helped me to clarify the conceptual inquiries I have embarked on.

I need to thank the editors and publishers of the following books and journals for giving me permission to adapt large portions of the following published essays for the present book: "Sports as Human Enterprises," in *Sport and the Humanities: A Collection of Original Essays*, edited by William J. Morgan (Bureau of Educational Research and Service; Knoxville: College of Education, University of Tennessee, 1979); "Zen, Yoga, and Sports: Eastern Philosophy for Western Athletes," *Journal of the Philosophy of Sport*, IV (1977); "The Knowing in Playing," *Journal of the Philosophy of Sport*, V (1978); "The Varieties of Cheating," *Journal of the Philosophy of Sport*, VIII (1981); "Review Essay of *The Zen Way to the Martial Arts* by Jean Taisen Deshimaru," *Journal of the Philosophy of Sport*, XI (1984); "Representation and Expression in Sport and Art," *Journal of the Philosophy of Sport*, XII (1985); "Is 'Choking' an Action?" (Presidential Address), *Journal of the Philosophy of Sport*, XIII (1986); and "The Preservation of Sport," in *Topical Problems of Sport Philosophy*, edited by Hans Lenk (Cologne: Bundesinstitut für Sportwissenschaft, 1982). These essays have been significantly rewritten with an eye on each other, on *Sport Inside Out: Readings in Literature and Philosophy*, edited by David L. Vanderwerken and Spencer K. Wertz (Fort Worth: Texas Christian University Press, 1985), and on *Philosophic Inquiry in Sport*, edited by William J. Morgan and Klaus V. Meier (Champaign, Illinois: Human Kinetics Publishers, 1988).

Talking a
GOOD GAME
Inquiries into the Principles of Sport

INTRODUCTION

Chasing Paradigms

I

PHILOSOPHY since the mid-twentieth century has undergone many twists and turns to arrive where it has in the nineties. In the next few pages I shall try to explain where this book fits into that story and how I got involved with its subject matter. A global picture of philosophy will be sketched here, and a more detailed view will follow in chapter 1.

In his *Philosophical Investigations*, Ludwig Wittgenstein (d. 1951) directed our attention to language and its importance in understanding the concepts that make up our webs of belief or our conceptual scheme. So instead of looking for meaning *outside* language (such as in behavior or ideas), he directed our attention *within* language—to look at how certain words are used or function within a given language or specified realm of discourse. Such a description Wittgenstein called "a language-game." This insight into the nature of meaning and language and its application to philosophical problems became known as the Linguistic Turn.

Soon after this revolution there came a correction, because these philosophical investigations had become simply semantic ones that had little reference to life and its activities. Philosophy had quickly turned into theoretical linguistics. With the newly found emphasis upon language, we had lost a vital part as Wittgenstein had pictured it: "I shall call the whole, consisting of language *and the actions into which it is woven*, the language-game."[1] Philosophers soon realized that they had abandoned an important part of Wittgenstein's holistic project, so we took another course. This

1

time it was known as the Pragmatic Turn. We began to look for needy areas to apply our skills of conceptual clarification. We were now interested in understanding *actions* along with practices, institutions, and conventions founded on those actions. Applied philosophy became a major concern among a great many philosophers. Some of them began entering hospitals to talk with medical personnel about ethical problems in health care. The kind of literature produced from such an encounter was truly pragmatic: it faithfully reflected the concerns and problems medical staff faced in dealing with the sick and chronically ill. But it also tied theory to practice and consequently made theory more useful and accountable. Philosophers wanted to be helpful and wanted their work to be useful and a reliable companion in difficult times—times of philosophical decisions.

Some of us, having witnessed the success of medical ethics and the impetus it gave applied philosophy, began looking around for other needy areas to apply our philosophical (especially analytical) skills. Not having ventured far from the playing field, I became interested in analyzing the actions, practices, institutions, conventions, and talk of the sports world. By "sports" I mean games that depend upon the exercise of physical skills, and I include the spectators as well as the participants and the officials of these activities. So I set out to examine the playground, although this time primarily as a philosopher and secondarily as an athlete. In high school I had lettered in almost every sport, and in my senior year I practiced the martial arts. Judo changed the way I thought about the world and myself. In a way it prepared me for my major in college, philosophy, which included Oriental thought. After ten years of study I returned to pursue a philosophical understanding of those activities that have meant so much to me over the years. This book represents my passionate concern for both sport and philosophy. With the reluctance of a mother letting her child enter the world without her for the first time, I set this book before you. As Plato says in the *Phaedrus*: "Once a thing is put in writing, it rolls about all over the place."[2] I just hope it is ready to roll in the directions I have anticipated.

If nothing else, I think the time is right for the appearance of this book, because sport has undergone a major transformation. This "revolution" took place primarily in the mid-seventies, but it has continued in the eighties and nineties. In the remainder of this introduction, I shall describe in broad terms the transformation sport has undergone culturally as well as philosophically. This account is admittedly simplistic, but the overview will serve to unify my inquiries. The chapters in *Talking a Good Game: Inquiries into the Principles of Sport* will give some of the details of this cultural transformation or revolution, although this is not by a long shot the whole story   the notes and the selected bibliography are other places to look for further philosophical investigation. This book is my interpretation of what happened in the realm of sport during my professional career in philosophy thus far. If I generate further interest, I will consider my inquiries here a success.[3] Let me remind the reader that my interpretation has been along the lines of the traditional areas of philosophy. The sequence also follows the order of the evolution of sport in this century. Metaphysics or theory of reality sets the agenda in chapters 1, 2, and 5; ethics (primarily examining the decline in moral values in sport) in chapters 3 and 4; epistemology or theory of knowledge in chapters 5, 6, and 7; and finally aesthetics (primarily examining the ascent in aesthetic and artistic values in sport) in chapters 8 and 9.

By "revolution" I have in mind the sort of activity that Thomas Kuhn described for the history of science.[4] I am employing the more global use of "paradigm" below; Kuhn elaborates: "It [the term "paradigm"] stands for the entire constellation of beliefs, values, techniques, and so on shared by the members of a given community" (p. 175). The paradigm may also be used as a model or example in place of explicit rules for the solutions of remaining problems or issues, especially in an area of interpretation I am exploring ("sport") in which there are no explicit, agreed upon rules. *Paradigms work in place of theories.* Earlier Kuhn says that the "lack of a standard interpretation or of an agreed upon reduction to rules will not prevent a paradigm from guiding research. . . . Indeed, the existence of a paradigm need not even imply that any full set of rules exists" (p. 44). Both of these senses of "paradigm" are used in my study.

Margaret Masterman did a careful elucidation of Kuhn's conception of paradigm and found over twenty distinct uses of this methodological term.[5] She divides them into three categories (p. 65): (i) metaphysical paradigms or metaparadigms, where "paradigm" is equated with a set of beliefs, a myth, a way of seeing, a map, a standard, an organizing principle governing perception itself, or something determining a large area of reality; (ii) sociological paradigms, where "paradigm" refers to a recognized scientific achievement and Kuhn speaks of it as being like an accepted judicial decision or a set of political institutions; and (iii) artifact or construct paradigms, which Kuhn speaks of as tools or textbooks ("classics") and as actual instrumentations. Such diverse uses of the term, however, should not be viewed as a setback. The complexity of meaning helps capture and organize the extremely diverse phenomena we are talking about here, because it can be parsed into multiple levels or dimensions. (Chapter 9 addresses this and related issues.) But equivocal uses of "paradigm" can lead to confusion. As Kuhn reflects:

> For it [the sociological sense of the term] I should now like some other phrase, perhaps 'disciplinary matrix': 'disciplinary', because it is common to the practitioners of a specified discipline; 'matrix', because it consists of ordered elements which require individual specification. All of the objects of commitment described in my book [*The Structure of Scientific Revolutions*] as paradigms, parts of paradigms, or paradigmatic would find a place in the disciplinary matrix, but would not be lumped together as paradigms, individually or collectively. Among them would be: shared symbolic generalizations, like '$f = ma$', or 'elements combine in constant proportion by weight'; shared models, whether metaphysical, like atomism, or heuristic, like the hydrodynamic model of the electric circuit; shared values, like the emphasis on accuracy of prediction . . . and other elements of the sort. Among the latter I would particularly emphasize concrete problem solutions, the sorts of

standard examples of solved problems which scientists encounter first in student laboratories, in the problems at the end of
chapters in science texts, and on examinations. If I could, I
would call these problem-solutions paradigms, for they are
what led me to the choice of the term in the first place. Having
lost control of the word, however, I shall henceforth describe
them as exemplars.[6]

So Kuhn reserves the term "paradigm" for (i), metaphysical
paradigms or metaparadigms, since he later describes (iii) as
problem-solutions paradigms or exemplars and (ii) as disciplinary
matrixes. Paradigms work in place of theories in certain realms of
discourse, and this is especially true of the region of sport, and it is
also a realm where multiple paradigms are at work. The rich complexity of "theory" or modeling is captured by the three senses of
paradigm as they are operative in the sports world. They should be
kept in mind as we turn to other methodological issues.

Kuhn conceived of major historical change or revolution as a
critical transition from one paradigm to another. He takes "paradigms" to be universally or at least generally recognized achievements that for a time provide model problems and solutions to a
community of practitioners. When a paradigm is displaced by another, that transition or revolution alters the perspective of the
community that experiences it, and that change of perspective
should affect the structure of postrevolutionary thinking, writing,
and talking. One such effect is the shift in the distribution of technical literature or concepts, and it is to be studied as a possible index
or barometer to the occurrence of revolutions. The popular and
technical literature on sport of the seventies and eighties provides
such an index for philosophers and other scholars to describe and
analyze part of a broad cultural change in the world today. Something like this happened in the world of sport, and this book is an
account of that revolution or transformation.

In the nineteenth century, the British or Eton view of sport
held sway. It extolled the virtues of amateurism, sportsmanship,
and the conventionality of sport. These elements are what I call the
old paradigm. In Kuhn's terms, the old paradigm forms a shared set

of assumptions that we use to perceive the world, to explain it, and to predict its behavior.[7] As Adam Smith says: "When we are in the middle of the paradigm, it is hard to imagine any other paradigm." The old paradigm of sport gradually changed and developed until the early twentieth century, when profound technological developments and the economic growth associated with it created a series of crises in the world of sport. Late in the nineteenth century, the emerging paradigm had undergone significant change with the growth of professional sports. We began to see the corruption of sport and the eroding of those values, especially moral values, associated with the Eton paradigm in the mid-twentieth century, but it had been threatened earlier. The recent erosion is discussed in the early chapters of this book, especially in a section of chapter 2, in most of 3, and in 4. Communities operating in the middle of the Eton paradigm are basically conservative and reinforce the values of the Establishment. Once a paradigm is in place it doesn't change easily; there is vested interest at stake. People cling to tradition and seek guidance from the past.

The new paradigm in sport to emerge in the mid-seventies came from Oriental philosophy.[8] In the words of Adam Smith, sport became a Western Yoga. Katsuki Sekida published the long-awaited *Zen Training: Methods and Philosophy* in 1975. A year earlier Tim Gallwey began the "inner game" movement in the semitechnical, popular literature on sport: first it was *The Inner Game of Tennis*, and soon followed books dealing with the inner game of other sports—golf, skiing, running, and so on. Chapter 5 examines this literature and discusses its more important philosophical ideas. In sum, Asian thought made its unexpected popular arrival by way of the sports world. The clash of these two paradigms has led to a transfiguration of sport from a dominance of moral values to one of artistic and aesthetic values. Chapters 8 and 9 discuss these controversial values in sport. This alteration has not only changed our thinking about sport, but changed ourselves. Perfection and excellence came to replace equality and fairness as central concerns. Winning, unfortunately, rather than the performance itself, became the measure of perfection and excellence for many.

6

However, before we discuss the change in the value structure of the sports world, we need to explore the realm of philosophy, since it is that area which analyzes those structures in our multiple worlds. Chapter 1 discusses the philosophical methodologies employed throughout the book, although I have a few words to say about them here. In 1975, when I started examining philosophical issues in sport, I was startled by the rich diversity and fertility of the problems I encountered. Cases taken from the sports world generate novel ideas and connections rarely seen or appreciated in other worlds, such as the art world. In other words, there are phenomena uniquely or characteristically associated with the world of sport. A flood of philosophical questions enter our discussions when we contemplate these phenomena. Students and colleagues alike have begun to see that sport is indeed an important area for philosophical investigation. I hope to convince skeptics of this claim through the ensuing chapters. Some of the questions that continue to challenge our thinking about the sports world are: What is sport? (This is a fundamental question to which we keep returning.) When does sport cease to be sport and become something else, like criminal conflict or an art form? What is cheating? Can stalling in a tennis match or in a basketball game be considered cheating? Can one cheat at surfing? What are the concepts of winning, losing, competing, and the kinds of knowing necessary in playing? Is "choking" in the psychological sense an intentional action? Upon examination, there appear to be several good answers to these questions. Many of them make up the very fiber of the world of sport.

The controversy that often fills the sports pages of magazines and newspapers can in many cases be traced back to the two paradigms. This book is an attempt to develop these paradigms into perspectives from which sport is viewed and critically examined. Many of the chapters employ "cases" from the pages of magazines and newspapers for philosophical analysis. In large part, "ordinary language" or analytic philosophy is practiced here because of the reliance upon sport-talk.

Ordinary language philosophy is a method of doing philosophy that developed in the mid-twentieth century in England and quickly spread to the United States. (Wittgenstein and his teacher, Bertrand Russell, plus their students were instrumental in its growth and acceptance by a large part of the philosophical community.) It is still commonly practiced in one form or another among philosophers today here and abroad because it offers a way both of obtaining results and of judging the merits or success of those results. Before this revolution in philosophy, philosophers appealed to introspection, intuition, reason, common sense, experience, or human existence to justify the claims they made about the world. They still do make these appeals, but ordinary language, at least, has provided some ground for agreement, and appeals to that ground could be made along with the more traditional ones. I have been eclectic in my approach, borrowing whatever seemed to be called for at the moment: pragmatism usually dictates my route. Kuhn's idea of using a community's literature as an index for judging important changes in thinking enhances the method of ordinary language philosophy.[9] Indeed, Russell's dream of a philosophy that would be truly a community endeavor could be realized in practice as *criticism*.[10] Needless to say, there are problems, especially methodological ones, associated with ordinary language philosophy and analytic philosophy generally, but they are inconsequential compared to the results that can be established by such a pragmatic philosophy. The study of the language of a given subject, like sport, yields important truths and interpretations of that subject, from which to develop philosophic perspectives.

So, what is sport? The Wittgensteinian answer is that sport is what commonly passes for sport in the sports pages of our newspapers and magazines. Of course, not all sport-talk is equal; some of it is better, more interesting philosophically, than other kinds of sport-talk in those pages. Philosophers must dig their way through the salary disputes, strikes, polls, trades, scandals, and gossip. They must discover intelligence and ideas in the midst of all these columns. Thus, the way to achieve a degree of moderate success in philosophy is to trace the way that a given phenomenon is experienced and discussed, and to show where and how other philosophers who have analyzed it have gone astray or have hit the mark, or to provide such an analysis if it is absent. An analysis of cheating, the subject of chapter 3, is a good example of the procedure.

On the basis of sport-talk, and the experiences it interprets, the philosopher's job is to build perspectives. The world of sport may be a better or worse place because of our awareness of these perspectives. But at least our consciousness of them places us in a position from which we can change those conventions and institutions that make up the world of sport. Some of the book's perspectives are broad, embodying major cultural differences, as evidenced in my use of paradigms like those of the East and the West and old and new, while others are more narrowly focused on specific families of sport actions, for example, "choking" in chapter 6.

The world of sport is very much like those of the humanities and the arts. If one wants to see what is going on in the world of sport, one has to be appreciative and sympathetic in order to penetrate what Michael Novak called "the inner life of sport."[11] One must look below the surface of games and look at what surrounds them to find what is valuable to analyze and to discuss. For the key to understanding the games lies in seeing them in the proper surroundings or context: think of Wittgenstein's language-games with games themselves, just as he did but in greater detail and with more elaborate analysis. His initial insight led to a development of a field of study. The meaning or sense sport has is discerned from its context. Much of this is missed unless one is "tuned into this world," to use a phrase from the contemporary German philosopher in the existential/phenomenological tradition, Martin Heidegger.[12]

Essentially the same point can be made from the literature of the analytic tradition. In "Logic and Conversation,"[13] H. P. Grice describes language or discourse in the following manner:

> Our talk exchanges do not normally consist of a succession of disconnected remarks, and would not be rational if they did. They are, characteristically, to some degree at least cooperative efforts. Each participant recognizes in them, to some extent, a common purpose or set of purposes, or at least a mutually accepted direction.

Grice goes on to call this general feature of discourse the Cooperative Principle (C.P.). The point I wish to make is that in order for interesting and intriguing concepts to be found in the sports world, it (C.P.) must be present: sport-talk must have a certain rationality to it. There must be something *there* to "tune" into, that is, interesting ideas that are relevant and applicable to our experience and understanding. For the most part, those concepts require a participant who is cooperative, interested, and involved. Otherwise, the magic and the excitement of sport will be missed. In this respect, the language of sport is like the language of art: it acts as a clue and as an initial starting point in one's inquiries. In "On the Inner Nature of Art" (1844), Arthur Schopenhauer expresses essentially the same idea in this fashion:

> The co-operation of the beholder . . . as demanded for the enjoyment of a work of art, depends partly upon the fact that every work of art can only produce its effect through the medium of the fancy; therefore it must excite this, and can never allow it to be left out of the play and remain inactive. This is a condition of the aesthetic effect, and therefore a fundamental law of all fine arts.[14]

What Schopenhauer says of art applies to sport. A fundamental law of sport is that there be the cooperation of the beholder or spectator. Every sporting event will produce its effect only through the medium of the imagination. But that imagination must be an appreciative, sympathetic, and honest one. The best writing or reporting on sport will exhibit these characteristics. The last chapter explores the textual dimension of sport.

Clever philosophers can try their hand at analyzing the language of sport without having an experienced, "inner" (imaginative) understanding of the philosophic in sport. But they only abuse sport. One needs to know the directions or purposes, as Grice labels them, in order to get at the "rationality" or inner life of sport. That life lies behind or surrounds the language of sport; it is what Wittgenstein referred to as the actions woven into the language. But we must first be tuned into that world. A case will illustrate these points.

II

WHAT is the language of sport? How is this the domain of the philosopher? Have you ever seen any language in the sports pages that needed a philosopher's explanation or analysis? Such a time might be when we need a clearer view of what we already know, or when we do not know what to make of the facts we already have. Let us look briefly at a very simple example that leads us quickly into metaphysics—into questions on the nature of reality. It will also aid us in answering the above questions.

In the 1982 United States Open, Pam Shriver upset top-seeded Martina Navratilova in the women's singles quarterfinals, 1-6, 7-6, 6-2. Shriver said, "In the third set, I was zoned. I've never used that word before."[15] The newswriter explains: "The zone refers to the never-never land players float into occasionally, and Shriver was up there for 24 minutes. She got 80 percent of her first serves in. She came to net—Navratilova territory—and used her long reach to take away Navratilova's game." The metaphors, phrases like "never-never land" and "floating into it occasionally," do not help explain what the zone is. What Shriver did while in the zone—command the net and serve that high percentage of first serves in—does help. But what did Shriver mean by the term? She never had used it before, but she still knew when to apply it to her experience. She knew, from others' applications of it, how to apply it to herself. We learn the application of words to our own experience by first learning the words from others and by applying them to others. But this process is never unproblematic. As Wittgenstein reminds us, "what confuses us is the uniform appearance of words when we hear them spoken or meet them in script and print. For their *application* is not presented to us so clearly. Especially when we are doing philosophy!" (p. 6). Shriver is attempting a philosophical explanation of what happened; *in one word* she has given us her interpretation of an aspect of the sport experience. What she is attempting to explain is one of those things that set the sport experience off from other sorts of human experiences.

Let us try to unravel her use or application. Shriver obviously was not using the word literally. This moment was not one in which she was commercially zoned or sectioned by the city officials. This was not some sort of objective demarcation she had undergone. Rather, this is players' jargon for a particular subjective region that is set off as distinct from other areas of the sport experience. This region is what I call "sport samādhi" (*samādhi* is the Sanskrit term for "concentration" or contemplative awareness) in chapter 5, and it designates a type of consciousness uniquely associated with the performance of athletic skills.

Notice again that Shriver said she had never used that word before. In all the time she has played (about ten years), she had never been in the zone. "Zone" has a specific use and the players *know* when to apply it to their own performance or to someone else's. And what does the zone refer to? The zone is that subjective region where play or execution takes place effortlessly and without conscious intervention in the physical performance of sport. "Playing in the zone" describes a performance in which the development of the game comes about of its own accord. The game dictates what is to be done rather than the player consciously doing so. The zone is where play becomes "involuntary," in the sense that each move has been dictated by the game itself without any admixture of intention and reflection. Such play is sometimes described as that of genius or inspiration. (Schopenhauer would surely have given such a description.) When the gaps between understanding, technical skill, and routine have been filled, brilliant play results. In sport, reflection, intention, and deliberate selection are necessary supplementary work that recede in consciousness as the activity itself replaces them in consciousness. This is the zone Shriver referred to.

Philosophers who examine terminology such as this are attempting to describe or analyze what she could have possibly meant by such a term. How can something voluntary be involuntary? As inquisitive beings, we sometimes confront paradox in the way we conceive the world or our activities. We have here a classic question for the metaphysician and the action theorist. As Stanley Cavell remarks: "This is not a question of cutting big ideas down to size, but of giving them the exact space in which they can move without corrupting."[16] This is not easily accomplished when the term covers another realm of perception and being. We must marshal the assistance of Oriental philosophy to adequately deal with this particular avenue of sport-talk. Shriver has given us some metaphysics to think about.

In the zone, there is no thinking about what one is doing; one is just doing it. It is as if something has happened to a person rather than his or her having brought about that given action. It is this aspect of the experience that probably led Shriver to use the passive verb "zoned" rather than "zone." As Wittgenstein says: "A whole cloud of philosophy [is] condensed into a drop of grammar" (p. 222). It is like "being breathed," rather than "breathing."[17] The game's processes become one's own processes. The game and the player blend into one event. How is such a transformation possible? Answers are not that easy, but this is what happened to Pam in that region. It is one of the hidden dimensions in the experience of sport, and it is much talked about by those who have experienced it. The careful articulation and development of the concepts involved in the sport experience and its linguistic counterparts are dealt with in some of the following chapters, but for now let us look at philosophical method as it is practiced in this century, since I constantly employ it in my handling of questions and in the development of answers or solutions.

PART ONE:　THE REGION

ONE

Philosophy of Sport:
The Three Traditions

I

PHILOSOPHY OF SPORT today is where philosophy of history was in the early fifties. In explaining what philosophy of history consists of, W. H. Walsh had to begin with a section on the current suspicion of the subject.[1] Those philosophers who choose sport as their area of inquiry have a similar task—to address the skeptics. The general consensus is that the group of problems that belong to the philosophy of sport are those associated with the nature of the sport experience and with analysis of the language used to describe it. These problems arise when we reflect on the activities and assumptions made in sport and in the reporting or discussion of it. An abundance of theorizing occupies the sports pages—most of it unchecked and undisciplined. It is in need of philosophical scrutiny. The skeptics have not seen or appreciated the problems because they do not believe that sport has any genuine philosophical problems. They think, instead of looking. Their reasons usually embody a naive view of sport. Most of the skeptics think that sport is merely entertainment, amusement, diversion, or recreation. For them, sport is simply time off from things that really matter, from those things that are a product of the human spirit. But wait—sport can be one of those things too.

Philosophers are generally thought of as reflective thinkers who seek to describe, interpret, and illuminate lived experience by making more precise the vague expressions of ordinary communication. When precision is achieved and we step back to assess the results, no

17

verification process is used as in the validation of some scientific theories. To estimate the adequacy and viability of philosophical theories or propositions, we compare their elucidatory power with that of other alternatives.[2] This statement of how philosophers perceive their activity most aptly applies to philosophers of sport. They begin their inquiry with sport-talk, but it does not end there. Sport-talk is transformed into positions and perspectives. Ordinary language is not the wherewithal by which we judge positions and perspectives, but it is a beginning. It serves as a useful guide.

Much of my work has been inspired by Nelson Goodman's recent work, especially in the philosophy of art. What he tries to do for art, I have attempted to do for sport, which is to "harden" its study.[3] The hardening of sport studies begins by seeing that sport is a part of a symbolic process. Sport symbolizes, because sport-talk implies structure, conceptualizes experience, and ascribes properties.[4] Even though sport may be relatively free from representation and expression, it remains a symbol—it can stand as a sample or exemplify something; see chapter 8 for a fuller discussion of these ideas. A given sport performance illustrates, rather than just names or describes, relevant kinds or types. More importantly, sport must be taken no less seriously than the arts and the sciences as a mode of discovery, creation, and enlargement of knowledge in the broad sense of the advancement of the understanding. Hence, the philosophy of sport should be conceived of as an integral part of philosophy, notably of metaphysics and epistemology.

The view of sport offered in this text, one shared by many others, is the exact opposite of Paul Weiss's view.[5] Weiss's view is that people are *less* than what they can be—the intellect is all that is needed for people to reach their full potential. By contrast, my view is that people can be *more* than what they normally are when they engage in sport. To refine my earlier definition of "sport," I principally mean participant sport and secondarily spectator sport. "Sport" does not equal watching the National Football League on television. Weiss begins his book *Sport: A Philosophic Inquiry* with the pronouncement that he was never an athlete. It is no wonder that he thought people are less than what they are capable of:

18

watching television does not place one within the inner life of sport. (Of course, participating in sport doesn't guarantee that one will appreciate its inner life, but one stands a better chance by so doing.)[6]

Possibly the most important decision someone can make on any given day is whether or not to engage in sport. How can this be? Generally, we find that work debilitates, dehumanizes, and subordinates us to certain roles.[7] But in sport, we can experience self-satisfaction, self-expression, courage, beauty, excellence; develop the ability to endure pain; learn to handle stress and pressure; and ventilate rage and other powerful emotions which, if not channeled in the right directions, explode into violence. We get a chance to do something for its own sake rather than doing something instrumentally. Such activity is rehabilitating: we become better-tempered, better-balanced people. Like Novak, I tend to distrust people who have never tempered their thinking with the emotional and physical experience of sport or exercise. Maybe we even become better philosophers. Does this sound absurd? Only initially. We see, upon examination, that engagement in the philosophy of sport can make us better philosophers, because we will be reflecting on an area of human activity that makes us more real, more genuinely human, in addition to dealing with more complicated cases than are often dealt with. These values and cases need to be analyzed and developed into a philosophy. But in turn, sport gives philosophy an "ecological validity"[8] in requiring that its theories and results relate to what people do in real, culturally significant situations, rather than merely deal with cases like "raising one's arm" in action theory. Understanding human action as it occurs in a given environment, like sport, can lead to a better understanding of natural, purposeful activity. Philosophy loses some precision and clarity in dealing with more complicated life situations, but its relevance and importance are reaffirmed by those who seek its assistance. So other areas of philosophy can be enhanced by such an excursion to the world of sport. A philosophy cannot be indifferent to culture, which some recent analytic philosophy can be accused of doing, if it wishes to be heard by those who can profit the most from it. Our culture has come to identify sport as one of its major expressions; of all our cultural activities it is one that is in the most serious need of philosophical reflection. Philosophers can no longer afford to ignore this region, if they are to be perceived by the public as scholars performing tasks that have relevance to the public's interests.

The reconstruction offered here is not merely the product of runaway speculation. It is checked by seeing whether it is in accord with actual sport practices. Such a concept of sport is tied to cultural heritage. Even though the significance of our inquiries may ultimately transcend a given culture, a preliminary understanding of the cultural setting of sport helps one to grasp the concepts behind sport. In a way, I am offering a Kuhnian "history" of sport with the internal workings those of philosophical analysis. However, this process is a two-way street. A reconstruction can also serve as a reform for some of those practices that are corrupt. It shows us that an alternative exists, that as an old paradigm crumbles, there emerge new ones to take its place. Of all the multiple, actual worlds that are in need of philosophical understanding, the need is perhaps greatest in the world of sport, mainly because of the attention devoted to it in our culture, and further because it has had few previous dealings with philosophy.

Any adequate philosophy of sport needs to reflect the sport experience and the sports world, and to enable us to better appreciate the interaction between the individual and his environment. In a way, then, Weiss's book does not even qualify as a volume in the literature, since his work is that of a non-athlete. (Weiss's book was the first in Anglo-American philosophy on the subject, although it is admittedly speculative or essentialistic.) What is philosophy of sport, then, since I have just excluded a volume considered to be a classic in the field? How does philosophy reflect experience and the world—a specific world at that? What is the nature of that reflection? To answer these questions, we must come to see that the way in which philosophy understands its own reflections has changed in recent years.

A commonly accepted way of showing how philosophy mirrors the world and experience can be illustrated by the following diagram.[9]

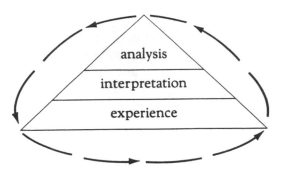

Figure 1.   Levels and circling of consciousness

Following the diagram, consciousness serves as the link between sport and philosophy. Sport occupies the levels of experience and interpretation, and philosophy occupies the levels of interpretation and analysis. Interpretation (discourse, language, talk) is that level of consciousness which is central to understanding both human endeavors. Philosophy traces the movements of consciousness here by means of sport-talk, but not exclusively so. Logical analysis and thought-experiments (*Denkenexperimenten*) are means to assist in deciphering sport-talk. Philosophical discourse is more than description; in this case, it is a description of a particular kind of experience that is shaped by method and analysis. Principally, then, philosophy deals with the levels of interpretation and analysis. Below we shall discuss how these levels are themselves interpreted by philosophers.

Several key terms and ideas about the sport experience, moreover, are problematic. The very fact that they present difficulty is one of the reasons why philosophy of sport exists. Consider: winning, competition, the good game, chance, sportsmanship, cheating, knowing, rules, play, game, sport, athletics, training, practice, strategy, learning, momentum, physical skills, body, mind, and so on. Sportscasters, sportswriters, fans, spectators, and others formulate "theories" concerning these terms whether or not they are aware (i.e., fully conscious) of doing so. Some of us find this process of theory construction demanding and urgent. We become most acutely aware of the need for analysis when our own interpretations (i.e., unconscious discourse) break down or become inadequate.

Communication becomes difficult in such situations, and understanding is replaced by frustration and suspicion. Analysis thus becomes an intellectual process for rebuilding our interpretations to adequately reflect our experience and to restore communication. The result of this process is then to communicate our ideas and experience to others, or perhaps only to ourselves. If we see our experience as significant enough to interpret, because we wish either to avoid it in the future or to experience it again for the pleasure we derive from it, then some analysis is called for. When we single out those elements that we deem important, this process is labeled "interpretation." Other features of our experience are ignored. The same process of selection takes place between analysis and interpretation; some terms are more significant than others. To be adequate, each of the levels of consciousness should be related to the others. Philosophy should be built on experience (the movement up the pyramid in the diagram), but it should also be "verified" or confirmed by experience (the return movement down the pyramid).

Within philosophy we have several alternatives available as to how interpretation and analysis are composed. We shall briefly look at these before moving on to the language of sport, where the term *language* includes the "rationality" and inner life of sport.

II

THREE TRENDS have emerged in the discipline of philosophy today, and these—not surprisingly—are practiced by the majority of writers who are preoccupied with the philosophical problems of sport. Their methods in dealing with these problems are markedly different, yet there appear from time to time commonalities and affinities among them. The territory these "camps" occupy is not completely hostile, and in the past decade, especially in the last five years, these philosophical schools have grown together and have profited from their interaction. This situation is reflected in my account of the three traditions below. Also, the better, more significant works in the area are ones that do not fall easily within these categories: as with most classifications, there exist noteworthy exceptions. I shall discuss each of these movements in the order of their recent emergence in the philosophy of sport.

The first trend is the speculative tradition. As I mentioned above, its best-known representative is Paul Weiss. He is principally interested in the metaphysical problems of sport; for instance, in games as a solution to the problem of the one and the many, and in the nature of a team.[10] His works are attempts to locate sport within the dimension of societal reality. Another of the main functions of speculative philosophy of sport is its attempt to deal with sport as a whole, trying to define or state the "essence" of sport and asking questions like "Does sport have a meaning or purpose?" This question has generated much discussion. Josef Pieper argues against the notion that sport is "meaningful in itself." The question remains open: "By what virtue does an act possess the inner quality of being meaningful in itself?"[11] Pieper convincingly argues that no affirmative answer can be given. Or, our initial question may pertain to symbolic meaning. What is the meaning of sport? What is the meaning of the body? What is the meaning of play?[12] Shirl Hoffman thinks most of us have missed the meaning of sport.[13] He, too, has seen meaning below the surface of what transpires on the playground. He seeks *form* in the events of the field. Hoffman seeks the essence or substance of sporting events.

Questions of meaning give way to questions of being. Many writers are concerned with the ontological issues and address themselves to the "reality" of sport. Sport can become another realm of perception and being. These metaphysical notions can be used to uniquely define the world of sport and separate it from other worlds.[14] Oriental philosophy is concerned with these issues, too (see chapter 5), but much of what is done here also belongs in the next philosophical tradition. In sum, speculative philosophy of sport deals with substantive issues and makes substantive claims about the activity itself. Some sports commentators and writers would do well to listen to the speculative philosophers' reflections or recommendations.

The second trend in philosophy of sport is the existential/phenomenological tradition. The literature here is more extensive. I will suggest just a few of the questions and problems these philosophers deal with.[15] Instead of raising questions concerning the essence of sport, these writers try to portray what human existence in sport is like from the standpoint of human subjectivity, i.e., of the experiencing subject. Speculation gives way to involvement—something Weiss and the speculative tradition tried to avoid. In describing the existential tradition and the athlete, Mihalich says:

> The point is that sports and athletics subsume an artistry of consciousness and bodily presence that must be perceived in terms of lived experience rather than conceptual analysis. There is a spontaneity and inventiveness (without arbitrariness) in sports and athletics and the athlete's being and acting. This is much more than mere instinctive actions and reactions: it is the measure once again of the existential athlete's attunement with the experiential world. The existential athlete does not think about space and time in the world—the athlete lives space and time in the world in his or her uniquely acute expression of consciousness-in-the-world-with-a-body. (p. 80)

The significance of the hyphenated clause is that the existential tradition stresses unity and rejects dualisms like mind/body, self/world, subject/object. The emphasis upon being and acting is an interest shared with speculative philosophy, but the existential tradition rejects systematic accounts and the search for essences. In place of essences it substitutes existence as a lived experience. Reflection and analysis must be the servant of the lived experience rather than the other way around. Maurice Merleau-Ponty, the French existential phenomenologist, outlines the program of the continental tradition thus:

> The phenomenological world is not pure being [as the world is conceived of in the speculative tradition], but the sense which is revealed where the paths of my various experiences intersect, and also where my own and other people's intersect and engage each other like gears. It is thus inseparable from subjectivity and intersubjectivity, which find their unity when I either take up my past experiences in those of the present, or other people's in my own.[16]

The phenomenological world is a world that is already there—a world given and constituted by human consciousness, guided by its intentions. The task of the followers of this tradition, which stems from Edmund Husserl (the founder of phenomenology who wrote his most important works at the turn of this century), is "to locate, describe, and analyze the grammar of experience: the elements which comprise our world of everyday existence."[17] In the area of sport, the phenomenologist charts the elements that comprise our world of sport existence. Existential reality in sport is the object of the phenomenologist's reflections: what set of intentions make up this distinct realm of consciousness? In chapter 4, I shall discuss Jean-Paul Sartre's phenomenological description and analysis of the experience of skiing. Sartre's discussion will serve as an example of this type of philosophical reflection.

The third trend in philosophy of sport is the analytic tradition. Following Bertrand Russell's program, the "big" questions are divided and then conquered. The piecemeal analysis of key terms and concepts is the domain of this tradition. Many of the writers in the analytic philosophy of sport follow some variation of ordinary language philosophy, but there are a few, like Hans Lenk,[18] who subscribe more to a pragmatic "formalism," that is, to an ideal (logical) language philosophy approach to sport. This latter approach is one of systematic theory construction, and when successful it recommends alternative schemes for the world of sport to those currently in use.[19] Analytical or critical philosophy of sport of either variety attempts an analysis of sport ideas; for examples, the ideas of the well-played game and sportsmanship. It charts the character and presuppositions of sport thinking; it analyzes the language we use to talk about sport. Instead of attempting to deal directly with reality or lived experience, analytic philosophers discuss these by examining the language and the concepts used to talk about them. This "detachment" from its subject matter has produced promising results in the field of philosophy, and has contributed to the realization of Russell's dream; but analytic detachment is not like that of speculative philosophy. Many have seen this Linguistic Turn as a step away from introspection and intuition, a move away from subjectivism. Concerning the language of sport, sport reporting is of particular interest. Writers in the analytical tradition are concerned with its (sport's) objects (by way of analyzing predicates and attributes). Problems tend to fall into the following categories: sport and other forms of knowledge, the role of value judgments in sport thinking, and the detection of various "myths" that underlie such thinking. I shall have more to say about the analytic tradition below, since my method stems primarily from these philosophers.

III

AS THE PREVIOUS section attests, the tradition most heavily relied upon in this book is the analytic tradition. I have, as I have mentioned earlier, been somewhat eclectic in my approach, taking whatever paths are demanded by sport-talk and tracing these paths from the three traditions when necessary. Each has made its contribution to the field, and I have tried to heed these contributions when the occasion arises in my selective narrative.

In the introduction, I briefly characterized "the language of sport" as sport-talk that exhibits the inner life of sport or that reveals life (or value) perspectives. So the instances of the language of sport that interest a philosopher are those that provide food for thought. How are we to identify those cases? This is not an easy question to answer. With the help of J. O. Urmson and Hans Lenk, I will attempt an answer. The cases that philosophers single out are those that satisfy Urmson's definition of "field-work": "By doing field-work I mean studying examples of people actually trying to decide whether a certain judgment is or is not esthetic and observing how they most convincingly argue the matter."[20] If we take Urmson's concept of field work and expand it to include other sorts of judgments, this can be used as a "guide" for investigating the world of sport. But what I have in mind is not some random mapping of "family resemblances." Following Wittgenstein, Robert Fogelin charted the territory of sport, and what he found of greatest interest to record is its diversity.[21] If we substitute "sport" for "games" in Wittgenstein's passage from the *Philosophical Investigations* below, we get a fairly clear picture of what Fogelin and others who follow Wittgenstein come up with. The latter writes:

> Consider for example the proceedings that we call "games." I mean board-games, card-games, ball-games, Olympic games and

so on. What is common to them all?—Don't say: "There must be something common, or they would not be called 'games'"—but look and see whether there is anything common to all, but similarities, relationships, and a whole series of them at that. To repeat: don't think, but look!—Look for example at board-games, with their multifarious relationships. Now pass to card-games . . . and so on until we . . . can see how similarities crop up and disappear. And the result of this examination is we see a complicated network of similarities overlapping and criss-crossing: sometimes overall similarities, sometimes similarities of detail. I can think of no better expression to characterize these similarities than "family resemblances." . . . And I shall say: "games" form a family. (sections 66–67)

The result, then, is reading a complicated network of similarities, and that is all. No principles or ordering result from such an examination. It is questionable whether Wittgenstein himself followed his own advice, much less his most enthusiastic followers. He wanted so badly not to see commonality and essential structures that indeed he didn't.

Even though I have indicated that I follow Wittgenstein's advice on several points, I have several fundamental departures from his use of language-games:

Our clear and simple language-games are not preparatory studies for a future regularization of language—as it were first approximations, ignoring friction and air-resistance. The language-games are rather set up as *objects of comparison* which are meant to throw light on the facts of our language by way not only of similarities, but also of dissimilarities. (p. 50)

As we have seen from his discussion of the concept of game, he stresses the dissimilarities more than he does the similarities. His antiessentialism also led him to be exclusively preoccupied with them—so much so that the similarities, especially with sport, have been missed. Hence, I have emphasized the analogies between sport and other aspects of life that are drawn in the sport litera-ture. Another reason for my doing this is that there has been a long-standing assumption in the literature (from Huizinga on) that one of the important characteristics of play is that it occupies a separate, distinct world with its own rules and demarcations.[22] These characteristics have been transferred to sport, and part of the justification of its development in the mid-twentieth century has been made on the basis of this premise. This "separateness" of sport led to its deterioration and ultimately to its widespread corruption. I try to correct this tendency here by emphasizing sport's similarities with other categories of experience so that it will be viewed as part of the mainstream of culture and its associated values: ethical, aesthetic, artistic, religious, epistemological, and metaphysical. My preoccupation with these values led to these inquiries. How these values are historically expressed also led us to perceive sport's uniqueness in our culture and experience.

In the contemporary dialogue *The Grasshopper*, Bernard Suits attempts to counter the Wittgensteinian approach, by constructing and then testing a definition of game playing.[23] Word is still out, but indications from its initial reception have it that he has made a formidable challenge to Wittgenstein's antidefinitional (antiessentialistic) stance in philosophy.[24] With the Pragmatic Turn in the analytic tradition, we find an increasing dissatisfaction with the Wittgensteinian approach because it does not get in touch with the pragmatic problems of sport. And a philosophy isolated from practice tends to turn out too abstract to be really meaningful.[25] This Pragmatic Turn has led analytic philosophy back closer to some of the aims of philosophers in the speculative tradition. Speculation has led to pragmatism. Lenk puts it this way:

> Analytic philosophy has already done and will, as well as should, increasingly do the same in developing substantial approaches, in considering historical and cultural traditions, in contriving language reform proposals and in critically reflecting scientific results . . . since definitional problems only make sense if pertaining to a theoretic framework, to problems and language. Fogelin [see above and note 21] suffers from a negative definitional fallacy and from a too simple theoretical isolationism. Concepts of a family resemblance character like

28

"sport" only function and work, if they are integrated into a seemly theoretical and/or pragmatic framework. Then, actually, one will find out that sport is indeed not "the sort of thing written about on sport pages." He who only knows the sports pages does not know very much about sport. He certainly gets a distorted definition and interpretation.[26]

Lenk has summed up the anti-Wittgensteinian movement in the analytic tradition, and he has made an appeal to more formal, in addition to more pragmatic, studies in the area of philosophy of sport. I should note that I feel that my work here belongs to this movement. I have tried to blend practice and theory, pragmatism and formalism, because philosophy, if it is to be useful to other disciplines, needs to offer results that can be useful to the social sciences. So conceptual analyses, stipulative definitions, and the like, are needed to help solve the urgent problems of sport.

To avoid a potential misunderstanding, let me remind the reader that what I mean by "sport-talk" and "the language of sport" is much more than what Fogelin means by "the sort of thing written about on sports pages." Concepts can be found in the sports pages, but in the philosophically interesting cases they usually need explication. To this Wittgensteinian approach I have added Kuhn's paradigms and his theory of historical change to account for cultural traditions that have been transformed in recent social history, especially in this country. Ideally, it is conceivable that sport could be just that which is found on the sports pages, but this does not usually happen. In the eyes of journalists, this is not how one sells newspapers. One must dig through the gossip to find the ideas and the more profound issues in sport. Novak expresses my sentiments regarding language in the sports pages of our daily newspapers:

> When I read the sports page, I'm not interested in big business, wheeling and dealing, money; all that is part of the mundane world of everyday and belongs on the other, boring pages of the paper, to be read from a sense of duty. On the sports page, I seek clear images of what happened; or, in advance, what is likely to happen in athletic contests. I expect guidance in learning afterward exactly how it happened. I

would like sports reporters to be, in this sense, better news-men. I would like them to give probing, intelligent, and artis-tic accounts of the one world that here interests me: the events on the field. (p. 261)

This state of affairs usually entails that philosophers keep their eyes on theory and practice in the context of sport when they begin to examine sport-talk. Such pragmatic procedures can provide a philosophy that will be helpful to the sportsperson in addition to the physical educator. If philosophy of sport is to be truly pragmatic, it must reflect the inner life of sport—those things that matter most to those who really know what sport is all about. The language of sport must speak to those who really care. And to do this, analytical philosophy must get beyond the sports pages to discern the form in the activities taking place on the field. So in following Lenk's lead, I have attempted to construct a viable and relevant work on sport for those who care, but also one that I hope will convince the skeptics that this area of philosophy is as important as any of the others. We should expect more from philosophers in this tradition than an examination of "sport" like that Wittgenstein gave of "games." The language of sport forms more than family resemblances. It forms substantial proposals if it is done well, and these are generated on the basis of careful field work. Paul Kuntz initially started some field work in this area by examining how aesthetics applies to sport as well as to art.[27] Kuntz begins by discussing Neal Sharter, a Georgian gymnast who conceived of his sport as artistic performance, and the resistance he met from the sports establishment. Kuntz explores his reasons and discusses what kind of impact this case has had on the world of gymnastics, and indeed on the world of sport at large. I have continued this endeavor in chapter 8.

In a later piece, Lenk applies Kant's famous statement "Thoughts without contents are empty, intuitions without concepts are blind"[28] to sport studies, arguing that "philosophy of sport with-out sociology of sport (including social psychology of sport) is (socially speaking) void; sociology of sport without philosophy of sport (including philosophy of science) would be blind regarding a) methodological questions and b) problems of meaning."[29] He goes on to make the plea for a necessary integration of philosophical and social science approaches to the scientific analysis of sport, and to that extent Lenk's proposal fits in with the recent philosophical movement known as "postanalytic philosophy," in which the discipline tries to "de-disciplinize" itself by aligning itself to other fields (see note 30).

The other formal elements found in the language of sport, besides the aesthetic and the artistic discussed in chapter 8, are described and analyzed in the last chapter. We now turn from the nature of the philosophy of sport to the nature of sport itself. Where does "sport" belong in our mental geography? In the next chapter we shall try to chart its course on our philosophical map— where the word "sport" rightly abides in our web of belief or conceptual scheme.[30]

TWO

The Nature of Sport:
Three Conceptions

I

IN THE PHILOSOPHIC literature on sport, notably Graves,[1] Caillois,[2] Suits,[3] and Schmitz,[4] there is a distinction drawn between sport as recreation and sport as a profession or as a way of life. This distinction has a long and troubled history, partially because the distinction forces us to think in terms of the extremes of a continuum. Indeed, those engaged recreationally and professionally are playing the same game, as Suits reminds us, but more attitudes and ideas are involved than are encompassed by these two views. Neither one of these traditional perspectives is suitable for the majority who engage in sport today. There must be some middle conception for those of us who are not professionals and who feel awkward in answering individuals who snobbishly ask, "Do you still play that game?"; or "Don't you have better things to do than play soccer?" Or when asked if they still play, they smile amusedly and say, "Oh, I don't have time for that anymore; I have more important things to do." Comments such as these are difficult to respond to because the inquirer presupposes that sport is merely recreation; in particular, a mode of amusement or diversion. The skeptics do not see commitments and tests in sport. They mistake the surface of sport for its depth. So the ideas of commitment and test need to be incorporated into another perspective of sport,[5] one broader than the recreational concept but significantly narrower than sport as profession and way of life, which applies to only a select few gifted athletes. This synthesis, which has affinities

33

with both traditional views, I develop below into a thesis which I label sport as human enterprise.

Several philosophical examinations of sport have resulted in theories that attempt to explain the individual activities ordinarily referred to as "sports." At the turn of this century, the first modern thesis concerning sport was advanced by an Englishman, H. Graves, who analyzed the idea of sport as recreation. In the late fifties, Kenneth Schmitz developed a second but related thesis depicting sport as suspension of the ordinary, and his essay is essentially an updating of Graves's philosophy. Both of these views contrast sport with work, profession, or way of life. In this chapter I shall offer another view that I hope will answer some of the objections raised against these two, and it will reflect the present state of sport better than they do. Sport has grown to meet new human needs, to reflect different attitudes, and has, for many people, taken on a new significance not accounted for in the other two perspectives. Some individuals may become involved in sport for recreation or a suspension of the ordinary, but there are other motivations also.

I shall argue that sport is no longer merely a form of entertainment or amusement on the part of the spectator or participant; indeed, for some it never was. I propose, rather, that sport is a distinctive form of human enterprise. Before discussing the notion of an enterprise, I want briefly to summarize the two theories mentioned above so that we may have them to compare and contrast with the one I develop below.

II

PERHAPS the most prevalent view of sport is that it is a mode of amusement or entertainment. That sport is to be viewed as recreation is one of the oldest conceptions articulated about the activities denoted by the term. We can find it at the beginning of the Western intellectual tradition and stretching down to the present day. We find it represented in recent television commercials such as the AMF advertisements for sports equipment. The weekdays are for work; the weekends are for play—an appealing notion and one that is true for many people. These individuals engage in sport in order to be amused, entertained, and diverted. Sport provides a suspension of the ordinary, as Schmitz labels it. Play and involvement in sport can be releases from the pressures and drudgery of work and daily routines. There are times when we escape these dehumanizing influences by moving into the "separateness" of the *Spielwelt*, the play world, the world of sport.

The word's etymology even suggests this: the verb *disport* means to divert or distract. Sport diverts or distracts us from our daily concerns; it re-creates or creates us anew. Recreation (re-creation) restores us to health; that is, it restores our strength and revives our spirits. But how is this done? And what are the conditions by which we re-create ourselves through sport?

The characteristics of recreation are that it is accomplished through the influence of pleasant surroundings, and that the pleasure a participant derives is from the "attempt." Graves terms these two marks of recreation *the conventionality of sport*, which, he says,

> proposes for its object not to kill the bird, hook the fish, destroy the fox, win the match, but to derive, and perhaps afford to others, pleasure from the attempt to do so. If the object ostensibly aimed at be attained by a skipping of corners, by the use of illegitimate and unconventional means, by the maxim of "win, tie, or wrangle," in fact by any means which diminishes the pleasure to be gained from participation in the pursuit, then the result achieved is considered foreign to the nature of sport. Otherwise, we should take guns to our foxes and poison to our fish. Our aim should be not so much to win as to play the game. (p. 8)

In other words, one of the purposes of the set of conventions that governs a given sport is to help guarantee that the activities remain pleasurable ones. So Graves argues that a code of ethics is common to all branches of recreation in order to insure that sport is undertaken for pleasure and in a legitimate manner. This may sound puzzling at first because what is recreation for one person may not be for another. The code of ethics is contained in the idea of sportsmanship. He concludes: "Sportsmanlike conduct would appear to lie in such practices as conduce to the pleasantness of a sport, and unsportsmanlike conduct in such actions as tend to spoil it by making it less pleasant." What Graves probably has in mind are the "spoilsport" and the cheat—not individuals who "bend" the rules or employ gamesmanship, although these individuals, too, might be considered unsportsmanlike. Also, he thinks that if the game is taken too seriously with the objective to win at all costs, then the conventionality of sport is violated. This British or Eton view of sport views competition as a social, cooperative undertaking where one plays or strives to play well in order to bring about the best in others as well as oneself. One wouldn't strive to surpass all others— this conception of competition is a more recent American view than Graves's turn-of-the-century view. Why didn't the Eton paradigm take hold in America and become resistant to corruption? Sport historians argue that there was absent a conception of amateurism in sport because sport was conceived of as recreation in Puritan New England.

Another point I wish to make about Graves's discussion of the conventionality of sport concerns his statement about the nature of play: "The true sportsman plays for the love of the game, the sense of mastery, the sheer *joie de vivre* which he feels in playing a stroke well, and not for the mere honour, or still less the profit, of a victory." This is still a popular view of the sportsperson, but it ceases to carry over into athletics. The collegiate athlete's primary aim in the game is to win; victory is essential to his endeavor, whereas with the sportsperson it is not—and for the reasons Graves gives. What is important for me as a sportsperson is that I play as well as I am capable of playing. People ought to ask me how well I played after my tennis match rather than asking if I won. Thus I would know that they understand the order of priorities and value judgments that I place on these activities.

Another major characteristic of recreation is that it must be undertaken purely for the sake of pleasure, as distinct from business. A recreation is "a relief from the hard necessities of life" (Graves, p. 10). In detail:

> Once the idea is imported into sport that a man's subsistence depends upon it, then the pleasantness of sport as a recreation ceases, and we import into it the bitterness of the world's

struggle for existence. There are things which a man will do when his back is against the wall, and he feels that his own livelihood or that of his wife and children are dependent upon him, which he would not dream of doing if this feeling were removed. (p. 9)

And elsewhere, Graves expresses the same point this way:

In so far as a pursuit is followed as a means of livelihood it ceases to be sport, and becomes merely a matter of business. Sport is followed for no other end than to afford pleasure to those participating in it, and a sportsman follows sport for no other reason than to enjoy that pleasure. (p. 8)

As I mentioned in the introduction, the Eton paradigm has undergone radical change with the growth of professional sports. Yet these two passages from Graves could have been written in this decade rather than the turn of the century. They undoubtedly have a contemporary ring to them, showing just how long the recreational concept of sport has been threatened by business or professionalism. The tension has been there from the beginning.

So what kind of pleasure is Graves talking about? Harold VanderZwaag provides the most succinct answer:

Recreation, in its fullest sense, carries away the individual from his usual concerns and problems. The attitudes derived from this are those involving feelings of relaxation. Contentment, not complacency, might best describe an attitude which is [the] product of a recreative experience.[6]

These marks of the spirit of play in sport are what make it recreation. As Graves recognizes (p. 15), this is not the whole story on sport, even though it is, and has continued to be, one of the most central. The shortcomings that this perspective fosters will be dealt with in the section on sport as human enterprise.

Schmitz articulates the options that lie in sport today better than Graves. Both see business and commercialization as basically foreign to play. However, Schmitz hints at what is later to come, when he states:

The deepest problems in our technological society center about salvaging, promoting, and developing truly human possibilities. Sport stands in a very sensitive position. It can be part of the drive to dehumanization, or in a very direct and privileged way, to the recapture of human values and human dignity. (p. 31)

One of the theses of this book is that sport has participated in both of these drives—that the one (dehumanization) has led to the other (a recapturing or a new awakening). When sport is associated with profession, way of life, or business, it is often seen as essentially negative. Profession takes on those elements or values that are the opposite of recreation. So dehumanization is commonly discussed in the literature. But a more positive view can also be made for the notion of profession.

III

PROFESSION is an idea that has not fared too well in the literature on sport. The views are all essentially negative, touching only briefly on the positive conceptions of sport implicit in the notion of profession. The best detailed statement, which is more sympathetic than most, is Schmitz's:

In professional sport [its binding force] does not lie in interest in the game itself but rather is reinforced and ultimately enforced by values not intrinsic to the game. Perhaps the clearest distinction is between the wage the pro earns and the win or loss of the game. Win or lose, for a time at least he is paid a wage for services delivered; but he gets the victory only when "the gods of the game" smile upon him. Play ceases when the primary reasons for undertaking it are alien to the values of the play world itself. Values intrinsic to the play world include not letting down one's own teammates in team games, not begging off the contest because of personal discomfort, taking pleasure in performing activities within the rules of the game, prizing the victory and its symbols. Values that lie outside the play world include agreement to deliver services for wages earned, abiding by a contract because of fear of being sued, playing out games in order not to be barred from further league participation, finishing out a sports career in order to achieve social and economic standing upon ceasing to play. These motives are not unworthy; they are simply not motives of play. (pp. 31–32)

Here we find a statement similar to Graves's, although the tone is not one of condemnation. However, professional values are still seen as alien to and outside of the world of sport. The elements of monetary corruption are usually the ones singled out as alien, potentially threatening the inner life and significance of sport.

Besides remuneration, what makes any occupation a profession? In common usage, a profession is first and foremost a calling requiring a specialized knowledge and a long, intensive academic preparation. This characterization has several items that should be emphasized. First, in the idea of a calling we see a religious analogy. Someone is being summoned by a deep set of beliefs and commitments about his or her life and the way it ought to be lived (one that requires a great deal of time and energy). Second, the epistemic requirement is manifest: a given activity is a profession in part because of the degree of difficulty involved in mastering its subject matter. And third, the lengthy practice of this knowledge as an art or a craft is essential to the concept of a profession. Activities that can be viewed as professions encompass specialized skills that are acquired and practiced. The most prominent examples are obviously medicine, the law, divinity, and teaching. These fields traditionally emphasize service rather than monetary gain. They also allow for extensive autonomy and self-regulation, although these are currently under attack in America. Jim and Tammy Bakker have not upheld the virtues of the ministry, to say the least. Hence there is a move to regulate publicly what has become an industry. Robert Churchill adds another condition: the professions expect their individual members to accept personal responsibility for their actions.[7] He continues:

This list [of necessary and sufficient conditions] works well for the traditional professions: physicians, lawyers, professors, and priests. The conditions seem to be necessary and, when taken

39

together, complete. But what about *professional* athletes? Re-
ferring to highly paid athletes as members of a *profession* violates the fifth condition, which pertains to service rather than
personal gain. But is this condition really necessary? After all,
some doctors and lawyers also enter their chosen fields primarily for monetary or personal prestige. We may not be able to
say whether the fifth condition or any one on the list [his list,
which is similar to mine] is really necessary. But thinking about
these conditions helps us understand what it means to be a
member of a *profession*.

To Churchill's discussion I might add that with the tremendous
growth of professional athletics, which has led to a deemphasis of
service relative to monetary gain, comes the loss of individual autonomy and self-regulation. Athletes are now extensively regulated
by drug tests and other league restrictions imposed on the players.
Also, because of the large amount of money involved in their
participation, they have become a commodity that is pushed from
one place to another as the busy schedule demands.

However, it should be noted that even on Churchill's fifth
point, society has a residual desire to treat sports professionals as
professionals, that is, we *want* to think of them as doing their work
for the love of excellence, we want them to be our cultural heroes;
and surely filling the hero role is very much a form of service to
society. As Arthur Ashe recently expressed it: "It is not that I believe
sports are not important. But I believe they have assumed a role
more than is significant. We have come to almost exalt our athletes."[8]

Sport can join the illustrious company of professions, though
for it to fulfill the above conditions, much in the world of sport
would have to be changed. However, there are a *few* individuals
who do satisfy these conditions. Sport, too, can be a principal
calling for individuals who spend a great deal of time training and in
"academic" preparation. An athlete who carries out these activities
truly aspires to a profession. What makes his or her attitude toward
sport a professional one is more than just the monetary or working
conditions. It is, rather, dedication, commitment to a certain way of
life, commitment to certain values, and a willingness to practice

one's skills within the institutional setting that normally accompanies this particular calling.

Further refining the concept of profession, Renford Bambourgh has drawn a distinction between profession as *techne* and profession as a natural craft.[9] Building on Aristotle's insights, Bambourgh describes profession as *techne* as something that fulfills or corrects a deficiency and is primarily perceived as a service. The medical community would be an exemplar here. There is the necessity of qualifications, which are established by testing and are formally stated in licenses to practice. By way of contrast, for profession as a natural craft an informal apprenticeship is all the "training" that is required: a poet is an exemplar. A profession in this sense can be natural and is expressive. The tensions that can be seen within each of the professions may be analyzed as a development of *techne* that is resisted by some members of the community, who wish to keep some of the elements that make a profession a natural craft. Sport has undergone such a transformation in its practices. Games between professionals today are struggles of technology more than of natural human abilities: football is a prime example. The change in equipment has led to a very different game from the one played in the thirties, when athletes relied more on natural ability than on *techne*.

The terms of employment are those features that most philosophers have seized upon in order to illustrate the social distinction between sport as recreation (avocation) and as profession (vocation). But this can lead to a misrepresentation of the player's attitudes. A case in point. The sports pages in the newspapers and the television sportscasters focus on the money athletes stand to make, leading us to believe that playing a given sport is the players' sole livelihood. But there are many—a great many—athletes who play professional golf, for instance, but earn a livelihood from other business interests. This might not be true at the beginning of a sportsperson's career, when that individual does not yet have the reputation or leisure time away from the tour to pursue those monetary interests that allow golf to become less work and more play. But this situation usually does not characterize the entire career, much less the individual's attitudes and motivation. Lee Trevino, the professional golfer, was once asked how he could possibly putt as boldly as he does when one stroke is worth $50,000. Trevino replied that it was easy, because it wasn't his money. Trevino's point was that only afterward would the money be his. Money that is included in the prize is viewed by athletes as just that—the prize. Trevino does not think about the money when he putts, only about putting and the rest of the conditions in that particular sport situation. For golfers, tennis players, football players, and so on, professional playing is still play. Martina Navratilova was asked recently why she continued to play tennis on the circuit. It is not that she needs the money or the prestige. She continues to think that she hasn't reached her full potential; she is striving to improve, to be better than she was yester-day. Navratilova comes perilously close to embodying what I have called a human enterprise.

IV

THE NOTION of a human enterprise is a particularly fruitful one to apply to sport because enterprises can be both individual and collective.[10] Looked at as an individual enterprise, sport poses for the participant a set of problems and exciting goals. The person then develops tasks and long-term procedures by which he or she can solve those problems and can realize the goals. In this way, he or she achieves a sense of mastery over the fundamentals of the game and begins to experience the game and himself or herself, as a player, as extensions of each other. At this point the game becomes a project, or an undertaking, of an individual. The game becomes a possibility for perfection; one sets goals or ideals that are circum-scribed by the rules of the game. Charles Frankel calls this process of planning and the attempt to give substance to one's idea *an enterprise*.[11] The work and achievement on which a human enter-prise is founded give us a sound estimate of the way the richest kind of happiness in human life can be found. A sense of great reward is there for the taking in sport. It seems to me that sport, as practiced by many people today, fits this description and perspec-tive. Sport provides structure or meaning in an individual's life; it organizes his or her experience and creates a relation to the world. An individual's orientation to the world and to himself or herself becomes markedly different when sport is viewed as an enterprise. Why? When the skills and goals of sport bear some relation to those of the rest of the world (which at least in some cases they do), then the sport enterprise creates purpose or meaning in relation to the rest of a person's world.

However, enterprises may be collective as well as individual. The institutional setting of sport plays a dominant role in the notion of a human enterprise here. Through sport, people can share problems, common needs, and similar ideals, can join together to accomplish what they could not accomplish individually. Competitive structures like tournaments can provide the environment needed for individuals who share this vision of sport. Obviously team sports or endeavors illustrate the characteristics of collective enterprises better than they do individual ones, although the two interface with each other, one making the other possible. Collective enterprises encourage an extra dimension of community, of comradeship, of fellow-feeling. The joys of sport are the fruits offered us through engaging in such an enterprise with others. Thus, those collective enterprises that are successful usually become institutions. They reflect the development and history of sport. These institutions are manifested by the sets of rules and expectations, collections of codes and norms, by which individuals regulate their behavior toward one another.

Moreover, there can be an interplay between individual and collective enterprises. Sometimes an individual's enterprise (for instance, personal style in sport) offers a unique, interesting solution to or direction for a collective enterprise. When this happens it becomes part of that institution—part of the game. For example, peculiar styles of play such as the two-fisted backhand in tennis or a new technique for the high jump are incorporated into the repertoire of the sport. The individuals who popularize these and capture the imagination of other players or participants are those written about in the history pages of sport.

This interplay between individual and collective enterprises may take place at the professional end of the sport continuum, or it may take place in the recreational sport of a small, country town and go unnoticed except by those involved. But the condition for the social interplay that takes place in enterprises is *project*. A project in its fullest sense is a conscious undertaking that is difficult, complicated, and risky. When we reflect on the notion of enterprise and contemplate the word's use, we immediately associate it with business; a business organization is a project or undertaking that is difficult, complicated, and risky. In business the risk is a financial one; assessing the market successfully is difficult and immensely complex. In sport the participants risk personal injury, perhaps even their lives, and in a lesser way their pride. To conceive of sport as enterprise is to construe it as systematic purposeful activity whereby an individual can engage in daring action. The conceptual key to the idea of enterprise is found in the notion of a project. As Robert Solomon reminds us, such an intentional activity is not just a projection on our part, but a project.[12] It involves a set of hopes and expectations that may be fulfilled or unfulfilled. A project is a way in which we try to change the world and ourselves. The one realm marked off by ideal conditions in which individuals may take the situation as a project and an undertaking is sport.

When an individual participates in such a project, constrictions and limitations are imposed by institutions and collective enterprises. They initiate him or her into a broad complex of purposes more varied than his or her own. As Frankel says:

> They offer him a basis for discipline, for a consciousness of the world that is broader and deeper, for the complex and enduring kind of fellowship with others that is based on diversity and difference and not on a monotonous uniformity of ideas and tastes. In brief, they are instruments for educating and civilizing him. (p. 8)

This civilizing dimension is an exercise of intelligence. Novak says, "One joy in sports today is its engagement of intellect: criticism and countercriticism" (p. 105). Recall Russell's definition of philosophy as criticism: there are greater affinities between philosophy and sport than one preanalytically thinks.

Intelligent viewers of sport ask questions such as the following, and seek appropriate answers in what they are watching: Is this strategy better than that one? Is this the best decision for the coach or manager to make at this point in the game? Why did the quarterback pass in that situation? Is one particular defensive formation better than another? And so on. The fan, the spectator, and the participant have recently emerged as thinking beings. And sport, for them, has become a repository of certain codes and disciplines, of bodies of knowledge, of a manner of behavior, and of an image of civilized life. Sport exists to perpetuate these codes and disciplines, this knowledge, manner, and image, and to renovate them, as Frankel suggests. This textual dimension of sport I return to in the last chapter.

Leisure, construed now as a human enterprise, is moving in the direction of self-improvement and regeneration, and not toward recreation or amusement.[13] Skiing is a good example. Its popular image is that of a dashing, dangerous, expensive sport—one performed in romantic, far-away, mountainous places. Power lifts take people up and gravity brings them down. There is not much to this except a strain on the pocketbook. There is more exercise to be found almost anywhere than here. However, a new breed of skier has emerged on the scene. This is the earnest cross-country skier who "walks" or "skis" for hundreds of miles contemplating fitness, safety, and the promotion of health and well-being. This is one kind of skiing that improves the skier. People in sport today, furthermore, are not satisfied by merely playing golf or tennis. They want to take lessons. They want to measure their progress and their improvement. The health spa craze of the past decade is a sign of this change in social and personal consciousness.

B. J. Diggs recognizes the point I am attempting to make here when he says, "Games make new goals, new pursuits, and new skills available to men."[14] The player derives pleasure from a kind of instrumental activity that the rules of a game make possible. So even though game rules are not themselves instruments, they support a considerable amount of instrumental activity. To play a game, then, is to follow the rules of a game, but also to engage in a variety of instrumental activities, like the ones I have described above. However, games have a variety of problems or obstacles built into them that demand new kinds of ingenuity. Work does not always promise this. As Glover says, "Work may have more point if it fits into some great cause" (p. 354); or more generally, it makes a difference if what we are doing is a contribution to something larger than ourselves, but the larger context is not always necessary. Individuals who *need* this larger context are ones who choose collective enterprises as manifested in sports. The latter are only significant if individuals *want* to carry them out or have them within the "circles of our lives: We eat and rest in order to be able to work, and we work in order to earn money for food and rest, and so on" (ibid.). The "and so on" includes *sport*; for many, it is as important as any of the others.

What America is doing today with sport has not gone unnoticed. Sport as human enterprise has been written about in many different ways, but their similarity lies in the fruitful notion of an enterprise. Let me list a few authors who have attempted to capture this philosophical movement, some of whom we shall look at in greater detail in later chapters. Sport has inspired a revolution in thinking. Indeed, there is so much philosophizing about sport in our popular culture that it has made possible books like these. For instance, George Leonard, in *The Ultimate Athlete*,[15] published in 1974, was one of the first to offer a semiautobiographical account of the martial arts as providing a lifelong project. A few years before, Michael Murphy's half-comical, half-mystical *Golf in the Kingdom* contained the seeds of what was to emerge later.[16] Though much less mystical, Novak's *The Joy of Sports* works in here, too, with his emphasis on the inner life of sports (chs. 3, 7–10). Also Viktor Frankl's piece entitled "Sports—The Asceticism of Today"[17] is a fine example of viewing sport under this sort of perspective. The list could be amplified. What this list shows, and this chapter theoretically extends, is an alternative to the superficial view of sport as entertainment or amusement and its counterpart, professional occupation. This latter view is ultimately dangerous, I think (and here I agree with Novak), because it can destroy the inner life and significance of sport. Human enterprise is one way of capturing the rewarding attributes sport possesses for those who wish to undertake it.

V

WHAT I am proposing here is nothing novel. The term "enterprise" has been used in conjunction with sport before, for example, in David Aspin's contribution to *Readings in the Aesthetics of Sport*.[18] Joseph Mihalich talks constantly about the sporting enterprise.[19] And there are many others who followed in the eighties.[20] However, the implications of such an association have not been worked out. I have presented here a social theory of human enterprises to help account for sport as one segment of our population conceives of it.

Are there alternative theories that are similar to the one above? One that comes to mind is Earle Zeigler's continuum of amateur-semipro-professional.[21] Such a scheme has its merits, because there are semipro teams (like the Ashville Chiefs—a semipro football team that plays in its own league), but it has at least two drawbacks. First, it stays within the traditional framework and ideas of the distinction, and hence does not move us very far from present conceptions. Such a continuum as Zeigler's is also not cross-cultural, because of its reliance on "professionalism" (in the sociological sense), whereas mine is cross-cultural since it is independent of this and other culturally bound notions. Second, the idea of "semipro" and the term's use (as I am familiar with it in tennis circles) is a derogatory one. Attitudes and consciousness as exhibited in sport today are more than just a combination of these old conceptions. They are new and take us in a new direction. Measuring one's progress and marking one's self-improvement are important new values that have emerged.

Jane English labels these values as the basic benefits[22] of sport. And people see themselves as possessing the right to construct a strategy to achieve these values and goals. The handicapped in sport are a case in point today; they want to experience these things themselves. Tennis tournaments have been expanded to include the handicapped; the officials have added a men's wheelchair division. And recently paraplegics have climbed some Oklahoma mountains to dramatize their rights to the basic benefits of sport. Such strategies are captured by the idea of a human enterprise. The risk of physical pain and injury might be added to English's list. As Novak points out (p. 198), hard physical challenge, taking pain, and being hurt are important ingredients in sport. In sport today we are not escaping risk as Graves suggests; on the contrary, we are seeking it. The challenge of daring action is captured in sport as elsewhere in life. Many people today make sport an integral part of their way of life. Some individuals have consciously replaced the "work ethic" with a "sport ethic."

So what is sport? This question can be answered by a series of analogies. Sport is recreation, enterprise, profession, and much more. We have just started to clear the avenues for better answers to that philosophical question. More analogies wait for us in the chapters to come. In part II, I consider those values normally associated with the Eton paradigm. Chapter 3 analyzes some of the corruption of those values and chapter 4 examines their possible preservation and restoration in sport. Consequently, in Kuhnian fashion, I am as preoccupied with conceptual change when it comes to examining the next realm as I was in the last; in other words, it was natural for me to find myself looking at the *decline* of moral values and the *ascent* of aesthetic/artistic values in the sports world. The "mechanics" that account for that transition or movement "upward" are the subject of the middle chapters (part III).

PART TWO: THE ETHICAL

THREE

The Varieties of Cheating

I

WHAT IS CHEATING? The simplest and most immediate answer is that cheating is breaking the rules. In the end this commonsense view of cheating is not far from the mark. But as it stands, it is neither a conceptual characterization nor an adequate definition. Any human activity has underlying principles and ideas that can be discerned by analysis and seen as governing its process, and cheating is no exception. This chapter will attempt to clarify the underlying principles and ideas of the activity we call, and so easily recognize, as cheating.

Cheating is not limited just to the play world, for we frequently hear of someone who cheats on her income tax, of a businessman who cheats his customers, or of the student who cheats on an exam. We learn of referees cheating a team out of a win,[1] or of a referee in boxing who delays the count.[2] We also hear of spectators being cheated, as at one of the Duran-Leonard fights when Duran did not finish the fight.[3] We frequently read in the newspapers of coaches who cheat in recruiting.[4] Do these uses of the verb reflect a literal sense, or just a figurative one? It appears clear from these usages that cheating cannot be distinguished by virtue of belonging to one class or set, like that of the play world, or to one particular group, such as participants.

Generally speaking, the mere idea of breaking the rules will not do, for there are instances in games and sports where I may break some rule, such as tripping my hockey opponent or roughing the passer in football, which we would not call cheating. The

51

rules I break in these games are regulative rules; when they are violated, precisely weighted penalties are assessed. Penalties are established to deter players from certain actions which constitute unfair playing, but which are not, strictly speaking, cheating. All cheating on the part of participants in a game or sport is unfair play, but not all unfair play is cheating.[5] Some unfair play is designed to be part of the games. Stalling or biding time in football or basketball is part of those games. However, the action of stalling may be either an illegal "delay of game" or a legal using up the clock. Taking undue advantage of persons—for example, roughing the passer or kicker in football—is another instance of unfair play, but one not ordinarily labeled as cheating, except in special instances. Clearly, players who slam their helmets to the ground in protest of an official's call are guilty of unsportsmanlike conduct, but this is not considered cheating. And what about an inadvertent grab of the face mask in football? The official usually judges this act. Although we may not know the basis of the umpire's decision to throw the flag, we do know that unfairness is no measure. Consequently, the idea of unfair play will not do as a definition of cheating because it is too broad.

If this account will not do, then it must be that breaking only certain rules constitutes cheating. But which ones? Cheating actions, I submit provisionally, are those rule violations by means of which a player tries to change and take control of the outcome of the game, or the structuring of factors that will lead to the outcome of the game being naturally in his or her favor in ways that are not permissible by the rules or conventions that govern the game. In other words, the game's insured equality for the participants is undermined. For example, in American football a player is not supposed to tackle with the intent to injure another player. The action of tackling has its boundaries, and any individual who exceeds them is cheating. Unnecessary roughness in tackling a quarterback (say, the only one left on the team) in order to eliminate him from the game is cheating if this intent (whether consciously carried out or not) accompanies the action of tackling. A player who does this is obviously attempting to change the outcome of the game along the lines I just outlined. When such violations of the (prescribed) boundaries of legal actions occur in sport, the elements of chance are no longer operative, but are controlled for the advantage of one player or team over another. The idea of an equally matched contest is lost.[6] In other words, cheating occurs whenever a player, or any other participant, such as a referee, in a given contest, attempts (by actions not defined as part of the game), through breaking a rule, to control the elements of chance (in the sense of contingencies) that contribute to the outcome of the game.

When I break constitutive rules—the formalized rules that make up the fundamental aspects of the game—my actions constitute cheating.[7] This proposed characterization is too narrow, however, for I am capable of some actions in certain games where rules (that is, constitutive rules) are not broken, and yet cheating occurs. For example, when playing bridge, a player could see the reflection of the cards in someone's glasses and utilize that information in the game. No rule in *Ainslie's Complete Hoyle*[8] lists the above state of affairs. Nonetheless, tacit agreements, such as not peeking at another's cards, are understood regulative rules governing game behavior. Thus, we can still say that a rule has been broken—only this time, it is an unspoken regulative rule belonging to a class of rules that restrict players' conduct. The same may be said of the football example just given. Even though these agreements or "rules" are tacit, they seem to concern the fundamental nature of the game—and no penalty is assigned for them. Most of those we could view as "tests" of a person's character.

When we ask ourselves for the paradigms of games in which cheating is possible, several classes of games immediately come to mind. The first is those games that Caillois (pp. 17, 74ff.) classified as *alea* or games of chance, or those games that involve *alea* ("chance"). Games such as dice, roulette, slot-machines, and baccarat are paradigm cases, because they have nearly perfectly defined characteristics and precise, arbitrary, unexceptionable rules that must be accepted by all the players and must govern the game at all times. In *alea*, cheating usually occurs when the instruments or equipment of the game have been tampered with; for instance, altering the dice, changing the slant of the roulette wheel, or marking the cards. In contests or competitive games—ones Caillois classifies as *agôn*—cheating is usually accounted for by one's actions within the game, for example, picking up a card in the deck that is not the one on top in a game of poker or gin rummy, rather than by the instruments or equipment as in *alea*, although this may also occur. Let me give some instances of *agôn* where cheating occurs with equipment modification. In tennis the International Tennis Federation recently had to make a ruling dictating racquet stringing patterns. The "spaghetti" strung racquets were banned from sanctioned tournaments. In golf the calibration of the width of the grooves on the club face is strictly enforced by the United States Professional Golfers' Association. In the 1979 Indianapolis 500 race, rookie Dick Ferguson was "disallowed for deliberately attempting to override the mandatory pressure relief valve."[9]

One of the nearly perfectly defined characteristics of the above games, in either category, is that playing them involves uncertainty. When cheating occurs, the doubt that remains until the end of the game is replaced by the assurance of winning, or something close to it. This is incompatible with the nature of play. Not only is its form violated, but also its spirit. Caillois expresses this point in the following way:

> In a card game, when the outcome is no longer in doubt, play stops and the players lay down their hands. In a lottery or in roulette, money is placed on a number which may or may not win. In a sports contest, the powers of the contestants must be equated, so that each may have a chance until the end. Every game of skill, by definition, involves the risk for the player of missing his stroke, and the threat of defeat without which the game would no longer be pleasing. (p. 7)

In circumstances like these, cheating attempts to remove the element of chance. The risk and the threat of defeat are no longer present or are minimized by such actions. Consequently, the pleasure derived from situations in which they are present is lost: those recreational aspects of games, which we discussed in the previous chapter, are dissipated. There is no doubt that some players derive what might be called pleasure from cheating. For some, cheating provides the pleasure and motive for engaging in game-playing. But I would question whether there is cheating so subtle or so much a part of the game that it does not detract from the overall pleasure of games. On this issue concerning pleasure, I would agree with Caillois. Obviously cheating destroys more than just pleasure; it destroys the whole illusion of a world of even chances, an "alternate world" of sport, and so on.

When we move from games and sport contests that share the properties of competitive structure with fixed, rigid rules to those activities that do not, we find the absence of this kind of cheating. Nature sports, like skydiving, surfing, skiing, and boating (noncompetitive sailing), which have imperfectly defined characteristics, have no fixed or rigid rules. The absence of rules takes away the desired goal or prize and the standards of how to obtain it. The activities that make up nature sports are unregimented basic skills or movements performed for their own sake: gliding, jumping, riding, climbing, sliding, navigating, and so on. Of course, these sports can be participated in competitively for prizes at times. But competition is something superimposed on these activities; it is not integral to them. In nature sports, individuals can fail to meet the potential challenge, but their actions are not rightly labeled as cheating. These actions would be better grouped under the heading of personal failures. The use of "cheating" in cases such as these would be in an extended, metaphorical sense. So we can add to Progan's list of the characteristics of nature sports[10] the impossibility of cheating.

Perhaps one of the appeals of nature sports is their noncompetitive structure and all that goes along with it. One cannot cheat at surfing or skydiving; i.e., one cannot alter the laws of nature. Rather, one has to play in accordance with natural laws. What Schmitz says about the play world as a distinctive order applies especially to nature sports: "The laws of natural forces are put to use in an extraordinary way within an extraordinary world inspired by a motive that has suspended the ordinary interest of everyday life" (p. 28). The extraordinary may not be "dominance-oriented," as in other sports; nature sports by contrast are measured by being "challenge-" or "excellence-oriented." These two orientations are different ways in which one may approach a given activity. One can strive competitively to dominate others, or one can strive toward excellence and the challenge that the situation offers to test oneself. (More on the two models later.) Taking shortcuts or underachieving may be ways in which "the extraordinary" in nature sports is compromised, but shortcuts or forms of underachieving are not varieties of cheating.

In Caillois's classification of games, cheating may occur in *agôn* and *alea*, or in a mixture of these, but it is absent in *mimicry* and *ilinx*.[11] When these designations are placed on the continuum between *paidia* and *ludus*, we find that the latter component, *ludus* (that is, conventions requiring effort, skill, patience, or ingenuity), contains properties that make cheating a possibility not present in *paidia* (that is, frolic activity which is spontaneous and usually free of rules and conventions). One cannot cheat when frolicking. Moreover, because children's games tend to fit *paidia* and the categories of *mimicry* and *ilinx*, there is a notable absence of cheating in children's games. If cheating is present in children's games, it tends to have a disruptive influence, that is, the game ceases. Hence, a partial explanation of cheating or its absence is provided by Caillois's categories.

Nonetheless, more needs to be said about the concept of cheating, at this point, before more can be said about classification. Can one cheat oneself? Can the cheater and the cheated be the same individual? My initial response to these questions is yes, but not for the reasons already entertained.

The card game solitaire is the game we immediately associate with the possibility of cheating oneself. It is a competitive activity in which one competes against the particular layout of the cards or the game of solitaire, rather than competing against a rival or an opponent. If one can compete, regardless of what it is with, one can cheat oneself. It is this underlying principle of competition that makes self-cheating possible. Let us look at a not-so-obvious case that allows for self-cheating—running. In running, when a person sets up individual goals, such as besting a previous time, then he or she brings the activity into the realm of self-competing.[12] Failure to obtain the goal people set for themselves is not self-cheating, as, for example, when runners have not trained well for the run. Besting one's time by artificial means, however, like taking drugs beforehand or hedging on the time or distance, would be clear cases of self-cheating. The goal is obtained by means other than those prescribed by the activity: namely, by altering the spatial, temporal, or individual parameters.

Ultimately, in all actions of self-cheating, the cheaters rob themselves of the rewards provided by the rules of the game: a measure of skill, superiority, esteem, pleasure, pride, self-confidence. A broad, extended sense of "cheating" will cover these challenge- or excellence-oriented activities, although they are not cheating in the constitutive, rule-breaking sense, which involves only dominance-oriented game-playing situations.[13] Caillois's classification of games helps to clarify why the presence or absence of cheating occurs in sport. Self-cheating may occur in game-playing in either the strict or extended metaphorical senses. However, any adequate definition of cheating needs to cover specific cases of self-cheating, for they are clearly legitimate and important uses of the term.

II

IN *The Moral Rules* Bernard Gert considers various likely candidates for the characteristics of cheating.[14] He asks if cheating is a subclass of deception. It seems in most instances of cheating that deception must be present because most people simply will not tolerate overt cheating. Or, perhaps individuals cheat, as Moody suggests,[15] because no one else is looking or they think they can get away with it; for this reason, they might do that which they probably would not do otherwise. A case in point: if there were two different prices on a commodity in a supermarket, a person might scratch off the higher one—provided the above conditions are met. But if this is done, it is usually done with finesse and subtlety. Cheating, however, is not always deceptive. If people think they can get away with it, many will cheat openly, like the boss who plays golf with subordinates, or a tennis player in a match witnessed by others. Some people—here called "Machiavellian cheaters"[16]—may even think that this is just one of the ways of the world. Gunther Lueschen distinguishes between open and secret cheating in sport.[17] By "secret" cheating Lueschen means undetected forms of social deviance. The most imaginative and ingenious rule-breakings in game-playing surely come from this class of actions. Undetected forms of cheating will fit the challenge- or excellence-oriented model of sport, as well as the dominance-oriented model, so that these forms will be minimally covered by the extended sense of the term. Also, some undetected form of cheating may apply to the cheater and not just to those who can potentially observe his or her behavior. In "open" (that is, detected) cheating, however, the cheater's manner of cheating may be deceptive or not. A man may try to conceal his actions, or, on the other hand, he may be a rather brash fellow. While cheating may involve deception, deception is not a logically necessary ingredient of the class of actions labeled as "cheating." This observation agrees with some other consequences established later on in the chapter.

Cheating involves the violations of standards or rules in order to obtain some goal. Might the violation be like that of breaking an implicit promise? If so, then cheating would be just a special case of promise-breaking. Here again, Gert shows us that the answers to these questions are negative. Promises are always made to a particular person or group. People bind themselves by a speech act to carry out an action for some individual or others. In promising, they verbally place themselves under an obligation to do (or not do) something.[18] The act of adultery, for example, would be the only instance of cheating that would fit the "promising" model. Here one cheats on the vows one has taken in entering the institution of marriage rather than on the partner. But this case may be an exception to the rule governing the promising model. In the other cases, it is clearly one's partner or opponent that one cheats on. Gert also sees adultery as a form of cheating.

K. M. Pearson thinks that in an athletic contest "a player has entered into a contract with his opponent for the mutual purpose of making that determination" (that is, to determine who is more skillful in that particular game).[19] Such a legal paradigm, if interpreted literally, would make no sense whatsoever of game-playing. Pearson's account could be true only in an extended, metaphorical use of "contract." Athletes do not make explicit or even implicit agreements of this sort just by playing a game or entering a field or court to play. Furthermore, contracts are thought of as lists of promises.[20] No verbal commitments or promises are made in play, and players' actions surely do not constitute such commitments. We cannot "read" that much into them. This is not to deny that an athlete is supposed to make a very strong implicit commitment to follow specific rules. What I deny is that this commitment is of a contractual nature—only in a Hobbesian or fictional nature would we talk about a "contract." The situation is more like what David Hume explained in *A Treatise of Human Nature*:

> This convention [of abstaining from taking the possessions of others] is not of the nature of a *promise*: For even promises themselves, as we shall see afterwards, arise from human conventions. It is only a general sense of common interest; which sense all the members of the society express to one another, and which induces them to regulate their conduct by certain rules. I observe, that it will be for my interest to leave another in the possession of his goods, *provided* he will act in the same manner with regard to me. He is sensible of a like interest in the regulation of his conduct. When this common sense of interest is mutually express'd, and is known to both, it produces a suitable resolution and behaviour. And this may properly enough be call'd a convention or agreement betwixt us, tho' without the interposition of a promise; since the actions of each of us have a reference to those of the other, and are perform'd on the other part. Two men, who pull the oars of a boat, do it by an agreement of convention, tho' they have never given promises to each other.[21]

Hume's rowing example is analogous to what I am claiming about game-playing in general. On the sports pages of newspapers, we do not find games being interpreted along these legalistic lines, and I think with good reason. Indeed, if such interpretations were made, they would be logically odd. For these reasons among less obvious ones, then, playing is not a species of promising.

When I play I am not also by that very act or set of acts promising anything. Let us look at another case that might be construed that way. In basketball when officials explain to players what will and will not count as fouls, they are not promising or contracting anything for themselves or for the players. The players, when acknowledging these interpretations, are not thereby promising not to violate or commit these actions. The officials are simply making known that certain interpretations of actions will be given if they occur. These are indeed agreements, but they are not examples of contracts; these are more like decrees. Not all agreements are contracts; Hume's explanation makes this point abundantly clear. Some "agreements" are more informal than others, and those that occur in games are examples that fall under this less formal interpretation.

Furthermore one can cheat another without the claims of a promise being present. In some cases of cheating there is no particular person or group to whom one has implicitly promised anything. This claim of a promise involves a convention that is too overt and whose boundaries are too rigid. The most we can say is that one is expected not to cheat, not that one has promised not to. Cheating is failing to live up to certain standards or rules expected by all those who participate in the activity. There are certain social expectations for persons entering the play world as players. So cheating is more of a social phenomenon than a personal one, although it does have a personal dimension too. The personal dimension is most clearly seen in the extended metaphorical sense of cheating that involves the challenge-excellence model. The social dimension primarily evolves from the dominance model in the analysis of cheating; again, see Hume's explanation of the nature of human conventions.

The notion of entering the play world is very far from the notion of placing oneself under an obligation. I am not obligated not to cheat, only expected not to. This point, which shows the social dimension of cheating, demonstrates its proximity to deception, because these expectations are social relations. What one does to others and to institutions is more important in cheating than what one does to oneself, although this personal dimension is significant to the individual in question.

The first provisional characterization of cheating presented by Gert is that cheating occurs only in voluntary activities that have built-in goals and well-established standards for their achievement.

Gert then asks us to imagine two different cases of cheating to test or challenge this characterization. The first case is justified or retaliatory cheating, and the second case is unintentional cheating, which we shall discuss momentarily. First, he asks, can we imagine a case of justified cheating? Gert presents an implausible case in which one is justified in cheating someone at cards who says he or she will kill one's family if he or she wins. This case does not fit his own definition because one would obviously be involuntarily engaged in such an activity. In this circumstance one is *forced* to play and to cheat, so by definition neither activity is really undertaken or would be categorized as *play*. In extreme cases the situations seem counterintuitive and their plausibility is also questionable. These cases sound more like rationalizations than defenses. "Everybody is cheating. So if you expect to win, you have got to do it, too." In *Right and Wrong* Weiss and Weiss argue against the notion of justified cheating, regardless of circumstances.[22] Morally, the two ideas cancel one another out. Sissela Bok agrees with the Weisses in the case of lying.[23]

But what about other game examples where the stakes are not quite as high? Can we say that one is justified in cheating another player because that player cheated first? Is it an honorable motive to cheat a cheater in order to make him or her stop; that is, to follow the moral rule that one should not cheat? Or does it give the other player(s) license to cheat if others do, again, in return? If one is inclined to answer "yes" to these questions, then one's conception of rules corresponds to the *lex talionis* conception of law as an eye-for-an-eye and tooth-for-a-tooth affair. However, if one's moral sensitivities are offended by such practices (and Bok's would be), then the notion of rule is governed more by a deontological conception of what is right. (In ethical theory, deontology is the view that takes duty as the basis of morality. Kant's ethics, in addition to Bok's, are good examples.) One might be inclined, from this point of view, to say that retaliatory cheating is just a further corruption of the sports world. It is a further erosion of the trust and honesty built into games. Below is a good example of this kind of cheating:

"Sure I hit guys on purpose," Don Drysdale said, when asked about the 154 batters struck by his pitches when he played for the Brooklyn and Los Angeles Dodgers. "When I knew they [opposing pitchers] hit our guys on purpose, I had a rule—a 2-for-1 rule—two of theirs went down for every one of ours."[24]

So the question of justifiable cheating becomes a question of the function and kind of moral rules that lie behind one's action. That is, is the moral rule to be interpreted within a retributive or a deontological framework? Such a framework is an element in an individual's philosophical perspective on sport. Obviously, Drysdale, for one, looks at such situations from a retributive point of view.

The second case we are asked about is whether there is such a thing as unintentional cheating. Gert (pp. 108–109) claims repeatedly that there is not. However, in the next section, I will produce cases from sport which I think show that one can reasonably label some instances of cheating as unintentional. Moreover, the question of intentionality is of central importance in arbitrating cases of possible cheating in games—something that many writers on the subject have overlooked or are unaware of. These are in need of analysis.

Gert claims that there is no such thing as unintentional cheating, primarily because one is expected to take reasonable care not to break or violate the standards or rules governing the activity in question. This notion of "reasonable care" is sufficient for such cheating to be a subclass of "intentional" or, at least, antithetical to "unintentional." Gert describes a case in which one breaks a rule unintentionally or unknowingly, discovers it later, but does nothing about it. Would he call such a case unintentional cheating? The case does involve deception, which many instances of cheating have, because there is concealment of the fact. But does it fit Gert's previous provisional characterization of cheating? It does not seem to, because the violation of standards in order to attain goals is a sort of violation that needs to be made consciously. In other words, one's motive or reason for cheating is to obtain the prize or to win. So if one consciously or otherwise violates the standards this way, then this is clearly what we mean by cheating. But this may be a question of semantics or of the way in which we categorize phenomena. I agree with Gert about not being sure whether to call such a case cheating, or unintentional rule-breaking, or possibly neither.

Uncertainty leads us to look briefly at another example. Suppose in playing a hand of bridge I think I am void of the suit just led, and so I slough cards in another suit. Then I come to discover that I have one card remaining in the initial suit. Was I cheating when I sloughed those cards; or was the act an instance of cheating only upon my discovery of that singleton in the given suit; or do I cheat if and only if I do not reveal what I have done? These questions raise what can be called the time lapse issue. In this instance, I may not have cheated earlier in sloughing the cards, but would be cheating later by remaining silent, after I discovered the singleton in the suit I thought was void. The time lapse issue is an interesting one, but it is one we shall put aside for now.

One last item in Gert's analysis requires discussion. He takes cheating to be the model for immoral action in general. This is clearly reflected in his definitions.

> (D1)   Cheating in its basic form involves violating the standards of an activity that one is participating in voluntarily in order to gain some advantage over others participating in that activity.

And,

> (D2)   Cheating is participating in a voluntary activity and acting in a way that all rational persons participating in that activity would publicly advocate that no one act.

Thus one needs only to remove the reference to voluntary activity to get a general definition of immoral action.

Lueschen (p. 7) has provided us with a definition that reflects game-playing:

> (D3)   Cheating in sport is the act through which the manifestly or latently agreed-upon conditions for winning such a contest are changed in favor of one side.

Lueschen states further that accidental violations of rules and norms do not qualify as cheating because such acts are neither intended nor planned. So the phrase "the act" (D3) omits accidental, unintentional, or unplanned actions from the domain of cheating. I shall argue that this definitional omission is incorrect. I believe that there are actions that do fit these exclusions. Further we must ask how it is that the conditions are changed in favor of one side. It seems evident that many conditions change, but only some changes constitute cheating. So a revision—an additional qualification something like that contained in (D1) and (D2)—is needed. A composite, formal account, then, will look like this:

(D4)   An agent J *cheated* at doing an A if and only if:
    (i)   J intentionally did an A; or
    (ii)   J unintentionally did an A;
    where *doing an* A is (was) an act through which the constitutive or regulative rules and conditions for winning a contest are (were) changed in favor of one side.

The way in which this action is accomplished is covered by the two clauses. Clause (i) covers J's belief(s), purpose(s), reason(s) for doing some A. Clause (ii) covers those cases in which J has some level of awareness, but in which J does not consciously connect[25] himself or herself as the agent who brings about an A. As Lawrence Davis puts it: "A person may do an A and know [in the sense of awareness] that he is doing an A, yet *not* be doing an A intentionally."[26] Davis's assertion would appear contradictory only if "knowing" were construed as a conscious state or act upon the part of J. Let us look at an example.

A member of a tennis team of an eastern state university is told by the coach that if she does not stop calling her opponent's good serves out in crucial games during a match, she will be removed from the roster. (The player sincerely believes that she does not cheat.) After such an incident with the coach, the player's calls improve. This case illustrates what I mean by "awareness," in that any given agent can modify his or her actions or behavior; in this sense one "knows" that he or she is cheating. We can refer to this as the principle of modifiability. In contrast, consciously knowing an A while doing an A excludes the possibility of there not having been a decision or other definite formation of intention on the part of J. We can add to this another refinement from Davis in that "it is possible to intend to do an A without caring at all whether, or when, one will succeed" (p. 74). If caring is associated with intending, this prevents the act from being unintentional. However, Davis separates "J intending to do an A" from "J caring about an A." In this instance caring is a second-order activity—something done by J when intending to do an A. So "Acting intentionally must be sharply distinguished from intending," again following Davis's exposition (p. 59). The sentences "J intended to do an A" and "J acted intentionally to bring about an A" have different analyses. The first sentence permits cases like the tennis player's actions. We can attribute intending to an agent's act without being committed to saying that "J acted intentionally in doing an A." Consequently Davis's analysis of intention makes room for the sorts of cases I am interested in here.

It makes sense to say that "agent J is perfectly confident that he is playing straight, and that he has not discovered that he is cheating his opponents." The argument I develop for clause (ii) in (D4) is in accord with the generalization that all human actions are volitions or desires and intentions, the word "intentions" conveying, among other things, the meanings of the verb "intending." Part of the confusion here lies in the extreme economy of the English language, which cuts across important conceptual distinctions and does not reflect them semantically. (D1) fits closer to the description in (D3) than does (D2) because rationality does not fit prominently into the picture due to the conditions stated in the second clause. The reason for this can be seen in Davis's account: "Volitions are attempts, and attempts—tryings—are doings" (p. 17); this class of actions contrasts with desires, which are states. (This characterization of desire looms large in my analysis later.) In addition, (D2) is stated negatively, which is something of a definitional defect; it also reflects more the social constraints on participants, rather than being a description of the behavior prescribed by rules. Also (D4) is a revision of (D3) with the above considerations.

III

WE FIND, in instances of cheating in games and sport, some interesting characteristics that do not show up in the standard analysis.

For one thing, we frequently find that when cheating is reported or alleged in the newspapers, the word is set off in quotation marks. This is no accident on the part of sportswriters, for they purposely draw attention to the fact that a given case is controversial. In the 1978 Indianapolis 500 race, Johnny Rutherford claimed that two qualifiers pulled away from the field under the yellow caution flag.[27] (Drivers are supposed to slow to 80 miles per hour and not try to improve their standing during yellow caution periods.) In the 1981 Indy 500, Andretti, Johncock, and Foyt claimed that Unser "bent the rules" by passing seven cars under a yellow caution flag instead of blending into the traffic after a pit stop. In these instances it seems quite appropriate to ask questions about intention and deliberateness. In an activity like automobile racing, where one's energies, concentration, total awareness, and actions are caught up in driving in the race itself, one could improve his or her standing without intending to do so. One of the elementary aims of racing is to improve one's position, and the driving that results in the completion of this goal is not totally or consciously controlled. Racing consists of a complex set of habits and physical skills that are more closely related to perception than to thought. Because of this, it is quite possible that the drivers would refuse to concede that they had intentionally cheated. Cheating is an *interpretation* of an action or event—not an action or event itself, or one action or event superimposed on another. Remember Rutherford said he *saw* cheating.

Is my account of cheating here plausible? Do people really distinguish between intentional and unintentional cheating? Why talk about "intentional cheating" unless one thinks other varieties of cheating exist? Surely people think that this is an important qualification, and that the addition of the adjective does supply information and is not redundant.[28]

Let me give an example of unintentional cheating from the game of tennis. Some years ago I watched a Men's 45 singles final. The two gentlemen were involved in a close match and were in the third and final set. After a few games in the third set, one of the players signaled the other to the net. There he told his opponent that he knew he would not intentionally cheat him, but that he had best watch his line calls. He added that he was going to beat him (his opponent) anyway, regardless of the calls, which he did. After the match the loser complimented the winner on playing a fine match and said that he hadn't given the winner anything—that the winner had earned the win. An example like this clearly shows that perceptions are alterable by thought. If a player is even so much as accused of cheating, he or she will usually "monitor" his or her calls or actions.

Let us turn to a famous, ambiguous case from the game of baseball. In the 1978 World Series, controversy erupted in the game that evened the Series at 2-2 between the New York Yankees and the Los Angeles Dodgers, who eventually lost the Series. Sportswriter Hal Bock detailed the crucial play at the center of the controversy:

> With the score 3-1 and runners at first and second, Piniella lined a shot to the shortstop side of second base. Bill Russell gloved the ball for a moment and it seemed like a sure double play with Munson trapped off second base. / But then Russell dropped the ball. He recovered in time to step on second and it appeared he still might complete the double play with a throw to first. But the throw struck [Reggie] Jackson, who had ventured only a few feet off first, in the right leg and bounced away. / That allowed Munson to score. The Dodgers argued that Jackson had interfered with the throw, but the umpires disagreed. It was ruled a fielder's choice and Russell got an error on the throw. / "Reggie saw the ball coming," said Russell. "He moved right into it. That's interference." / First base umpire Frank Pulli of the National League understood Russell's argument. / "I couldn't tell whether Jackson intentionally interfered with the ball or not," he said. "I was back maybe 15 feet because there is the possibility of a double play happening and I take that call in fair territory. If he moves in the way of the ball, then we have intentional interference."[29]

It is interesting to note that the rule describing interference (7.09) makes no reference to intentions. It simply states that when any batter or runner who has just been thrown out hinders or impedes any following play, the player on the following play shall be declared out for interference. Pulli was asked to comment on the rule and said: "There has to be intent in the judgment of the umpire." Why did Pulli think this to be so? Probably because there has to be something on which to base a decision; that is, one needs to have some sort of evidence in order to make a judgment or an interpretation of such actions. For Pulli, intention was the best criterion for distinguishing between interference and noninterference. However, Dodgers' manager Lasorda was incensed by the call and claimed that Jackson's move was interference: "He stood there. He's got to get out of the way."[30] But Jackson did not.

This incident inspires a whole series of questions. Why didn't Jackson move? (Here we can apply Gert's "reasonable care" clause.) He may have thought that he did not have to move because Russell had dropped the ball, and consequently, there would not be enough time for a double play. Did Russell's actions lead (or mislead) Jackson to do what he did? Russell said: "I didn't drop the ball intentionally. You can't think that quickly. If I had had time to think, I would have dropped it on purpose."[31] Might this have confused Jackson? Further, if a player confuses another, does that nullify the chance that the other player will draw a penalty? Who is responsible here, Jackson or Russell? Should the Dodgers have been awarded the double play, or should Munson have been brought back to the base from which he started? The umpires, as usual, had the last word, so Pulli's controversial judgment call stood. This is about as clear as mud; it shows that the rules of baseball leave great room for interpretation, and perhaps need careful rewording to avoid situations like this.

What is interesting about this case is the question of whether certain actions are intentional or not. Russell's comment suggests that one of the characteristics of unintentional actions is the element of time. Most games are simply too fast for actions to be accounted for in terms of intention, where the meaning of "intention" covers deliberate, purposive, calculated, conscious actions on the part of the agent.[32] Perhaps here the umpire Pulli was relying on a concept that did not apply. If not, we at least need to draw a distinction between intentional and unintentional actions in order to make the rules clearer in cases like this. (The chapters in part III will help to clarify the mix of conscious/unconscious and intentional/unintentional in sport actions.) And yet there are actions that nonetheless should be labeled as "interference" or "cheating." In other words, I claim that Jackson interfered—that he cheated, but perhaps unintentionally. Reggie's action had the effect of controlling the outcome of the game. Jackson was already out, so why wouldn't he have done what he did? No other penalty would have been assessable. See (D4) for more details. But maybe Jackson just standing there was the result of not paying attention to the matters at hand. So he still cheated because he should have been paying attention in a situation where the game was riding on that particular play.

Now let us consider some borderline cases to the above philosophic considerations pertaining to unintentional cheating. Dan Jenkins reported an incident in golf that occurred at the 1979 Arbor Day Open.[33] Golf professional Lon Hinkle took a shortcut on the number eight hole; instead of driving conventionally down the 528-yard, par 5 hole, he drove down the adjacent seventeenth fairway and from there hit a couple of low iron shots, shortening the hole by 75 yards. He birdied it repeatedly. Was this cheating? We would generally answer negatively in cases like this because they are numerous in the world of sport and appear not to violate any regulations. Hinkle had simply "outsmarted" the USPGA officials (the rule makers or enforcers). One is expected to follow the particular layout of the golf course, but Hinkle chose not to. Obviously, the officials did not interpret Hinkle's ploy as cheating because they simply set up obstacles; for example, a 25-foot Black Hills spruce tree was planted in the gap that allowed the shortcut during the championship. (This kind of measure had never been taken before in the history of golf!) This was done to "protect the integrity" of the eighth hole. If instances such as this were to become numerous enough, the USPGA might be led to establish a rule stating that players must follow the layout of the holes on the course. In that event, subsequent similar episodes would be labeled as "cheating." The conditions or rules for cheating stipulated in (D4) are absent in Hinkle's tree incident. Further institutionalization of the conditions surrounding this case would be required for cheating to be identified. One wonders why the Arbor Day Open officials went to so much trouble when they could have stipulated a rule that would have done the job much better than their tree-planting did.

A more recent case is Greg Norman, the Australian pro golfer, who disqualified himself from the $625,000 Daikyo Palm Meadows Cup held in Brisbane, Australia, during the second week of January 1990. Norman stunned tournament officials when he said he had breached Royal and Ancient rules by taking illegal relief during his opening round. Several days after playing this round he was advised that he had been in breach of the rules. "I had no intention of deliberately cheating," said Norman. He had hit his tee shot into the water on the tenth fairway and *believed* he was entitled to take total relief from what he *thought* was a lateral water hazard.[34]

Thus far we have mainly discussed participants. But what about the spectators and umpires who also enter into play? Their behavior can affect the environment of the game, sometimes unfairly so, and this can be viewed as a form of cheating. Tennis players who are not European dread playing in the Italian and French Opens because of the biased crowds and officiating. This raises the question of whether *rooting* (Novak's category, see his ch. 9), in its extreme form, should be viewed as cheating. This aspect of sport can be corrupted and distorted beyond permissible limits, just as the others can be.[35] During the 1980 football season, television announcers informed the viewers that they could expect calls to go the way of the home team. Has pressure from the fans and players on the referees resulted in a subtle form of cheating? It appears to be just that; in addition, as we see next, there are other subtle forms of cheating.

If players keep their mouths shut, are they cheating? Suppose an infielder misses a tag, yet the umpire mistakenly calls the runner out.[36] Is the player cheating by saying nothing, or is it that the arbiter's word is law, and a player who confessed to the miss would then be cheating his or her team? On the other hand, arbiters in sport are present to eliminate or minimize cheating. They do not let Connors or McEnroe make their own calls in tennis matches. But Connors and McEnroe try nonetheless to influence the arbiters by their antics, and in the worst incidents, attempt to make their own calls anyway. Behavior like this is just another form of corruption in the world of sport.

IV

IF the tennis players, race car drivers, or baseball players did not intentionally cheat, then what happened that would allow a plausible interpretation of these actions? Precisely what did they do? In answering these questions, our concern may not be simply whether they intentionally cheated or not. Pearson's discussion of deception, sportsmanship, and ethics hinges on the criterion of intentionality—whether actions like fouling are committed accidentally or deliberately.[37] She asserts that "the intentional commission of a foul in athletics is an unethical act" (p. 461). Deliberate interference is the standard she proposes for judging whether a given action A is to be considered as cheating or not. Lueschen (p. 68) and McIntosh[38] are others who adopt the same criterion. All of this is too neat, however; the more complicated, interesting cases are left unaccounted for by this criterion.

Perhaps the kind of cheating covered under clause (ii) of (D4)—unintentional cheating—is an example of what Davis (p. 72) calls *irresolute behavior*; a person intends to do an A, yet fails to do so when the time comes, even though nothing has prevented the action or changed his mind. This characterization would surely cover some instances, but obviously not others, such as the case of the tennis player and her coach in which the player was not consciously aware of her behavior, but was able to modify it on subsequent occasions. Other acts would not qualify as irresolute behavior either; therefore, it is necessary to look elsewhere.

One proposal suggests that some acts may be more intentional than others.[39] We do talk about firm intentions, final intentions, and primary intentions, but "not about impossible or utopian intentions."[40] There can be other qualifications, too; for example, "momentary" intentions. There may be degrees of intention as well, but even this does not provide an adequate answer. The notice of degrees of intention is much too complicated and conjectural to be considered here. For the sake of argument, we can agree with the

71

premise shared by the theorists that a given action A is either intentional or it is not.

By "unintentional" acts, I do not mean that agent J performed actions accidentally or contrary to J's intentions. Obviously, one cannot cheat accidentally. It would be absurd for a cheater to respond, "Yes, I did cheat, but look here, it was an accident or a mistake." The cases of unintentional cheating I am considering are not ones of "mistaken" intentions, either, even if it makes sense to talk about mistaken intentions (and I think there are serious objections to accepting this as a species of intentions). What I wish to illustrate by these cases is that instances of cheating occur in which there is some awareness yet no intention of doing it, and perhaps no intention of not doing it.[41] One can act from ignorance in such cases, yet some degree of awareness must be ascribed to the agent. By "unintentional," I also wish to refer to instances of action sentences such as "I intended not to cheat, but I did anyway."

In cases like the ones previously cited, tennis players really do see, or think they see, the ball out; whereas, in fact, it lands on the line or inside it. How can this be possible? Perception is not something objective—totally void of subjectivity—that we passively register at the appropriate moments.[42] Rather, perception is conditioned by our interest in and the intensity of our experience at that given moment. Individuals can be so absorbed in the sport experience at hand, with winning and accomplishment foremost in their minds, that they "color" what they see, thus determining how they call the shots or the plays. This "fact" is acknowledged by Nick Powell in his Code: "Some players will insist that on occasion even though a ball is good they want it to be out so badly that they will unconsciously call it out."[43] Foot faulting in tennis is another good example. Players who foot fault may not know or even think that this is what they are doing. As Powell says, "Foot faulting is just as surely cheating as is making a *deliberate* bad line call" (p. 4, my italics). However, it may not be the case that we can automatically ascribe intention to an alleged case of cheating, in the sense that the violation occurred deliberately, knowingly, or consciously. If the ascription of the intent to cheat is immediately made, then this overlooks an important element in the sport experience. As Ortega y Gasset reminds us in *Meditations on Hunting*, the experience of hunting and its analysis is to be found in the notion of the hunt—not in focusing on the hunter or the hunted.[44] I think the same applies here to understanding cheating and its related question of intention. It is the action itself that should be at the center of discussion, and the other elements linked to it—not the other way around.

The sport experience may be an all-absorbing one that has as its ruling passion the fruits of victory, thus demanding one's total energies and attention. One becomes an instrument of the game, ceasing to consciously and deliberately carry out the mechanics of play. Such a state will influence one's perceptions and actions at that time. Because of this, the sport experience can be "ambiguous"; that is, during the experience things can be altered without one knowing it. Sport is not so tidy that we can label a given act as intentional simply because it is an instance of "cheating." Experiences—especially sport experiences that are close to what psychologist Maslow called "peak" experiences[45]—are more complex and intense. Cases such as those presented in section III of this chapter are good examples of this situation. In situations like these, I think it is appropriate to ask whether an alleged incident of cheating was intentional or not. Or perhaps those who have to rule in situations like these should try to determine whether such actions are intentional or not. Either instance of cheating (intentional or unintentional) is blameworthy; but one is more excusable than the other. Perhaps a less severe penalty should be drawn for unintentional cheating. Still, cheating is a morally questionable type of action; the player cannot escape responsibility by claiming that he or she did not do it intentionally.[46] This ploy in moral reasoning is a *non sequitur*, a fallacy.

Next we need to consider the problem of people who just don't see straight. In response to this, I am reminded of Barry Tarshis's little tennis tale:

> I remember watching a couple of 13-year-olds play in a tournament last summer, and I mentioned to the woman beside me that one of the boys just made a terrible call on a deep forehand.

73

/ "I know," she said. "He's my son." / "Oh," I said. "How come you never say anything to him?" / "He can't help himself," she said. "He has a perceptual problem. But don't worry. He calls as many against himself as he does against the other player." / And you know something? She was right. (p. 74)

She may indeed have been correct, but this did nothing toward solving his perceptual problem. We may feel a certain amount of sympathy for the youth, but just as individuals must be held responsible for their problems, this boy and his parent should have been responsible for his, too. Perhaps with the right help, he could improve his perception.

Playing the game with intensity can have an effect on a player's ability to see, call, and make decisions involving the outcome of the game. This applies to the race car incident and others mentioned earlier. Moreover, these episodes are not isolated instances that rarely occur; the same point applies throughout the realm of sport. The issue of cheating in a given game or sport is usually controversial and difficult to resolve adequately for the parties concerned. Determining intention, I submit again, is not one of the ways leading to resolution. It does, however, establish the degree to which we are to hold the individual responsible. There may not be degrees of intention, but there are degrees of responsibility that we can assign to actions. Some acts of cheating are more morally reprehensible than others. A violation of a rule or of some standard in a game may result from actions that are unintentional and nondeliberate, yet irresponsible and blameworthy.

Within the context of sport, what are the consequences of my argument for the standard analysis? One is that the link between cheating and ethics, or more specifically, immoral action, is not as close as has been supposed. The traditional literature has us believing that correct definitions of cheating are ones like "sinning against the gospel of sportsmanship."[47] With a long history of thinking like this, it is not too surprising to find Gert (p. 110) suggesting that cheating provides in miniature the nature of immoral action. This may be true so long as we look at the kind of cases Gert examines, but not all cases lend themselves to this moral analysis. I am not sure

74

whether standard ethical practices enter into this at all; or, if they do, perhaps only to a small degree. I have tried to supply other kinds of cases from the sports world, which would illustrate the difficulty of imposing such standards. Should we look with moral indignation upon the player who cheats in order to make the opponent stop cheating him or her? No, we might not; we might take this action as an attempt to *restore* the play world. (Restoration is the subject of the next chapter.) The restoration might be thought of as more important than the specific act of cheating that brought it about. This may serve as a reminder that a player needs to take more reasonable care in making calls, keeping score, maintaining his or her standing in a race, or arriving at other game decisions. This situation recalls Gert's original condition of "reasonable care," but this time it is not linked to "intentions" in the conscious, deliberate sense. It also makes us pause to reflect on the deontological position; that is, that an individual would not cheat because it is his or her duty not to.

There seems to be a conceptual domain between acts of cheating and acts that are not. We can carefully distinguish between actions whose agents are *responsible* for doing an A and those that are *accountable* for doing an A.[48] An illustration of accountability in sport can again be taken from the game of tennis: Suppose that an individual plays carelessly, paying little attention to the regulative rules (for example, serving behind the baseline), and distracts his or her opponent by talking during play, thus demonstrating little or no regard for the strict enforcement of the rules of the game. This individual is a weekend player who plays just to fill some free time and to have a good time. He or she does not really try to win the points, games, or match, but is interested only in trying odd spin shots and the like.

My suggestion is that this type of player be held accountable, but not responsible, for the same violations that the regular player is. The regular player, responsible for breaking the rules, is considered to be a cheater. But if a player is held to be only accountable for breaking rules, is he or she then also what we would call a cheat? This is a difficult question to answer because the participant is not adhering strictly to either the means (the rules) or the end (winning the game). The cheat, as Suits (pp. 36, 46) puts it, is not really playing the game, because his or her behavior exemplifies an excess of zeal in seeking to achieve the prelusory goal; that is, his or her desire to achieve the prelusory condition, the condition that stipulates winning, is so great that he or she violates the rules of the game. Suits distinguishes between two types of goals: prelusory and lusory. The first are actions that have to be done in order to win; for example, crossing a finish line in races or capturing a certain number of tricks in bridge. And the second are the ends that really characterize game-playing; that is, trying to win or playing the game. A player must exhibit a lusory attitude toward the rules of the game in order for his or her actions to be considered playing. He or she must not be just following the rules of the game, but consciously and intently applying those rules to the playing situations in which he or she finds himself or herself. In actions implying accountability, other excesses are present besides the prelusory goal in cheating situations. In urban adult softball games, fun and camaraderie are in excess, too, which seems to balance out the single-mindedness of the cheat in overbalancing the other elements of the game. If participants (that is, opponents) view fun and camaraderie as cheating, then the other team has learned something about the attitude of its opponents; namely, that the former team—the team who views these actions as cheating—is taking the game more seriously than the latter team and that their excesses are not viewed as fun and camaraderie, but as cheating. Such a situation would propel the game back into its competitive structure, balancing the gaming attitudes, and perhaps restoring the world of sport to a less chaotic affair.

Is (D4) out of the mainstream of philosophic thought on sport? I do not think so. My analysis and definition is compatible with Suits's explanation of cheats in game-playing. The cheater's desire to achieve the lusory goal of winning (whatever counts as winning) is so great that he violates the rules of the game in order to do so. However, "violation," for Suits (pp. 161, 77, for examples), seems to be interpreted along the lines of "intentional behavior." "Cheats," according to Suits, "are pursuing a goal whose attainment overrides obedience to the rules" (p. 147), where the overriding concern is something consciously aimed at, something done purposely. Here, volitional action is discussed in the context of beliefs and reasons. If this is what Suits takes intentions and desires to be—emphasizing their cognitive dimension—then this account of cheating is different from my own. It is the noncognitive aspect of desire I wish to draw attention to in this chapter, specifically in clause (ii) of (D4). I follow Davis's lead in understanding desire to be primarily a state rather than mere doings (p. 17). In any event, Suits's treatment of cheating has affinities with my own because of the emphasis upon excesses and desires.

Weiss and Weiss (in note 22) speak of cheating, lying, and violating the ordinary code, all in the same breath. Suits claims: "In terms of their dependence upon institutions, cheaters at games are precisely like liars in everyday life" (p. 46). Is this the case? Let us look briefly at Bok's study of lying to see if this is so. I shall examine lying in relation to what has been established here on cheating, since, curiously enough, Bok does not deal with cheating at all in her discussion. Admittedly, the two concepts have some things in common. Her major description of lying, like others that have dealt with cheating, involves the notion of intention: "A lie is any intentionally deceptive message which is stated." Further, "All deceptive messages, whether or not they are lies, can also be more or less affected by self-deception, by error, and by variations in the actual intention to deceive." These three factors she calls "filters," and to complicate matters further, suggests that individuals can work to deceive others by manipulating them in subtle and discreet ways, "until it [a deceptive message] is almost unrecognizable even though no one may have intended to deceive" (pp. 13, 15, 16).

This last situation, perhaps, parallels instances of unintentional cheating. Recruiting in collegiate football is a good example: here the corruption and confusion running throughout the system regulating the sport permits much of a morally questionable nature to be passed off as part of the system. This is only a "parallel" situation, however. Most of Bok's analysis corresponds to clause (i) of (D4). Deception is integral to lying. Clause (ii) reflects actions and circumstances that fall outside of her framework for lying. Yet there is a class of actions that fits an area covered by clause (ii). This area is dubbed "moral shortcomings" and is best described by Patrick Nowell-Smith. He makes the following relevant comment on moral responsibility and appraisal, using a golfer as his example:

> The player might have been bribed by the other side and have missed the putt on purpose, while pretending to try his hardest. Or, knowing that it was a critical shot in an important match, he may have been culpably negligent in its execution. (Negligence of this sort, thoughtlessness, lack of consideration, failure to see something in a situation that is morally relevant—all these, though different, belong in the same bag, and it is a bag which philosophers have not examined as carefully as they should; for nine tenths of our moral shortcomings will be found in it.)[49]

We have seen that much of cheating amounts to negligence in one form or another. In keeping with Nowell-Smith's example, let us take another example from the world of golf. In the 1980 Tournament of Champions, Tom Watson gave Lee Trevino a tip that he was playing the ball too far forward in his stance, and a microphone on Trevino's caddie picked it up, relaying the message throughout the television audience. Immediately a viewer phoned the country club and asked officials about the legality of such advice. PGA tour director Tuthill questioned Watson, then assessed him a 2-stroke penalty. But because Watson led by 5 strokes over the second-place finisher, he retained his title. Bob Green recounts the discussion about the incident afterward with the champion: "'It's a violation of the rules,' said Watson, accepting the penalty graciously. '*I just wasn't thinking.* If I'd led by one, I would not have won. The rules are there to follow. I violated them. It's a violation of the advice rule.'"[50] Watson added that he had done this out of kindness to Trevino. They are good friends and frequently play practice rounds together. Did Watson succumb to kindness? Is this why he was not thinking? Possibly. Here again we have a case in which wants or desires and emotions play a role in human actions, possibly taking precedence over more cognitive or rational activities. It seems that an emotion—kindness—was aroused, and complicated the situation by providing a possible motive for Watson's action. Even if this were not his motive, it is a likely analysis of what could have taken place. His thoughtlessness, carelessness—whatever it was—could have been brought about by emotions or desires. Part of the account of unintentional cheating would be explained by descriptions similar to the one I have given above.

This is surely the case in Andretti's reasoning as to why Bobby Unser did what he did in the 1981 Indy 500 race. Andretti said he could sympathize with Unser's denial of wrongdoing because he had had a victory taken away in the 1978 Italian Grand Prix, when he had wanted to win so badly because his teammate Ronnie Peterson had been killed earlier in the race. Andretti was reported as saying: "What can you say about a situation like this? You feel sorry for Bobby, yet he's not a rookie and you would expect he would know the rules. Maybe he wasn't thinking about it [when he came out of the pits]." Like Watson, in the above example, Unser did not think about the legitimacy of his actions; he had other things on his mind. (Instances of Nowell-Smith's moral shortcomings.)

In some instances cheating seems to be socially approved; retaliatory cheating is a good example. This kind of cheating involves a covert set of norms, because established social norms dictate against it. But we also find cases where "justified" cheating is approved. This is rather like "beating the system"; as Moody puts it, we see a David versus Goliath attitude on the part of many people who approve of such actions (p. 11). In short, cheating may be socially acceptable, and it goes almost without saying that just because a given action is labeled as cheating does not imply that the action is disapproved by others.

Two related issues on cheating need to be brought into sharper focus. One is the question of whether or not cheating occurs within the confines of the game, or conversely, whether cheating involves an imposition of something outside of or foreign to it upon the game. The second, related issue is the problem of evil. Is evil an integral part of sport, something that is ritualized and mysteriously celebrated in games, as Novak (ch. 16) suggests? Or is evil something that has nothing to do with sport? Some (Caillois, for example, pp. 64–65, 131), think that moral matters and problems have no part in the sacred playground where sport is performed.

I agree with Novak that evil is indeed present in sport, and even ritualized; for example, in various intense, emotive acts of violence in hockey, rugby, and football. As a consequence, cheating is a phenomenon integral to sport and is to be viewed within its rule structure. We reveal what we are and who we are just as much in play as we do in everyday matters. Perhaps we reveal even more of ourselves in play, because we are called upon to make decisions that do have moral import. To play fairly is to play by the rules, but this also informs us of the character of the player. Therefore, sport has a personal as well as a social dimension. Unfairness, like equality, is built into games, which are not exempt from evil (see, for instance, Truly, in note 28, p. D1). Cruelty manifests itself here just as it does in ordinary life.

I now wish to return to the question of figurative meaning. Examples of extended uses of "cheating" are not too difficult to find in the sports media. Let us look briefly at one from baseball. Rick Burleson of the Boston Red Sox said that he "cheated" to make the hard ones look easy:

> "I cheat," he said. "I cheat a lot. I know most of the hitters and pitchers now, and their tendencies. If I suspect something, I'll cheat over and most of the time I don't get caught going the wrong way. I like to think that I'm among the top three or four shortstops, in the American League, anyway."[51]

Burleson's actions do not satisfy the requirements of (D4), for there is no violation of games rules or established conventions. Although he may hedge on certain spatial restrictions normally accepted for a shortstop, this is part of knowing the position and playing it well. He is simply anticipating the play, which good shortstops are supposed to do. As Pearson (p. 460) states, this is just strategic deception—something not only permitted but encouraged in games. Actions of this sort are to be distinguished from those acts covered under clauses (i) and (ii) in (D4). In this instance, Burleson merely substituted the word "cheat" for "move" or "poach." He has used the word metaphorically and most of us know what he means.

In ordinary life we find that cheating grows with increased regulation and expands with technology, which has as its by-products social complexity and impersonal accountability. The more rules governing social institutions, like welfare, that we have, the more people try to defraud those institutions. Even the computer may be misused for this purpose (Moody, p. 12). However, such instances reflect the actions covered under clause (i). What about clause (ii)? Do we find any parallel instances in everyday life? Can self-deception "cancel out" intentions such that acts of cheating would fit clause (ii)? Could increased competition in schools and the marketplace become so intense that cheating would be accounted for (especially by lawyers) in a fashion similar to the cheating in these sport examples? These are thorny questions to answer. The intensity of emotions and the way in which they "color" actions would be one element of an adequate answer. Another would be the amount of responsibility one ascribes to agents who experience such emotional intensity and thus display excesses in their activities. Will these cases be treated someday by courts of law in the same way as temporary insanity pleas? Are they emerging as another sort of crime of passion? Perhaps cheating will be distinguished like killing: Is a given case L to be considered as murder or as manslaughter? Perhaps the way these instances are handled in the sports world will be an indication of how they will be handled in everyday life and the law.[52]

At this point, a summary of the previous analysis in relation to (D4) is appropriate. An agent J cheats at doing an A if and only if the doing of an A (whether intentionally done or unintentionally done) is an action through which the constitutive or regulative rules or conditions for winning a contest are changed in favor of one side. Notice that the case of self-cheating is covered because the definition does not report whether the change is in the cheater's or the opponent's favor. Also, the conditions for winning a contest can be interpreted broadly enough (see note 12) to include challenge- or excellence-oriented activities where they can be conceived of as "competitive" or as a contest with oneself. These would be extended, metaphorical senses of "cheating," but legitimate uses nevertheless. "Winning" would be construed as "challenging" or "excelling." The extended senses change the notion of cheating drastically, however, because some activities in nature sports become ones that could be loosely labeled as "cheating." But in the

81

strict sense of contest, activities conceptually associated with cheating are those games Caillois classifies under the categories of *agôn*, *alea*, or the *agôn-alea* combination.

The last items to summarize in the definition are the clauses on intentionally and unintentionally doing an A in acts of cheating. It is not claimed that all acts of cheating are jointly exhausted by the distinction between intentional and unintentional acts. There may well be a realm between these two domains. The distinction drawn in (D4) is centered on whether or not an agent J identifies himself or herself with the action being performed. This description is general enough to allow a diverse number of actions to fall under the ascription of unintentionally doing an A. This may be because J does not believe he or she has done an A, or J was not thinking about the game when A occurred, or J's lack of reasonable care resulted in an A, or J's excess of desire to obtain the given end resulted in an A occurring. These linguistic variations are but a few possible formulations of the sort of actions and situations that may fall under the category of unintentional actions. They form what I think are some of the most interesting examples of cheating.[53] And because they are related to other important ideas in the world of sport, they are worthy of philosophical analysis. Some of these other ideas will be described and analyzed in subsequent chapters.

FOUR

The Preservation of Sport

I

IN ORDER to discuss which ethical values are to be preserved or restored, we need to address some fundamental questions on the nature of sport. Especially we need to discuss (i) the purpose or end (in the teleological sense) of sport and (ii) the experiential method for attaining that end. To assist me in the former task, I call upon Aristotle.[1] Our initial question, then, becomes: What is the final cause of sport? Is it victory, as Keating (p. 20) says it is? To answer these two questions, we need to pause and to look briefly at Aristotle's doctrine of four causes. To know X, for Aristotle, is to know by means of causes the necessary elements of X, whether the X under investigation is a natural or an artificial object. In Book III, Chapter 3 of the *Physics*, Aristotle enumerates the four senses of "cause":

> In one sense, then, (1) that out of which a thing comes to be and which persists, is called 'cause', e.g. the bronze of the statue, the silver of the bowl, and the genera of which the bronze and the silver are species. [This is the *material* cause.] In another sense (2) the form or the archetype, i.e. the statement of the essence, and its genera, are called 'causes', e.g. of the octave the relation of 2:1, and generally number, and the parts in the definition. [This is the *formal* cause.] Again (3) the primary source of the change or coming to rest; e.g. the man who gave advice is a cause, the father is cause of the child, and generally what makes of what is made and what causes change of what is

changed. [This is the *efficient* cause.] Again (4) in the sense of end or 'that for the sake of which' a thing is done, e.g. health is the cause of walking about. ('Why is he walking about?' we say. 'To be healthy', and, having said that, we think we have assigned the cause.) [This is the *final* cause.][2]

G. B. Kerferd characterizes Aristotle's doctrine, using only Aristotle's first illustration throughout: "the material cause deals with the substrate, such as the bronze of a statue, while the formal cause is concerned with the shape of the statue. The final cause is the end or purpose for the sake of which the process of making the statue was commenced, and the efficient cause is that which initiates the process of change and so is its primary source."[3] Why would a statue be commenced? The most obvious answers would be to honor someone or something, to celebrate something, or to create something to appreciate or to enjoy. Any of these reasons would contribute to living well or to the civilized life for Aristotle. Let us look at another example, that of a city. Aristotle's analysis would proceed in the following manner. The matter or the stuff of a city would be the people. The form or plan would be its organization. The demographic data and plans plus various urban boundaries would be the formal cause. The final cause is living, or better yet, living well. Now only with the final cause in mind can we begin to give a decent description of the efficient cause. It would be, of course, the realization or acceptance of the final cause as desirable by most of the people. This urban example sheds light on how to analyze sport using Aristotelian categories.

The matter and form would be the same for sport as it is for city. The material cause would be the people. Pushing this category, one might want to include the equipment, the physical space or environment, and so forth. The formal cause would be the organization of the people involved. This would be the making of a team from an aggregate of individuals. With the execution of plans and strategies comes the unity and harmony of individuals' movements to form teams. Or in individual sports, a person is transformed into a player. The final cause, I submit, would be playing—playing well. Thinking of a city as a place where individuals merely survive is analogous to thinking of game-playing as an activity leading only to winning. This is an impoverished view of sport. Winning is only one of the consequences of playing well. Playing well enhances the quality of life for both spectators and participants. And how is this accomplished? One way to answer this question would be to view sport in the same way that Aristotle describes drama, especially tragedy, in the *Poetics*.[4]

Following Aristotle, we can suppose that sport imitates nature, as all human activities naturally do. Those things imitated in nature are harmony and rhythm in movement or action. The delight in seeing or in playing sport is that one is at the same time *learning*—gathering the meanings of things. If one cannot discern the meaning, then one cannot derive pleasure from the event. Pleasure, for Aristotle, requires both discernment or intellection and meaningfulness. So for sport to be pleasurable it needs to possess cultivated players and audiences—ones who are capable of exercising the above-mentioned activities. Cultivated players and audiences would then also be capable of efficiency, the efficient cause being the realization or acceptance of the final cause as desirable by all or most people involved. The cultivated players and audiences are present not just to determine a winner and a loser or to witness this, but to achieve or to appreciate excellence themselves. By contrast, the uncultivated audience and players watch and play only to win. Winning is only outcome or result; there is no excellence, mastery, perfection, or beauty: those appear on the journey or in the process of play. But these latter items are the sorts of things that cultivated audiences and players hope and expect to find. The final cause includes a sense of wholeness, a catharsis (an emotional release) on the part of the citizenry or the audience, who must be present in order for the final cause to be operative. The action in sport would be incomplete unless its reality of presentation were felt by those watching or playing. This idea is close to Schopenhauer's principle of art, in which the beholder's imagination works with the object to "complete" it as a work of art. The games purge the audience's and the players' emotions. Thus, athletics and games worthy of their names are akin to drama. In sport the actions are as nearly as possible one action or event, in which may be seen a sequence consisting of a beginning, a middle, and an end. The end represents the resolution of that whole action and is transferred to the audience by catharsis.

Here it is in theory. For the resolution to be a cultivated one, the unity of the game's action must be achieved by the players and appreciated by the audience. All of this is done within proper boundaries, which constitute, of course, the moral sphere to which Keating has drawn our attention. Following Schopenhauer's lead, I have added a second sphere, an aesthetic one, which will be developed in chapter 8. So, for the cultivated, there is a moral paradigm that governs and guides the games. For excellence and perfection to be achieved and measured, they must occur within the bounds of what Keating calls sportsmanship, to which I will turn momentarily.

Keating tempers his position that victory in itself is not enough for the athlete by suggesting that it must be coupled with something else. That something else is excellence (p. 21). Winning takes on whatever importance it has when opponents are equally matched and their effort is a masterful struggle of strength, endurance, and strategy. One other point I wish to make regarding Keating's discussion of winning is that there seems to be a distinction between winning and victory that he largely ignores. He uses the terms synonymously. However, there is evidence in ordinary language to support the legitimacy of the distinction. In German, *gewinnen* means to "win" friends or to come out the winner, or intransitively to acquire a win. Closely related to these latter two meanings is the noun *Gewinn*, which is *profit*. The dominance of monetary values in today's sports is ironically seen in German etymology. Here, "to win," is simply a question of whether the numbers (score) are in your favor; whereas *siegen* is etymologically related to *Sieg*, "victory," which suggests defeating, beating the odds, or "overcoming" the odds or a superior opponent. In English, "victory" also carries noble connotations—all those things that are brought to light by the Aristotelian perspective. In fact, the terms "victory" (*der Sieg*) and "victorious" (*siegreich*) are usually carefully used in the sport literature. When they are used, as in the sentence "We claimed a victory over the Tigers," the suggestion is that the win was achieved against great odds and in the presence of risk, pressure, and the exercise of masterful feats in order to overcome a seemingly superior opponent. Whereas if you asked me, "Did you win?" you are usually asking me for the results of a particular game. But rephrasing the question in terms of victory, such as "Were you victorious?" suggests appropriate and inappropriate contexts. You wouldn't ask a question like that of me after my regular Sunday afternoon doubles match. The question of winning is always appropriate, so there is a difference in meaning—one, I think, worth preserving. The minimal meaning of winning is the actual completion or end of the game; that is, that time runs out and/or there is the final succession of moves or score. Winning is gaining the upper hand of a struggle in a competitive situation. Looked at in this light, winning is always linked to victory; victory is a subset of the idea of winning. But victory embraces more than just winning. If we permit such a distinction, then the answer to our initial question becomes twofold. If victory is to carry connotations other than those of merely winning, then we might be inclined to agree with Keating that victory is the final cause of sport. But if we equate the two terms, there are serious reservations about this as a viable candidate for the final cause of sport.

Anyone familiar with the literature in the field of philosophy of sport will be aware of the ideas in Keating's essay (ch. 4) entitled "Sportsmanship as a Moral Category," which originally appeared in the journal *Ethics* in 1964.[5] Following the dichotomy he draws between athletics and play, Keating convincingly shows that there are two notions of sportsmanship that correspond to these diverse activities. In playful activities, "generosity and magnanimity are essential ingredients in the conduct and attitude properly described as sportsmanlike. They establish and maintain the unique social bond; they guarantee that the purpose of play—the pleasure or joy of the participants—will not be sacrificed to other more selfish ends" (p. 45). In athletics, the sportsmanlike conduct and attitude consists of a more legalistic interpretation of the rules (p. 50), in addition to fairness (p. 51). Keating concludes his discussion with the following comment: "The source of confusion which vitiates most discussion of sportsmanship is the unwarranted assumption that playful activities and athletics are so similar in

87

nature that a single code of conduct and similar participant attitudes are applicable to both" (p. 51). The moral value Keating finds in playful activities is *generosity*, which seems to color all the other moral qualities that may be found. The moral quality or value pervading athletics is *fairness*. Fairness is formulated as the constitutive rule or principle for sport; all the other rules or principles fall in behind it in order and magnitude.

Another moral quality Keating mentions, but leaves undeveloped, is *self-control* (pp. 45, 52, 73, 75). If there is a common link between athletics and playful activities, it is in the idea of self-control. Self-control is requisite to bring about the desired atmosphere and aims of the participants, whether it be in playful activities or athletics. I prefer to label this phenomenon "moral restraint," because this phrase seems to better capture the attitude and behavior of the individual involved, as well as emphasizing the moral sphere. Why were Bjorn Borg's and Chris Evert's court behavior and attitude universally admired by tennis players and fans? It is because we can readily see them exhibiting the kind of moral restraint we find underlying sportsmanlike conduct. Moral restraint is the guiding thread through the seam of conduct that should govern the actions of players, coaches, officials, and spectators. It is a value that finds expression in another constitutive principle of sport. When coaches draw technical fouls at basketball games because of unsportsmanlike conduct, it is due to their lack of moral restraint: Bobby Knight of Indiana University is the most vivid example. When a football team is penalized because of the crowd's reactions, the crowd has not exercised its responsibilities as a cultivated audience (to use Aristotle's phrase). Many individuals have forgotten this important element of game-playing. Moral restraint affects not only the rules, but also the spirit, of play.

There has been much discussion by Keating and others who view athletics as the pursuit of excellence. This view is similar to Paul Weiss's concerning the challenges that the body offers.[6] Also, like Novak, Keating chooses to discuss excellence by examining the Homeric image of life as an athletic contest (p. 55). The quest for superiority and eminence was a major goal in human life for the Greeks and Western man: perhaps the only aspect of our culture that resembles the ancient Greek ideal is sport. Athletes today are motivated by the desire to be number one, to stand apart from all the others. Keating records the personal accounts of Jack Nicklaus, Rod Laver, and Frank Beard in this regard. Speaking of the value of the pursuit of excellence, Keating remarks about judging one's maximal effort:

> The athlete speaks eloquently to this point [one's true limitations]. Great athletes never admit to their limitations; they must be painfully convinced of them. The chief value of any conscientious pursuit of excellence resides in its ability to reveal and exploit man's true potential. (p. 61)

It is here that we can speak of transcendence. Sport provides another realm of perception and being. Hints of what our future as a species may be lie in the athletic realm.[7] The essence of man, for Spinoza, the great seventeenth-century rationalist, is desire, and that desire on a grand scale is for perfection. We may be able to measure such metaphysical definitions best on the playing field.

II

WITH a general theory of value sketched above, we may now turn to issues pertaining to corruption and the decline of moral values in sport. We have seen some of corruption through the discussion of cheating in the previous chapter. Corruption or decline in sport values is due for the most part to a lack of reflection on our part. Activities such as game-playing require thoughtful conservation, but, unfortunately, we have lost the concern for what defines these activities. We are allowing actions that are not sport or game-playing activities to be passed off as such. Philosophy, however, will instruct us on the proper course to take if only we will listen. We have seen how Keating has assisted us in placing the key value concepts of sport into perspective.

Recent sport philosophers have envisioned their activity to be like that of the art curator: the preservation and restoration of their subject and its cultural milieu. The notions of preservation and restoration are certainly ones that dominate the sport philosophers' works. They think that sport is an area of human activity of positive

89

worth and value. Indeed, a sense of urgency is felt by anyone who reads much of the current literature. Preservation and restoration are ideas that suggest that something is in a state of ruin, or under threat thereof. Sport especially in America is in a state of ruin. Or less dramatically it is in a state of decline caused by outside, destructive influences. The philosopher's noble task is to set sport off and protect it from these negative influences by scrutinizing reasons and arguments given for these changes.

Keating has helped us begin this task by defining the key ideas that make up sport. Two things must be done to complete this task: first, philosophical analysis is to define the notions of competition, winning, amateurism, sportsmanship, excellence; second, it is to develop and appreciate the moral dimension surrounding these notions. Let us see how this works with competition and amateurism.

Competition is defined by Keating, who follows Lovejoy's analysis, as an attempt between or among rivals (according to agreed-upon rules) to excel or overcome each other to get or to keep any valuable thing, either to the exclusion of others or in a greater measure than others, with the provision that the activity excludes unbridled or criminal conflict or means. The proviso makes reference to the moral sphere. Ice hockey and football have frequently entered this realm of criminal conflict. Have they thus ceased to be games? Keating's proviso helps explain why Underwood's book on the death of American football has appeared on the scene.[8] Football has become so violent, so full of injuries, so disrespectful to players, fans, and officials that the activity is no longer a game, but is outright confrontation.

We have lost sight of the distinction between competition and deceptive, destructive conflict. The conditions under which competition takes place have eroded these games' moral sphere. We have sacrificed honesty for success. For honesty we have substituted deceit, lying, hypocrisy, cheating, and malice. Instances are so numerous in the sports pages of our newspapers that they hardly need to be cited in a discussion like this. The present state of intercollegiate athletics is so eroded that the reforms necessary to restore it have been proposed in the daily newspapers with frequent regularity. Equality and fairness lie at the heart of these reforms. But they go unheard because of the enormous financial gain possible for colleges with such programs.

Keating's definition shows us that there are proper bounds to activities that comprise sport, but that these bounds have been exceeded. There are several reasons why I think this is so. One is the prevalence of the success ethic. Americans are driven by the desire to be the best. And "the best" is measured by how much money one can make. When this is coupled with such intensity of competition, we have potential situations for corruption, because value is placed squarely on the success of winning. And that means winning at all costs. Another reason is that America is so materialistic.[9] Instead of spiritualizing activities as people in the Orient do, Americans tend to materialize activities. Sport is no exception. Professional sport becomes a commodity placed in a consumer marketplace. It is a bill of goods that is bought and sold. The sports and the business sections that usually appear in the same part of the newspapers have in some ways become indistinguishable. The business transactions of players' contracts or new franchises take precedence over the games. Talk of money in sport has replaced talk of the ennobling qualities of sport—what sport does for people. The humanizing aspect of these activities has been lost.

College athletics have also been equated with money. Colleges with Division I programs have accepted and now actively participate in the entertainment business. Most of these colleges have lost sight of their principal mission—to foster educational values. Let me give an example. Those who argued against Title IX and equal funding in women's sports have used this equation as the major premise in their argument, which goes something like this. Athletics, in particular college athletics, cost money to run. Those who produce the revenue, that is, the men or the "major" sports, ought to be the ones most entitled to it. Since women's sports, or the minor ones, do not create the attention or generate as much revenue, then they are not entitled to the same benefits. Therefore, disproportional amounts of funds are justifiable and fair. The main assumption behind this argument is the value judgment that the worth of sport or athletics is monetary. Athletics are treated as business, big business, and somehow we have come to tolerate and even accept this attitude.

91

However, this treatment and its supporting argument are ones we should challenge. Much of the corruption in sport and athletics can be traced back to the money mentality. The recent talk of creating super conferences—e.g., an expansion of the Southeastern conference—might have a positive value in restoring college athletics to its proper perspective by excluding a large number of colleges from sharing their conference revenues to the extent that they had in the past. Hence, if the college presidents won't initiate change from within, perhaps that change will come from without, by the formation of super conferences. It is ironical that change may be brought about by the very thing that caused corruption in sport.

American sport is not autonomous; it is heteronomous. It does not exemplify play, because "separateness" (Huizinga's term and one of his characteristics of play) is absent. In the communist countries sport is an expression of politics, whereas in America sport is an extension of economics. Money dictates where the growth or popularity of sport has and will take place. In the spring of 1980 an anonymous writer wrote on a Texas Christian University blackboard the following, which is very much to the point. "Curling isn't big in the U. S. because curling is hard to have a large audience for; it can't make money in our capitalistic society, so [it] isn't popular." This was truly a note from the underground.[10] Colleges and universities have forgotten the view that athletics are to be seen as a part of total university life—a life devoted to learning. Athletics make (or can make if permitted) a distinctive contribution of their own to the learning experience for both participants and spectators alike. The values associated with athletics here are those of competition, self-discovery, development of self-esteem and dignity, along with a host of others. The identity of sport and learning lies behind this perspective. When we engage in sport, we learn something profound about ourselves and others that cannot easily be discovered elsewhere. Sport has an indispensable role to play in the development of human character, and we need to regain the insight that this perspective affords.

Sacrifice is necessary if we are to restore sport to a moral setting—one that permits individuals to participate in living well, or learning to live well. The first step is to reject the athletics-equals-money equation and replace "money" with "learning" in that equation. Then the concerns become ones of what individuals are to gain from sport, and the decisions regarding which sports are to be supported or funded will depend upon understanding who is to engage in them. In fact, viewing the issue this way, women should be given a priority because they have been deprived of the learning experience that athletics and sport provide. (Perhaps this consequence is what critics of Title IX and other reforms fear the most.) The appropriate questions should not concern revenue production, available funds, and so forth, but rather should be questions of interest, equality, fairness, and growth. We cannot have it both ways—big-time intercollegiate athletics with amateur ideals.

The growth of professionalism has substantially changed collegiate athletics. Much has been written recently that sadly records the details of the decline.[11] Keating's own corrective policies are: (i) abolish all methods of compensation and reward, giving prizes only symbolic value;[12] (ii) prohibit all expense accounts and expect each competitor to pay all of his or her own expenses; (iii) make no effort of any kind to secure publicity; and (iv) do not charge admission nor employ any stratagem for the purpose of profiting from the tournament or competition, allowing entrance fees and/or a sponsoring organization to cover attendant costs (pp. 35–36). The second reform is the one most severely criticized—many argue that athletes should be paid. But how much, and how would it be regulated? Regulation of a current practice does not make it a morally acceptable one. Keating argues that we are caught on the horns of a dilemma:

> Employment of such policies would encourage greater equality in competition and the joyful, magnanimous spirit of play, but at a rather substantial price. Gone should be the drama, the widespread communal interest, the sense of importance which are inseparable from a well publicized and traditional athletic contest. Gone also would be the opportunity to cultivate and practice the virtues which are endemic to the agonistic life. You can't have it both ways. The values proper to play

93

and those proper to athletics are usually irreconcilable within the same activity. The futile and confused attempt to fuse diverse values lies at the heart of the amateur problem. The failure to recognize the important distinction between playful activity and athletics and the values proper to each is the heart of the problem of amateur athletics.

So here we have it. A rather austere program of reform. But Keating is not the only one; Novak has proposed a similar list (ch. 17), and Underwood has followed suit (pp. 71–72), as have many others recently. These writers are not content to give a description of the sports world. Like Keating, they envision their pursuit as revisionary; they are telling us what the structure of that world ought to be like. Will their proposals be enacted? If the institutions surrounding athletics are seriously threatened, then perhaps these reforms or similar ones will be put into effect. Novak ends with a good word of advice: "These reforms are proposed for purposes of stimulating discussion and careful thought. They grow naturally, I believe, out of present trends and possibilities. But in order to take root in reality, they must be refined, revised, and bent to fruitful shape" (p. 338). Is Novak suggesting compromise?

Another issue we need to address on a more personal level is the question of self-competition. Keating claims that there is no such thing as competing with one's self. He suggests that a better way to describe one's activity is as one's *improvement* upon past performance(s). This could best be described as self-actualization or discovery or improvement. When Wertz goes jogging and seeks to outdo his previous nine-kilometer runs by running ten kilometers, he is not competing with himself, according to Keating. He is, rather, attempting to better an earlier established goal. While this activity shares some common features with competing, it also has some essential ones missing. As Keating says, "Only when he seeks to exceed, surpass, or go beyond the best efforts of others is he actually competing. Competition in all of its forms always presupposes an other or others" (p. 3). While Keating stipulates this restrictive use of "competing," it is not in

conformity with ordinary usage. Why this divergence? No com-
pelling reasons are given. And as we have seen in the previous
chapter, there are uses of "competing" where the self is taken as
the object.

Another so-called misconception avoided by Keating's definition is that competition consists of "parallel efforts" of the competitors. (The German philosopher and sociologist Georg Simmel
held this view.) The consequence of this idea of competition is that
the "conflict in it is indirect." Keating develops a convincing argument against such a view and in support of the view that in sport,
as in economics and politics, most often competition is of a direct
kind. He says: "In all middle distance and distance races the competitors are keenly aware of the existence of their competitors and
usually, by the employment of their strength and speed, attempt to
get their opponent to run the type of race for which he is least
qualified." And, "Only in the short dashes can it be said that 'each
competitor by himself aims at the goal without using his strength
on the adversary and that he proceeds as if there existed no adversary'" (p. 5). But even in the shortest runs and hurtles, one is
pushed by his or her competitors if the races are close. The one
place where Simmel's "parallel effort" idea serves as a fruitful notion is where the concept of competition is thought of along the
lines of a cooperation or challenge, an excellence-oriented model
rather than a conflict- or dominance-oriented model.

There are many people who feel that the amateur ideal is
worth preserving and cultivating, especially in sport as a human
enterprise. "Through definition, they [including Keating and my-
self] hope to set it [the amateur ideal] off and protect it from
outside and destructive influences" (p. 27). Statements like this
suggest the view I mentioned earlier that philosophy has a role of
"policing" the concepts that underlie these activities we commonly
call the sports world. Philosophers point to the violations of the
fragile moral sphere that encompasses the sports world and remind
those who need reminding of the notions which make up that
sphere. Keating is one philosopher who has contributed to this
revisionary program. Amateurism, winning, and sportsmanship are

95

areas of his concern, in addition to competition and professionalism. Regarding amateurism Keating says:

> It is of prime importance, therefore, that we know who, or what, it is that we are trying to protect and, precisely, from whom, or what, it is in need of protection. Specifically, as applied to amateur athletics, what is sorely needed is a definition that will serve as an easily applicable criterion for the inclusion or exclusion of competitors in various contests. The reason why the French-flavored term "amateur" was chosen to characterize this aspect of human life is that its root or etymological meaning is "lover" and the distinctive feature of that human activity, thought to be in need of protection, is that it is performed out of love of the activity itself and apart from all pecuniary interest. (p. 27)

There are few such amateurs around these days, but that there are *any* is encouraging, and we should preserve high school and collegiate athletics where they will foster those things of the human spirit. "Sports are at their heart a spiritual activity," says Novak, "a tribute to grace, beauty, and excellence." But one must be made aware of that activity which is of intrinsic value—something undertaken for its own sake and not for the sake of something else. Although there may be a variety of reasons why people participate in a given game, participants themselves can be ignorant of their motives. So isolating attitudes or motives as the essence of amateurism is highly problematic. The confused values often found in today's sports must be sorted out along with attitudes or motives if the amateur ideal is to be salvaged. Some skeptics argue that the amateur ideal cannot be salvaged, but I would not go that far. I agree with Keating and the others on the reform issue for the preservation of sport.

III

I SHALL now turn to the second task of this chapter, which is to analyze methods for attaining the purpose or end of sport. How are the values in sport to be discovered? I shall attempt to answer this question by examining how human beings appropriate things from their experience. Appropriation is also one of the central ideas used by philosophers, mainly phenomenologists, to explain the distinctiveness of the sport experience. The concept was first developed in the context of sport by Jean-Paul Sartre and it has continued to be written about since 1943.[13] In many respects Sartre's view can be considered to be the Western or Occidental view of sport. Consequently it is worth discussing in some detail before we turn to the Eastern view of sport in the next chapter. This section does not pretend to be a complete discussion of Sartre's ideas on this subject. Rather what I have selected from Sartre's famous discussion allows us to focus more clearly on the fundamental differences that lie behind these cultural views and their respective paradigms. His view is rich in detail and difficult to summarize, so extensive quotation has been necessary.

Sartre uses as his example snow skiing—a sport at which he was an expert, and one that kept him alive during the Nazi occupation of France during the Second World War. He talks about an Alpine slope or a field of snow as an environment. "To see it is already to possess it. In itself it is already apprehended by sight as a symbol of being" (p. 581). The goal of the skier is to do something to the snow—to impose a form on it. Sartre describes the activity of the skier as changing the matter and meaning of the snow. He narrates:

> If I approach, if I want to establish an appropriative contact with the field of snow, everything has changed. Its scale of being is modified, it exists bit by bit instead of existing in vast spaces; stains, brush, and crevices come to individualize each square inch. . . . To ski means not only to enable me to make rapid movements and to acquire a technical skill, nor is it merely to play by increasing according to my whim the speed or difficulties of the course; it is also to enable me to possess this field of snow. (p. 582)

Sartre says that it is *he* doing something to the snow. He has a course to follow over the field of snow which has a continuity and unity from the point of departure to the point of arrival. In the descent, the skier traverses toward the point he assigns to himself. This "traversal," Sartre says, is not just an activity of movement but

97

"a synthetic activity of organization and connection; I spread the skiing field before me in the same way that the geometrician, according to Kant, can apprehend a straight line only by drawing one" (p. 582). Sartre continues: "At the same time I have chosen a certain point of view in order to apprehend this snowy slope: this point of view is a determined speed, which emanates from me, which I can increase or diminish as I like; through it the field traversed is constituted as a definite object, entirely distinct from what it would be at another speed" (p. 583).

In his commentary on Sartre's *Being and Nothingness*, Joseph Catalano gives a good summary of the consciousness Sartre believes is necessary for the skier to sustain his or her activity:

> Sartre notes that in skiing, the expert skier possesses the snow by continually creating it as the delicate support of his activity. By his proper turns, his lightness and swiftness of movement, he creates snow to be the very support of these movements and appropriates the snow to himself. The skier's ideal is again the ideal of every desire: to perfectly possess its object by a continual creation and at the same time to leave it unmarred and independent as the pure in-itself. Possession is the impossible union of the for-itself with the in-itself, which is the symbol of the desire to be God. [Catalano's footnote: "Sartre also notes the factor of 'conquering' in sport is related to mastering the other."][14]

What Sartre chooses to emphasize in this phenomenological description of skiing is the empirical ego, the self. It is *I* who change the field of snow. It is *I* who choose the route through the slope and the speed which *I* alone can diminish or increase as *I* like. It is *I* who master the slope; it is the self that does the appropriating. Sartre's dense metaphysical analysis continues along the above lines, with the point of subjectivity clearly focused on an autonomous self in conscious control of its actions.[15]

What is the nature of this autonomous self? The *I* appears in a reflected consciousness as Sartre has made it appear in his phenomenological description of skiing. For Sartre in *The Transcendence of the Ego*, there is no I in the unreflected consciousness

(p. 47): While I was skiing, there was consciousness *of* the slope, *of* the type (condition) of the snow, *of* the terrain, but the *I* was not inhabiting this consciousness. What kind of consciousness is this? Sartre answers: "It was only consciousness of the object and non-positional consciousness" (p. 47). However non-positional this consciousness may be, it is still centralized in that its source is "localized" by both its being in a body and its empirically constituted ego. The character of this ego becomes clearer when we see that it does make its way onto the unreflected level in a semantic or grammatical sense. Sartre clarifies this peculiar status of the *I* in the following passage:

> If someone asks me "What are you doing?" and I reply, all preoccupied, "I am trying to hang this picture," or "I am repairing the rear tire," these statements do not transport us to the level of reflection. I utter them without ceasing to work, without ceasing to envisage actions only as done or to be done—not insofar as I am doing them. But this "I" which is here in question nevertheless is no mere syntactical form. It has a meaning; it is quite simply an empty concept which is destined to remain empty. Just as I can think of a chair in the absence of any chair merely by a concept, I can in the same way think of the *I* in the absence of the *I*. This is what a consideration of states such as "What are you doing this afternoon?" "I am going to the office," or "I must write him," etc., makes obvious. (p. 89)

So I can think of *I* merely by way of a concept. I think of the *I* as the source of these reflected and unreflected actions. Sartre's skiing example bears this interpretation out. "The ego is the *creator* of its states and sustains its qualities in existence by a sort of preserving spontaneity" (p. 78; my italics), asserts Sartre. Simply put, the ego "*is* what it produces" (p. 80). Even though the *I* or ego for Sartre is a *fugitive* (p. 89), "The body there [in the skiing example, for instance] serves as a visible and tangible symbol for the *I*" (p. 90). Consequently, my actions when I ski are nothing more than those physical actions being realized in the world at a given time. How are they realized?

The ego or self that is present in skiing is there only as initiator or creator and is there only conceptually and not as an item of consciousness, the way the slope-having-to-be-overtaken is presented. After all is said and done, however, Sartre still has a view of the self or ego that is centralized and localized, primarily around the body. Sartre is so confident of his phenomenological analysis that he concludes: "No appropriation can be more complete than this instrumental appropriation; the synthetic activity of appropriation is here [the ski case] a technical activity of utilization" (p. 583). I agree with Sartre on the sense of completeness in which appropriation is achieved, but his analysis is only one possible model. Sartre doesn't quite escape his Cartesian tradition in that the self is still present as an agent, an initiator and creator in the world with its actions. These actions stem from the agent even though Sartre has replaced the substantial or transcendental ego with a conceptual ego; the ego empirically constituted remains.

However, this is only one way to look at how sport releases subjectivity or how appropriation takes place. There is at least one other way to view appropriation. The modification could occur in my being rather than in the field of snow. A total release of subjectivity occurs when outward concern dominates and inward concern is absent.[16] Sartre appreciated the dialectic of these concerns but interpreted them differently, that is, in terms of the agent. Nature—in this example, the field of snow—does the appropriating rather than the agent. It is nature (by way of unconsciousness) that does the releasing of subjectivity. Nature sports, like skiing and mountain climbing, ones Sartre called open air sports, make more sense to many by this analysis than by Sartre's humanism, because one of the benefits that nature sports provide the human being is the feeling of union with nature.[17]

Perhaps Sartre never felt this unity with nature in such a way that it was nature that initiated rather than the individual. The advocates of the Oriental view would argue that surely the experience of freedom and the release of subjectivity are more accurately portrayed from this ontological perspective than from Sartre's. Sartre relocates the experience in nature sports by construing it along the lines of competition and domination. His expression of it in *Being and Nothingness* leaves no room for doubt:

> Here [in skiing] the snow is identical with *the Other*, and the common expressions "to overcome," "to conquer," "to master," etc. indicate sufficiently that it is a matter of establishing between me and the snow the relation of master to slave. This aspect of appropriation which we find in the ascent, exists also in swimming, in an obstacle course, etc. The peak on which a flag is planted is a peak which has been *appropriated*. Thus a principal aspect of sport—and in particular of open air sports—is the conquest of these enormous masses of water, of earth, and of air. (pp. 172–173; his italics)

I shall argue next that an individual's involvement with nature in a nature sport does not always conform to the analysis of competition given by Sartre or the one earlier in this chapter. If we follow the wisdom of the Orient, in particular that of Sekida, the ego is to be eliminated along with the illusion that it is in control. This is almost done in Sartre's analysis, but he retains the ego or *I* as a concept to which he attributes agency. Sartre remains an example of the Western paradigm, which stresses the individual, domination, and action as self-centered and directed. The problem is that the self is tacitly (and sometimes even overtly) regarded as separate from or other than the world. But this model begins to break down when one attempts to apply it to nature. Other items in the sport experience seem to be emphasized under the Sartrean model than in the naturalism of the Oriental paradigm. Contrary to what Sartre says, unconsciousness is the link to being. This is the basic premise of Eastern thinking and it is one we shall examine shortly. Unconsciousness is how nature appropriates the individual. Sport teaches us how to do this type of appropriation on a smaller scale and prepares us to do that holistic appropriation on a grander, more metaphysical scale. Hans-Georg Gadamer is one of the few Western philosophers to appreciate the holistic dimension of play and that appropriation works in the opposite direction than Sartre supposed:

As far as language is concerned, the actual subject of play is obviously not the subjectivity of an individual who among other activities also plays, but instead the play itself. Only we are so used to relating a phenomenon such as playing to the sphere of subjectivity and its attitudes that we remain closed to these indications from the spirit of language.[18]

Notice the clue that the player is subordinate to the game is suggested by the language of sport. Gadamer reinforces this point by adding that phenomenologically, "The player experiences the game as a reality that *surpasses* him" or her (p. 98; my italics).

In sport samādhi, the game appropriates the individual; whereas under Sartre's model, it is still the individual who (*tries to*) appropriate the game. The link between being or nature and individual is distorted greatly when we try to conceive of it as being conscious and ego-centered, claim the naturalists of the Orient. They may be right, because that sort of awareness (that is, conscious, ego-centered awareness) usually brings about mishaps and miscalculations. Why? One's attention is on the self rather than the environment—that field of snow or slope. When the I makes its entrance into the experience, the action is no longer free and natural. This obviously doesn't happen with the better athletes, but they still cling to the notion that their sport actions are tacitly constituted by an ego—much like the one Sartre has posited. The alternative view is that the sort of control and mastery Sartre talks about in skiing come from nature—not the self.[19] One attempts to *attune* oneself to nature rather than to dominate it. Hence Sartre's theory is counterintuitive and lacking in the essentials that make up nature sports, and I will argue next that this is true of other sports as well. The Oriental view has a humbling effect on the individual who practices it, too. If American sportspersons had less of a Sartrean view of their sport experience and more of an Oriental view, perhaps there would be fewer violations of the moral sphere that encompasses the world of sport. Sartre's humanism suggests that the individual creates his or her own values. However, the East shows us another way that values can be created or sustained. Is the source of value the individual or is it nature?

To answer this question, we need to see alternatives to the Sartrean view more clearly, we need to examine the Oriental view in detail and to consider whether or not we can accept its argument. Our Western intuitions make us lean to the former, but this alternative has led to undesirable consequences, so the latter alternative looks at least initially more attractive. The next chapter has been designed to develop that position.

PART THREE: THE DOING AND KNOWING

FIVE

Zen and Yoga in Sport

An ambitious project—
Zen intends to control intentional creation.
It wants to control existence.

Katsuki Sekida

I

THINGS ARE HAPPENING to our wide world of sport. It has
expanded far beyond the original inventors' dreams. An apprecia-
ble movement toward scrutinizing the finer components concealed
in the sport experience is mushrooming around us. This exploration of the subtler aspect of inner awareness, which may produce
self-knowledge and spiritual stability, is the subject of one of the
regions of the language of sport, and consequently the subject of
this chapter. Our guiding questions, then, are: What is the nature
of this self-knowledge? How is spirituality a product of the sport
experience? We have seen in the last chapter that Novak claims
that the other values (moral and aesthetic) in sport stem from this
one source; that is, spirituality forms the core of *mythos* and *ethos*
in sport. So let us now see how these are manifest in the world of
sport.

Since I am developing a philosophy on the basis of sport-talk
and the sport experience, this extensive literature on inner awareness needs to be examined, especially for clues of a new paradigm.
One wonders if this recent focus on "inner awareness" is indeed a
fresh discovery, or if it has always existed, hidden beneath the
surface of other ideologies, purposes, and false pretenses concerning the true benefits of the sporting experience—awaiting its

timely discovery and articulation. Oriental philosophy has always been concerned with "inner awareness," and only recently has it been viewed as contributing to our understanding of sport. The chief aim of this chapter is to identify and illustrate the character of this "inner awareness" and the concepts on which it is logically dependent.

Some distinct inherent power, force, being, or energy labeled "It," if allowed the freedom from our ego-mind, can perform the perfect shot, throw, or game over and over—not just once or twice, but as often as one "willfully" desires.[1] The revelation of one's consciousness of oneself, in practice and in competition, is the essence of playing at one's best and the supreme achievement of an athlete. The East has always found this to be the goal of sport. In this respect sport is no different from other aspects of life. Sport is just another way (do in Japanese) of dealing with life (and death).

An example of this phenomenon is reported by Tim Gallwey. In a particular tennis match, he had split sets with his opponent; before going out for the third and final set, he meditated—attempting to center himself:

> By then it was dusk, and the lights had been turned on. I had difficulty seeing the ball in these conditions, lost the first game and was down 0–40 on my serve. But at this point my attention was not on losing or on the reactions of the crowd; I was concentrating on the ball during play and practicing meditation in between. I distinctly began to feel an energy building inside me, and I knew exactly what it was: That's who I am! I'm that energy expressing itself through this body! It's beautiful, aware, fast and accurate. It's not a bit worried about Tim Gallwey's image or the image of the Inner Game. It's perfect, and all I have to do is let it out! / And that's what I did. My tennis changed radically in that instant; I felt as fresh as if I'd just walked onto the court and had no self-doubt. I won the next five points and my serve. When I reached 0–40 on his next serve, I didn't let up as I normally might have, but went all out for the next point and won it. During the rest of the set

I lost only half a dozen points, and most of those because my opponent hit winners. I was playing out of my mind. / As we shook hands afterwards, my opponent looked at me in disbelief, as if to say, "Where did that come from?" I told him I was as surprised as he was. Sally said only, "That was really beautiful." Still out of my mind, I said innocently, "Wow, it really was!" as if speaking about someone else. The experience of fulfillment inside me was exhilarating; I had let out everything that was in me.[2]

But how such a desirable state is achieved and maintained or repeated at will has not been successfully known and taught until lately. Hatha Yoga and Zen training offer methods and exercises to help bring this about.[3] Some of these have been popularized by Gallwey and by George Leonard,[4] but they have left some of the philosophical ideas dormant. I shall try to flush these out into the open so they may be discussed and examined.

If, for individuals concerned with their individuality or potential as human beings, one of the purposes of playing a game such as golf or tennis is to "know themselves," then one must inquire about the nature of this inner self. This elusive entity has been tagged in the literature as the altered self, Self 3, reality, self-knowledge, spiritual energy, consciousness of "It," and more. When and if one is truly conscious of life, or recognizes his awareness—the inner man as in the Zen tradition—then he has found this entity.[5] As Gallwey summarizes it in *The Inner Game of Tennis*: "Every heightening of consciousness enables one to appreciate more freely the experiences which life offers each player. Changes in consciousness alter our lives automatically because it is only through consciousness that we experience life" (p. 140). There is no doubt that Gallwey feels tennis is an excellent mode of inquiry for the development of self-awareness; his experience described above convinces us of that. Sport as self-discovery has captured the interest of the public; there has been recently a television series based on the inner game. Furthermore, Gallwey is busy applying his version of the inner game to other realms of sport, so I am sure that we shall see these in the literature before long.[6]

What are the philosophical presuppositions and assumptions behind the inner game? As can be readily appreciated from the brief discussion above, there is more to the inner game than Gallwey makes out. To round out the idea of the inner game, we need the aid of the Zen "classics," especially those that pertain to sport. There are many pressing questions that need answering when one begins to critically examine Gallwey's ideas and those of the inner game generally. Does every "heightening of consciousness" enable one to "appreciate more freely the experiences that life offers each player"? Sekida thinks that this is extremely difficult to achieve. It is not automatic that given a particular heightening of consciousness, there will causally follow this free appreciation of life experiences and the altering of our lives. There are levels of consciousness, as Sekida states, and only in the highest, the fourth level, absolute samādhi (samādhi is the Sanskrit term for "concentration" or contemplative awareness), which is a condition usually attained only in a Zen student's maturity, does this freedom of mind in actual living come about. There are states of false or superficial samādhi, where the inner man is forsaken and becomes a victim at the mercy of outer circumstances. Gallwey is right about self-images and the ego restricting movements. But Gallwey's inner game is not the same as the inner man that Sekida talks about. In genuine or absolute samādhi the inner man is not on stage, but is wakeful inside; that is, he has the feeling of self-mastery. In detail (from Sekida):

> Jishu-zammai [the term denotes the samādhi of self-mastery] never loses its independence and freedom. It is spiritual power, and it contains within itself all sources of emotion and intellect. When you come out of absolute samādhi, you find yourself full of peace and serenity, equipped with strong mental power and dignity. You are intellectually alert and clear, emotionally pure and sensitive. You have the exalted condition of a great artist. (p. 75)

Or, in the context of our discussion, one who experiences this is in the exalted condition of a great athlete. Gallwey's experience fits the above description, but his claims about it throughout his books are grandiose at times, and his version of the inner game theory does not do justice to the sport experience, nor to the philosophical tradition it appeals to. More will be said about Gallwey's techniques in relation to Zen training methods and philosophy later in the chapter.

George Leonard has developed various ideas of the inner game from Aikidō, the highest Japanese martial art, into a program that can be applied to other realms of sport.[7] No matter what the medium, when individuals direct their abilities (potential or realized) toward activities requiring their total concentration, they find themselves able to "click"—to perform without analyzing every movement and to react smoothly, confidently, and well in any game or contest. The inner game helps to discipline the "mind" in order to bring about this kinesthetic feeling; or in terms of Zen, it disciplines the brain to let the "inner man" perform. What then is the "inner game"? It is a mixture of Zen, Yoga, and common sports psychology. And it also consists of an interesting set of concepts (body, self, time, ego, knowing, freedom, consciousness, thought, and so on), most of which I shall examine in the rest of the chapter. By the time we are through, we will have covered a large amount of the terrain of Oriental philosophy. This makes for marked contrast to the Western philosophy of sport (especially the Sartrean type), which I outlined in the previous chapter. In short, Oriental philosophy, as I conceive of it here, is a logic of cognitive states, a mapping out of the region of consciousness. Thus an Asian conception of sport (if I may be permitted to speak of such a thing) is a chart of various actions and cognitive states that bring about or account for the sport experience. An analysis of the stages and transitions in human consciousness is the subject matter of this area of philosophy.

II

USUALLY we think of the mind as being in control of the body, evaluating its performances—"Good shot"; "That's a bad serve"; "Keep your head down when you swing." What Adam Smith[8] and the others above suggest instead is that we make the brain an extension of the body through centering, or by concentration exercises that occupy our awareness with bodily processes like breathing. The only form of Yoga in Gallwey's works is to be found in the awareness exercises; there are no breathing, stretching, or centering exercises. Because of this, his books sometimes read as if they belong on the Positive Mental Attitude (PMA) shelf. If Gallwey (or someone) were to write *The Advanced Inner Game*, it would have Hatha Yoga exercises as part of its contents. Leonard's study or the Leuchs-Skalka manual could be viewed as this book, although I think it is yet to be written.

Tennis at one time was simple. There was just the one game. Then along came Simon Ramo[9] who showed us that there are really two, distinct activities taking place under one name, leading to insurmountable confusion. They are *pro tennis* and *ordinary tennis*. And now we have a third game, *inner tennis*, which affects us all, whether pros or hackers. We now have USPTA (United States Professional Tennis Association) instructors telling us that we, too, can win with Zen. The idea of the uncoordinated person, the klutz, is obsolete! The body has an intelligence—a language if you will—of its own and sport instructors are to employ techniques that awaken a person's native, intuitive ability. Analysis is out, awareness is in.

Inner awareness is not easily skimmed from the surface of our conscious minds. In a simplified, dualistic approach, Gallwey divides the person into Self 1 and Self 2. He interprets our problem as being with Self 1, the ego-mind, constantly directing Self 2, giving a running dialogue of instructions, reprimands, or put-downs and not trusting the Self 2, our unconscious self, to do anything by itself. This inner self can be found only as one quiets or stills one's mind and focuses Self 1's attention elsewhere on such objects as the lines in the tennis ball, the projected path of the next serve, or one's breathing. Or as Adam Smith metaphorically describes it, one must put on one's mental scuba gear. Following Gallwey, some writers have associated the two-hemispheres brain theory with the inner game. The right side of the brain—the creative, intuitive, non-linguistic half—is identified with Self 2. And the left side is identified with Self 1, the ego-mind with all of its calculations and judgments about its performance.

In *Inner Tennis* Gallwey describes an awareness exercise he labels "bounce-hit." At first the pupil calls out "bounce" as the ball hits on the court and "hit" as the instructor strokes the ball. After the pupil has this sequence synchronized, the same procedure is applied to his own shots. The calling out of "bounce-hit" keeps the player from thinking about whether he or she can hit the ball, whether he or she is in the proper position, has the right grip, and so on. In describing another exercise dubbed "Seeing the Trajectory," Gallwey observes: "The person who allows his mind to grow absorbed in the ball's trajectory often finds himself playing beyond his normal levels; totally forgetting about footwork and strokes, he is usually surprised to find himself returning ball after ball effectively and effortlessly. The art . . . is to completely lose oneself in the exercise and let the body respond spontaneously." Gallwey takes this bit of Eastern wisdom and its *limited* success with tennis, and further applies it to golf and skiing. His method is singular; it is only that of outward samādhi. Sekida describes this first level of samādhi as that state where we are quite forgetful of ourselves: "We are not self-conscious about our behavior, emotions, or thought. The inner man is forgotten and outer circumstances occupy our whole attention. To put it another way: inward concern is absent; outward concern dominates" (p. 72). This is like Gallwey's tennis exercises or the concentration in an actual tennis match. However, in Zen it is considered inferior to the seedless or absolute samādhi; the latter is a state in which the ego-mind is no longer functioning. It is unfocused, without source except from unconsciousness or nature.

According to the mystical sportsman, to play the game with the best effort is to play without effort. When one tries too hard, concentrates intensely on the game's progress or dwells on past mistakes, one is apt to make more mistakes. One loses the ability to play naturally, without tenseness or frustration. Trying too hard is the worst mistake a player can make in any game. In *The Inner Game of Tennis* Gallwey urges his readers: "Learn to love the tennis ball and scrutinize its seams as it hurtles over the net" (p. 92). Tennis teacher Vic Braden of the United States Tennis Academy disagrees; he thinks all one can see is a blur. My own experience suggests that most of the time the ball does appear as a blur, but there are moments in heightened perception when one *can* see the seams of the ball.[10] (Related experiences in football are described below.) Players

113

become so involved in thinking about every move they have made (past) and every move they want to make (future) that they fail to play the game (present), in the here and now. They eventually "psych" themselves right out of the game. We are told that we should stop listening to the constant criticism going on inside our heads—"Move your feet more, dummy" and "Lower your arm"—stop analyzing what we did wrong and approach our mistakes in a detached manner. Using the resources of Western thought, Ellen Gerber makes essentially the same point: "When one speaks of degree of involvement . . . it does not mean the whole person is involved to a greater or lesser degree, but that more and more of the person is involved, concentration and perceptions are more singly focused, until finally all of the person's powers are involved, and then it can be said that there is total involvement and intensity."[11] We shall simply become absorbed in the here and now of what we are doing because the good shots, as Gallwey suggests in *The Inner Game of Tennis*, "come when the mind is as still as a glass lake" (p. 31). Quieting the mind means to involve one's consciousness less with thinking, hoping, regretting, and to allow it to be totally in the here and now, the unconscious self automatically taking over, just as we do when driving a car.[12]

In a culture where to win is primary and to give one's all means to give one hundred and ten percent, one might suspect a philosophy of "knowing oneself, above all" would not draw support of any significance. Surely, the uninitiated would think, if a player moves through the backfield during a football game contemplating Herrigel's statement "What stands in your way is that you have a much too willful will . . . let go of yourself, leaving yourself and everything yours behind you so decisively that nothing more is left of you but a purposeless tension" (pp. 51–52), the fellow will be plowed into the ground! But just run the instant replay. Meditation on the field has caught on. As Adam Smith recounts, "Pros in football, diving, basketball, golf, and tennis now sound like Zen masters" (p. 48). The professionals are beginning to talk of getting into funny spaces, total concentration, energy streamers, and visions of the game in slow motion, ballet-style. Recall Pam Shriver's account of that third set against Martina Navratilova in the quarterfinals of the

114

1982 United States Open which I mentioned in the introduction: "I was zoned." John Brodie, a seventeen-year veteran quarterback for the San Francisco Forty-niners, describes the phenomenon explained in Adam Smith's article:

> Sometimes in the heat of the game a player's perception and coordination improve dramatically. At times, I experience a kind of clarity that I've never seen described in any football story; sometimes this seems to slow way down, as if I have all the time in the world to watch the receivers run their patterns, and yet I know the defensive line is coming at me just as fast as ever, and yet the whole thing seems like a movie or a dance in slow motion. It's beautiful. (p. 50)

However, such an experience is not limited to the pros. Gary Shaw describes a given moment in a late afternoon pick-up game of football that has many of the characteristics that Brodie describes:

> I have [had] experiences that go beyond victory. In fact, I've found that some of these possibilities [i.e., of Nirvāna, "enlightenment"] exist in sports. An example of this is the moment on a football field that for me soars above all others. It happened five full years after my last Texas workout. My lifelong friend, Dee Wilson, and I frequently spent our late summer afternoons running pass patterns and playing touch football. Some days I would be the quarterback and Dee the receiver, and on others it was vice versa. One September day we were playing two other friends on the otherwise empty field of a high school stadium. We were in good shape and had been playing for almost two hours. But now all of us were tired and it was getting dark, so we agreed the next play would be our last. Dee and I had been working on one pass pattern for a couple of days, and though it had been unsuccessful that afternoon, we had decided to try it again on this final play. What followed was an experience I'd never had before. At the end of this pattern, Dee was to be about thirty yards downfield angling for the corner of the zone. But as I dropped back and pointed my eyes toward his full strides into late

115

afternoon, I began to feel some inexplicable postponement of time. My mind was quick and clear, yet all physical movement fell into a lingering genus of departure. With a sudden calmness, I could see the whole field and the three small figures elegantly brushing its top. As I watched their grace, I could feel the empty stands and their suspension of a lost past. This changeless spell brought an acute sense of temporalness and the feeling of inevitably fading with the dusk. Yet just as acute was the sense that this present intimately belonged to both past and future. This time and our movements were one. As I released the ball with the giving length and completeness of my arm, I could see the beginning of its easy soft arc. And it somehow seemed perfectly coordinated with the stadium, the ground, early evening and the four of us. As the ball was coming down some thirty long yards into the distance, two figures in ballet stretched into the air to meet it. In one easy motion of symmetry, Dee took the pass and lissomely yielded to a surging turf. Then slowly and gently separating himself from the stadium ground, he turned to me and grinned. I knew we had connected.[13]

Now, imagine experiences such as these not only becoming repeatable, but also being willfully brought about by the right exercises and concentration. Gallwey, Leonard, and others suggest this as a distinct possibility. Moreover, coaches and physical education instructors would do well to pay heed to their suggestions. These instructions can lead to a distinct improvement in performance. If the coaches are skeptical, they should listen to the master Sekida.

At the start of the hundred-meter race, the initial spring of the runner's legs means a great deal. In fact, the starting dash is generated by the explosive release of energy from the contracted respiratory muscles. If these are tensed a fraction of a second too early or too late, the start will likewise be too early or too late. When you are experienced in the practice of zazen ["seated meditation"] you will naturally become aware of the moment at which the tension of the respiratory muscles begins to decline, and will spontaneously give an appropriate

116

contraction to them once more—automatically bringing about the bamboo method of respiration. (p. 88)

Zen training has much to offer the athlete. For almost every bodily movement, such as swinging, kicking, jumping, and running, there are appropriate (natural) moves. What Shurnryu Suzuki tells us of sitting and standing applies to any physical activity:

> Doing something is expressing our own nature. We do not exist for the sake of something else. We exist for the sake of ourselves. This is the fundamental teaching expressed in *the forms* we observe. Just as for sitting, when we stand in the zendo we have some rules. But the purpose of these rules is not to make everyone the same, but to allow each to express his own self most freely. For instance, each one of us has his own way of standing, so our standing posture is based on the proportions of our own bodies. When you stand, your heels should be as far apart as the width of your own fist, your big toes in line with the centers of your breasts. As in zazen, put some strength in your abdomen.[14]

The forms Suzuki tells us about are those that make up the exercises and practices of Zen. The key idea in this passage is that the forms are tailor-made by our own bodily proportions, so that each of us finds his or her own right practice and right action. Suzuki alludes to the basic patterns of human movement, whether they be standing or throwing punches and kicks. These have been formalized and ritualized in the martial arts, like T'ai Chi Ch'uan, the Chinese version.[15] For the principles of movement, Shurnryu Suzuki, like Sekida, thinks that Zen practice and training are *teachable*. They talk about method and philosophy. Together their outlook on Zen can be seen as a new movement or school. The "new school," as I shall call it, of Zen thought discerns a "method" in the conventions of the koan (a Zen poem or riddle), zazen, and the arts. Thinking of them is equivalent to meditation; that is, it is a good whereas with the old school (Herrigel and D. T. Suzuki), thinking is identified with calculation, that is, it is bad. The old school talks about Zen as mysticism rather than philosophy. Suzukian Zen manuals are esoteric; that is, they reveal to the uninitiated how the initiated experience Zen. And those initiates are elite, male, and few in number. There is no conscious effort to demonstrate to the reader how to experience the sort of things described therein; all is clothed in mystery and suspense. In contrast to this, the new school thinks that Zen should be practiced by everyone and that a master is not necessary for learning. Anyone can learn by himself or herself if they so desire, although this would be exceedingly rare and very difficult to do. Sekida has given the West the secrets of the old school. Now there is a body of knowledge available from the new school, and along with it a view of sport emerges which is very different from that commonly found in the West. Nonetheless, there are those Westerners who do know and have attempted to apply it to sport.

In his discussion of the energy body in conventional sports, George Leonard describes a game that employs the energy body concept and makes it possible to teach people of *average* abilities to recognize the energy surge that rises in the movement of a game. They can do this in a short period of time:

> Another energy game that has obvious application to conventional sports goes under the name "Walls and Doors." Again, ten players stand in a circle. One player volunteers to leave the room. Of the remaining nine, three volunteer to be doors; the other six are to be walls. The doors concentrate on the fact that they will open upon anyone's approach; they assume that their Energy Bodies will have door-like qualities. All the people in the circle, however, are to present relaxed, centered physical bodies. The volunteer then steps back to the center of the circle and walks forcefully toward a player assumed to be a door. If the decision is correct, the person playing the door will step aside and the volunteer will walk through. Otherwise there will be a collision. Three attempts are customary. Anyone who regularly picks all three doors must be considered a master at reading energy, and might apply such a skill to a number of team sports. In football, for instance, it would be helpful to know which

linemen were going to become doors, that is, draw or pull, on a given play. (pp. 100–101)

A more specific application of this idea is seen in the following passage:

> Take the matter of "momentum," for example. When a team develops a series of successful plays, it is said to have gained momentum, a powerful psychological factor. Simply by thinking of this momentum as a Newtonian force, coaches and players alike help make it into just that—a ponderous, physical juggernaut that can be stopped only by the greatest effort, or perhaps interrupted by calling for time out. In actual fact, though, the flow of a game can, and often does, change in the wink of an eye. A heavy object that is moving requires great force to stop, but a powerful electric current can be reversed by the flick of a tiny switch. By thinking in terms of such an energy flow, coaches and players may lose their fear of the opposition's "momentum" and find ways to turn the game around with relatively small amounts of force skillfully applied. The matter of "momentum" versus "energy flow" shows how language affects action, how metaphor shapes reality. No team in a major sport has yet applied the Energy Body concept explicitly, so far as I know. But there is growing awareness among sports experts of the importance of mental practice (of "imaging" and the like), and the concept coincides in many ways with what may well become a trend. Furthermore, energy awareness has been used explicitly and successfully in the teaching of golf, skiing, tennis and other individual sports. (pp. 101–102)

What Leonard speaks of has become a trend, indeed even a movement, in sport and its literature. It is a welcome sight because it has tempered the Western view of sport and its emphasis upon winning and domination. In the new trend, self-improvement and inner awareness are the values seen in sport. The desire to be number one has been replaced with the desire to know oneself. But it has also shown the West alternative ways to excel—new ways to practice and to exercise. Whether or not these can be applied to team sports remains problematic, but the energy game of doors for linesmen described by Leonard has been done successfully, so it warrants consideration by coaches.

The clincher for attaining inner awareness in sport lies in the difference in value attached to the meaning of competition and winning. Usually when a player measures his or her self-worth and significance by the final score, it is not surprising that he or she misses shots, plays poorly, or does what Gallwey calls losing self-control and confidence—"freaking out." People who worry about how they measure up to their friends and believe that to make and keep friends they must constantly be the best are never aware of anything but worry. In *Inner Tennis* Gallwey observes: "There is a crucial distinction between the reason for playing a competitive game and the goal of the game itself. The objective of the game is to win, but the reason for playing the game in the first place is usually different—to learn, to improve, to express one's full potential, for enjoyment or exercise, and so forth" (p. 142). When someone is truly involved in the exploration of one's own capabilities, one's level of performance, not trying to show others how well one can play, then and only then, as Gallwey claims in *The Inner Game of Tennis*, "can he directly and intimately experience his own resources and thereby increase his *self-knowledge*" (p. 22; my italics). Thus, only by competing with others with a detached non-judgmental attitude concerning his or her gains, misses, scores, and fumbles can a player discover the joy of his or her uniqueness and talents. To achieve this awareness, a player must allow a trust to develop between his or her brain and body. Gallwey explains, "It means maximum physical and mental effort. At the point one is going all out, he is most apt to slip 'out of his mind' into the unmatchable beauty of 'unconscious play'" (p. 124). (Recall Brodie's and Shaw's descriptions of the sport experience as beautiful.) The players and the play become as one through the competition and cooperation of all giving their utmost in competition. To perform at his or her best, one places confidence in his or her abilities and lets it ("It") happen. This sounds very simplistic, but more times than not, it is hard to be simple enough to be good.

Achievement of this elusive condition of selflessness requires practice and training. Only by experiencing an affective and effective performance, while the mind is still, is one encouraged to let go more often.

When one quiets the mind, one's self-awareness reveals itself via the body; it is then, as Gallwey notes in *Inner Tennis*, that "his full potential as a human being is allowed to unfold without interference from Self 1. He plays the rest of the game in accordance with his own given talents and circumstances. / He is free" (p. 141). Freedom is a prized notion of the Eastern view of sport. It is a freedom from the ego-mind, its worries and interferences, so that one has a freedom to experience one's full potential. This last kind of freedom Novak recognized as self-discovery—the last and innermost seal of the inner life of sport (pp. 157ff.). The West has started to aim at something that the East has incorporated all along. Playing games or participating in competitive events alerts players to their uniqueness, creativity, and individuality. In such circumstances the sport experience becomes a means of heeding the Socratic dictum "know oneself"—not just in the psychological sense, which is about all Gallwey suggests at times, but in the Zen sense. It is in a space such as this that the athlete and philosopher have found much to say to one another.

III

AT THIS POINT I wish to consider some objections that have been raised to my descriptive account so far, before dealing with the remaining basic concepts of the inner game of sport. There is a long-standing view that "Play is not only separated off from daily life; it is separated off from the fields of religion, art, and inquiry as well."[16] This point of view would obviously include Zen under the field of religion. What has been objected to is the tendency of the "inner game" proponents to reduce sport or play to a means, rather than an end in itself. The employment of the means/end distinction in thinking about sport may somehow jeopardize it as *play*. Play loses its freedom, spontaneity, and autotelic character. With sport as Zen, the end in question is self-knowledge or self-awareness (at times I am not sure which or if there is really a

121

difference), and sport becomes the means, which makes play participation chiefly instrumental. Weiss puts it this way: "Sport is, of course, not to be treated as primarily an agency for promoting health—or anything else for that matter—regardless of how important this is. Sport is an end in itself" (p. 228). This objection is I think a good one and difficult for this literature to answer. For Herrigel archery becomes *work* (see pp. 61, 68–69).

But accepting the objection would lead one to overlook two things that the "sport as Zen" theorists are attempting to accomplish. One is to offer the sportsperson a way to repeat those heightened moments in the sport experience. The second is to offer a way of freeing individuals from mental obstacles that prohibit them from fully expressing themselves and from achieving their full potential. These latter two desirable states need to be attained if self-knowledge and inner awareness are obtainable in sport. The only way sport can truly be like play is if these mental obstacles are overcome. For many, these psychological barriers are not overcome and sport does not have any of those desirable traits that play has. Zen in sport is one means of achieving this end. Also, with the overemphasis placed upon winning in sport today, perhaps viewing sport from a dimension like Zen could help *restore* those play-like qualities sport once had, when it was less institutionalized. Herrigel also suggests that one of the qualities of play—freedom—is obtainable: the "forms which he, the pupil, perfectly masters no longer oppress but liberate" (p. 63). So there is an interesting dialectic whereby through the work, the toil, involved in the forms come the qualities of play. The issue involving play is more complicated than it first appears with the Zen view of sport.

This is not to say that there are not any similarities between these broad cultural views of sport. Weiss reminds us that "one can become perfected by engaging in it [sport], but it does not have even that perfection as its aim. Perfection is an inevitable consequence of sport only when this is properly pursued in an enclosed arena where men and women find out what man [and woman] can bodily be" (p. 228). This may be true, but what if one wants to hasten that state or to repeat or maintain it?

122

Another one of "the inevitable consequences" of sport is that "man's play may prompt him to adventure and to learn truths about himself and things daily life partly obscures" (p. 139). This sounds very much like Gallwey and Leonard. However, in Zen training perfection is a goal, and the positing of that goal does not jeopardize the playful aspect of sport. Playfulness is found in Zen in various forms—art, humor, and koans. What is persuasive about this Weissian-type objection is that it is couched in terms of play—not sport. The means/end distinction, I would agree, does not do justice to play, but it applies without much distortion to much of sport proper, because the object is not something tangible—outside the player like the score. Sport—aside from play—has definite ends and purposes to which participants commit themselves. Sport is generally rule-governed, an institutionalized situation in which the participants are mutually engaged in instrumental and noninstrumental activities.[17] As Weiss has correctly observed: "It [sport] is a constructive activity in which aggression plays a role together with dedication, cooperation, restraint, self-denial, and a respect for the rights and dignity of others" (p. 185). In other words, when individuals enter into a game, they become mutual contestants—players—which means that they share goals, conventions, rules, and similar purposes. So with this observation in mind, it is difficult to see how the Zen view of the self in this literature would consider other individuals as means rather than ends in any perverse sense. (I cannot imagine what Kant's categorical imperative has to do with the internal considerations of sport situations.)[18] Consequently, Weiss's criticism of non-separation from other fields (like religion) is unwarranted, if it follows a path like that prescribed above.

In Zen the battle is with oneself; it is false samādhi if consciousness is directed toward the other in a demeaning fashion. This latter notion of competition is alien to Zen. (Note the vivid contrast with Sartre's view which we looked at in the previous chapter.) In fact there is no self—only a Humean succession (row) of events—one event following another, by which we become a unique part of the whole. So "self," "mind," and "ego," are just convenient names for a particular succession of events. There is no entity or substance

123

identified as the self. At this point in our discussion it may be time to supplement the idea of "inner awareness" in Gallwey's and others' writings. The state or stage of consciousness described by the athletes in the last section we shall label "sport samādhi."

When we are truly absorbed in playing a game, a state of *sport samādhi* is actualized. In such a state there is Sport pure and simple. The Sport fills up the whole field of existence. It is only after the sport is over, when we "come back" to ourselves, that we realize with a feeling of surprise that we have been completely "identified with" the sport. Sport, like music, has its own samādhi, and those who are truly accomplished at it have experienced it.[19] But when we actually realize it, the I and the sport are already split apart into two different "things." The experience of sport samādhi is for most of us a particular experience occurring only from time to time, on rare occasions or intermittently, like Pam Shriver's experience at the 1982 United States Open. For the person of Zen, experiences of this nature must be just ordinary, day-to-day events. There is no object of thought. Nor is there consciousness of the I as the subject. From no one knows where there emerges the play of sport. It does not involve the awareness of my "I," nor does it involve the awareness *of* the sport. But it is a pure awareness. And that Awareness *is* the sport.[20]

There is more to Awareness (in the Zen sense) than Gallwey makes "inner awareness" out to be. He never gets past his dualistic, Cartesian terminology to the stage of consciousness that most seriously preoccupies the person of Zen. A state of pure existence is there in sport as it is in other human activities or endeavors. However, "samādhi" admits of distinctions or levels of concentration. *Savikalpa-samādhi* is a state in which some duality of subject and object remains—Gallwey's third set tennis experience belongs in this category; whereas in samādhi as the last stage in deep concentration, the duality of subject and object disappears. In this higher mode of knowing, the mind becomes still and is transcended.[21]

Another objection is to the conception of *time* presupposed in this literature. The Zen-in-sport trend makes the present the crucial moment, which allegedly disregards the anticipatory or future orientation of sports activities. This claim simply is not true. Recall

124

Gary Shaw's description of his experience where past and future blended into the present moment. They became one continuous stream or flux of time, very much like what Henri Bergson pictured as the temporal flow of duration and consciousness.[22] Sekida expresses it in this fashion: "Moment after moment, only the present comes and goes during the period of samādhi, a continuous stream of the present. Only in the present can we be said to exist" (p. 121). Also, Shaw's and Brodie's descriptions resemble the experience of Kenshō in which one's awareness of the mind's purified state is projected onto the outside world (see Sekida, p. 95).

What Weiss has said about game time makes more sense to me than those who try to argue that the future orientation of games is the critical time moment: "In sport the largest present is the present of the game. In this we can isolate plays and moves only conceptually. The bunt and any other play is an organic, integral factor in the present indivisible whole of the game. The plays are, of course, also distinct units—as are the moves they encompass—each with its own present" (p. 164). The plays Weiss speaks of are what the players are or should be conscious of. If not, we will have a situation like the one Gallwey describes where those who think about their past shots or worry about the future ones fail to play in the present—where the game is going on. Perhaps, though, in games that are predominantly governed by time—by a clock—like basketball and football, players do play differently toward the end of the game than they do at earlier periods; but those moments still are in the present when they are played. My point, however, is that if players concern themselves with the clock, their concentration and play can be affected by such preoccupations. This brings me to the question of anticipation.

The phenomenon of anticipation occurs not in the future, but as part of the present moment. It is something a player lives through in the successful execution of a given shot, play, swing, or kick; it is something that every good athlete must possess at every moment within game time. For example, if I anticipate that my opponent is going to hit down the line while I am at the net, this is an act that I carry out in the present on the court; it is not some lingering future possibility to be realized. If all the objection amounts to is that the present moment in game time has a future dimension to it, then I do not think that there is a significant conceptual difference in these views of time.

Whereas Weiss speaks of the present time (Gallwey and I also do so at times), the student of Zen would speak of "no time." In absolute (and positive) samādhi there is no time; only the present. When we are completely absorbed in our work we are forgetful of ourselves and of time, "time" here meaning measured or clock time. There is only the present. When our attention is wholly on our work (or play) there is no room for reflecting consciousness. And psychological time is created and measured by the frequency of the reflecting action of consciousness.[23] Sekida draws the following parallel:

> In the same way, in the thick of battle you are forgetful of yourself, forgetful of time. In an emergency—an earthquake or a fire—rescuing people or things from a building, you have no time. There is only a continuation of the present. Present, present, present. This present time is interrupted if a reflecting action of consciousness occurs. You reflect upon your thought and recognize the difference between the moment ago and this moment. You notice the order of events, recollect the past, conjecture about the future. After a catastrophe, you go through the area once again and are astonished by the deeds that were accomplished that now seem remarkable and almost beyond human powers. (p. 120)

The sport experience is an intensified situation—like a battle or some emergency. Tennis matches (recall Gallwey's) are played like this: not letting up when one was ahead, astonished at one's own play later, and so on. Sekida's description of the present could very well be in a description of the sort of intense concentration found in sport situations.[24] We shall return to the concept of time later in the chapter.

IV

GALLWEY'S TECHNIQUE for teaching physical skills is an important one because it offers the sport community a viable alternative to the traditional one. By the "traditional" teaching method (and I know I am simplifying here) I have something in mind like Weiss's description:

> A complex act is more than the moves that can be distinguished within it. Not even all the necessary moves together can substitute for the act that encompasses them. To know how to pick up, hold, and swing a bat is not yet to have learned how to bat a ball. This is a single act stretching over those moves. But if one does not know how to bat a ball well, it may be necessary to concentrate on one or more of the moves. A correction of one of them may make a big difference to the quality of the whole act. (p. 42)

Gallwey (especially in *Inner Tennis*) and the others are challenging the conditional in this traditional view:

> (C) If one does not know how to bat a ball well, it is necessary to concentrate on one or more of the moves.[25]

I presume that "concentrate on" means "think about" in a reflective, calculative sense; not in a meditative sense or a Zen sense. The sort of concentration mentioned in (C) can slow learning processes of physical skills and become barriers to mastering them. But shifting one's attention to the ball, as in the "bounce-hit" exercise, one forgets about one's horrible swing or grip. (Many of the adjustments are made automatically by the body.) Gallwey tells of teaching an individual to play who knew nothing of tennis by using the precepts of the inner game: increasing awareness which in turn gives us the feedback (visual and bodily) from experience. The body will make its own adjustments on the basis of these messages. The three USPTA instructors who watched this were amazed to see what this individual had learned. They judged that it would have taken at least three lessons for that individual to have learned what she had in one of inner tennis.

Another thing that is challenged by the inner game and the Zen trend in the sport literature is the idea that all individuals who take up a game are to conform to a specific rigid model. One hits a forehand or a golf swing or handles the ski poles in just one way

127

and no other. One bats a ball with only one kind of stance, and so on. In the inner game there is individual adjustment of the game to the player rather than the player to the game.[26] Shurnryu Suzuki brought this insight to the West. Simon Ramo also independently realized it, but Gallwey has made it into a teaching maxim. As Herrigel recites: the tools of implementation are not as important as the mind (pp. 51, 55–56). Thus one of the major contributions of Zen is to learning theory in sport and sport skills. The Zen movement in sport has challenged the rationalistic model of learning.

It might also be objected that the Zen-in-sport literature *overrates* these awareness experiences and that they are not nearly as important as the normal, "average" sport experiences. Herrigel supplies an answer to this objection:

> I learned to lose myself so effortlessly in the breathing that I sometimes had the feeling that I myself was not breathing but— strange as this may sound—being breathed. . . . The qualitative difference between these few successful shots and the innumerable failures was so convincing that I was ready to admit that now at last I understood what was meant by drawing the bow "spiritually." / So that was it: not a technical trick I had tried in vain to pick up, but liberating breath-control with new and far-reaching possibilities. I say this not without misgiving, for I well know how great is the temptation to succumb to a powerful influence and, ensnared in self-delusion, to overrate the importance of an experience merely because it is so unusual. But despite all equivocation and sober reserve, the results obtained by the new breathing—for a time I was able to draw even the strong bow of the Master with muscles relaxed—were far too definite to be denied. (pp. 40–41)

And as Robert Fogelin would have put it, if these are not the paradigm cases of the sport experience, it does not really matter because the peripheral and extraordinary cases may show us something *more* about those conventions that govern our thinking and speaking about sport. "It is just in this area of so called vagueness that we can get our clearest insights into the conceptual structure of the notion under investigation."[27]

V

IN *The Zen Way to the Martial Arts,* J. T. Deshimaru puts forth an extended argument in which he tries to separate sport from Zen. Thus much of my discussion is put in jeopardy by Deshimaru's claims. His "objections" need to be examined before leaving the subject, so that what others have attempted in bringing Zen and sport together will not appear to be spurious. Many of his claims rest upon misconceptions.

Deshimaru was apparently unaware of the literature of the new school and of the more popularized literature of "the inner game," that of Gallwey and company. This becomes evident as we gaze at his whole text. He has written about something he is afraid is almost lost, extinct from the human race. The true martial arts, Budo (the way of the warrior), have become a formality (p. 15), an urban sport (p. 14). Etymology is important here. The word *do* means "path" or "way," but it is a special way. It is a path that is goalless, leads nowhere, and is pursued for its own sake. It becomes The Way. The character *bu* involves a pun. It literally means "war," but it also suggests to sheathe the sword or to cease to struggle. Paradoxes, like this one, are difficult for the Westerner to grasp, but they are a barometer of our enlightenment, as Murphy put it in *Golf in the Kingdom* (p. 164). Paradoxes are used to challenge and to transcend calculative thought. The spirit of Zen is foreseen in "*bu.*"

Deshimaru is attempting to separate the true from the false martial arts. Here is how he draws the distinction. For convenience, let me line these remarks up, because together they provide an indication of Deshimaru's perspective.

(i)   Its [Budo's] association with sports is a very recent development; the ancient writings are essentially concerned with a particular form of cultivation of the mind and a reflection upon the nature of the self: who am I? (p. 11)

(ii)   In Japan there is only: the way. In the West the "martial arts" are a fashion, they have become an urban sport, a technique, and have none of the spirit of the way. (p. 14)

(iii) The martial arts are not theater or entertainment. That is not the true Budo. Kodo Sawaki [Deshimaru's master] used to say that the secret of the martial arts is that there is no victory and no defeat. You can neither win nor be beaten. It is not the same as in sports. (p. 13)

(iv) In reality, *shin* —spirit—is what matters first; technique and body come afterward. In other sports, especially in the West, physical strength is the most important fact, but this is not so in the martial arts. (p. 29)

(v) Training must not aim only at developing the body. In present-day tournaments, of course, people are not fighting for life and death but for points, so physical strength and technique are enough, whereas in olden days things were very different because life was at stake and then, ultimately, intuition decided the outcome. It should be that way today: every fight should be fought as if life were at stake, even when you're fighting with wooden swords. Then the martial arts would find their rightful place again, and become the practice of the way. Otherwise, they are only a game. (p. 30)

(vi) . . . the general feeling [in Europe, the United States, and Japan] is that the principles and philosophy of Zen have nothing to do with the practice of the martial arts as sports. [These people are] . . . simply using the martial arts as playthings; to them they are sports like any others. (p. 38)

(vii) I have nothing against sports; they train the body and develop stamina and endurance. But the spirit of competition and power that presides over them is not good, it reflects a distorted vision of life. The root of the martial arts is not found there. (p. 38)

(viii) Sports are only amusement and in the end, because of the spirit of competition, they wear out the body. (p. 38)

(ix) Japanese Budo developed directly out of an ethic, philosophy, and religion, without any transition through or association with any sport. (p. 45)

130

(x)   The true way of the Budo is not through competition or conflict; it is beyond life and death, beyond victory and defeat. . . . It is no longer necessary to win victories over them [the opponents]. (p. 51)

(xi)   . . . the martial arts are not sports. (p. 71)

(xii)   There is nothing sportlike about training in those days [the period of Miyamoto Musashi, the greatest kendō master]; the samurai had a higher vision of life. (p. 72)

(xiii)   Zazen is not meant to make you feel relaxed and happy, any more than the martial arts are a game or sport. (p. 72)

(xiv)   These things [breathing, kin-hin] do have a connection with the martial arts—which are, I repeat, something other than sports. (p. 85)

(xv)   . . . today the martial arts are more like a form of gymnastics and have lost their original profundity. (p. 102)

The viewpoint that these statements afford is not unique to Deshimaru. It persists throughout the literary tradition. For instance Herrigel's master speaks the same way: "Archery is not a pastime, not a purposeless game" (p. 51; see also p. 19); "By archery in the traditional sense . . . the Japanese does not understand a sport" (p. 18; see also p. 17). Because of its persistence and the impressions it leaves of "sport," the perspective is worth singling out for brief comment. When Deshimaru's remarks are lined up this way, it is easy to see that sports and sport get a bad rap. The martial arts aren't what they used to be, and the attitudes behind sport are to blame, according to Deshimaru. But what attitudes does he mean? His characterization of "sport" as a game, entertainment, or amusement clearly reflects the concept of *recreation*. Now there are, no doubt, a large number of people in the West and Japan who have such an idea of sport. His claim in statement (vi) is well taken. But there is more to the generic concept of sport than the sport-as-recreation analogy. (There are other analogies at work in Deshimaru's perspective, and I shall turn to them in due course.) In fact, many of the things Deshimaru says of the true martial arts can be found in Western sport. So in the remainder of this section, I shall be preoccupied with similarities rather than differences between the true martial arts and Western sport. Also such differences need not be noted by me here, since they have been discussed by Carl Becker.[28]

Deshimaru's idea of the difference between sport and the martial arts is interesting; for one thing, because of his philosophical use of the concepts of time and thought:

> In sports, time exists. In the martial arts there is only the present. In baseball, for instance, the man at bat has to wait for the pitch, he has time; his action is not instantaneous. The same is true of rugby or football or any other sport. Time passes and there is time, if only a fraction of a second, to think about something, while waiting. In the martial arts there is no time to wait. (p. 23)

Deshimaru does not mean just "clock" time—conventional, measured time. He thinks there are moments of waiting built into games. He seems to be suggesting that such moments are not part of the martial arts. Consequently the martial arts and games (sport) are different because their respective actions are different. A little later he elaborates on how these actions are accomplished:

> [In the Japanese martial arts] it all happens in a flash. And in that flash the mind decides, technique and body follow. In all modern sports there is a pause, but in the martial arts there is no pause. If you wait, ever so little, you're lost; your opponent gets the advantage. The mind must be constantly concentrated on the whole situation; ready to act or react; that's why it is most important. There is no choosing. It happens unconsciously, automatically, naturally. There can be no thought, because if there is a thought there is a time of thought and that means a flaw. For the right moment to occur there must be a permanent, totally alert awareness, of the entire situation; that awareness chooses the right stroke, technique and body execute it, and it's all over. (p. 32)

On first reading, this explanation sounds convincing, but upon reflection, questions crop up. "Pause" is a relative term, and if it is equated with "waiting" (which it is above), then the same applies to the martial arts. The temporal, sequential language is inescapable: in a "flash the mind *decides*" (unconsciously), "technique and body *follow.*" Contrary to what Deshimaru says here, one has to wait for *suki*, opportunity. As he says elsewhere, "Opportunity is most important, and thinking cannot create it. Only consciousness can seize upon the opportunity for action, the empty space in which one must act" (p. 33). Isn't this true of sport situations also? A tennis player taking the net must wait for the right opportunity. In baseball the batter deciding to bunt must also wait for *suki*. The key is not to think while waiting. One must simply wait. "Consciousness" tells a player when to seize upon the opportunity for action. Time—real time or lived time—is moment.[29] The successive actions in sport should be instantaneous just as they should be in the martial arts. Overt thought impedes the proper successive movements of a given action.

Deshimaru asserts that "in a tournament, it is impossible to maintain the same intensity of concentration indefinitely. At some point the attention wavers and we show a fault, a *suki*, an opportunity, which the opponent must be able to seize" (p. 34). In games, the "faults" emerge as play proceeds, and mature, masterful opponents recognize and exploit them. Plays or strategies are built around such faults. Linemen in football watch their opponents to see a loss of concentration. And once it is spotted, they build a play around it. The following example of kendō, for which there may be no Western parallel, shows the importance of "waiting." Several years ago in Kyoto there was a contest between two kendō masters who were close to eighty years old. At the end of five minutes of absolute motionlessness the referee declared the contest a tie. As each master stood facing the other, he saw no opportunity to strike. Deshimaru comments that "the two old masters simply fought with their spirit, with and through their eyes" (p. 35). But even in this case there is time—the time of the match: after five minutes the referee ruled a tie. The match time was the present moment, which just happened to have the duration of five minutes.

Waiting is one of the activities of meditative thinking.[30] Herrigel's kendō master (Kenzo Awa) provides an image of the

right or true art, and in so doing gives us an example of meditative thinking—"waiting"—in his question-answer exchange with
Herrigel:

> "We master archers say: with the upper end of the bow the
> archer pierces the sky, on the lower end, as though attached by
> a thread, hangs the earth. If the shot is loosed with a jerk there
> is a danger of the thread snapping. For purposeful and violent
> people the rift becomes final, and they are left in the awful
> center between heaven and earth."
>
> "What must I do, then?" I asked thoughtfully.
> *"You must learn to wait properly."*
> "And how does one learn that?"
> "By letting go of yourself, leaving yourself and everything
> yours behind you so decisively that nothing more is left of you
> but a purposeless tension."
>
> "So I must become purposeless—on purpose?" I heard
> myself say.
> "No pupil has ever asked me that, so I don't know the
> right answer."
>
> "And when do we begin these new exercises?"
> *"Wait until it is time."* (pp. 51–52; my italics)[31]

This "waiting" is described by Herrigel in the following manner:
"And when, at lesson time, we again practiced with bow and arrow,
these exercises proved so fruitful that we were able to slip effortlessly into the state of 'presence of mind'" (p. 90). Learning to wait
is like learning the virtues of silence. As Deshimaru says, "body
and mind recover their natural unity" (p. 64) in silence. The natural unity of a person can be recovered in waiting. Deshimaru does
acknowledge time elsewhere: "In a contest the mind must be like
the moon unmoving, while body and time slip past, past, past
like water in the stream" (p. 22). Both Herrigel's master and Deshimaru think that one must learn to wait patiently, because only after
years (not days, much less minutes) of practice does one learn to
concentrate unconsciously. Patience and waiting are important
virtues and aspects of human activity in the Orient, although these
virtues also make their appearance in the West. In the preface to

Phenomenology of Perception, Merleau-Ponty appreciates the philosophical importance of silence: "In the silence of primary consciousness can be seen appearing not only what words mean, but also what things mean: the core of primary meaning round which the acts of naming and expression take shape."

Nonetheless much of what Deshimaru says about the martial arts is present in Western sport. As a paradigmatic case for sport, I shall use basketball, and my main source for discussion will be John McPhee's profile of Bill Bradley.[32] But much of what follows holds for other games and regions of sport as well. The great basketball player Bill Bradley, who played for Princeton University in the early 1960s, recounts through reporter McPhee: "When you have played basketball for a while, you don't need to look at the basket when you are in close like this," he said, throwing it over his shoulder again and right through the hoop. "You develop a sense of where you are" (p. 22). And later he adds, "The secret of shooting is concentration" (p. 24). The sort of concentration Bradley is talking about here is that which springs unconsciously from the mind: "Van Breda Kolff [the Princeton coach] says that Bradley is a great mover, and points out that the basis of all these maneuvers is footwork. Bradley has spent hundreds of hours merely rehearsing the choreography of the game—shifting his feet in the same patterns again and again, until they have worn into his motor subconscious" (p. 50). Bradley may not have meditated, but what he did before games shows a preparation not unlike that practiced in the martial arts. As McPhee reports: "During most of the afternoon, when any other player in his situation would probably have been watching television, shooting pool, or playing ping-pong or poker—anything to divert the mind—Bradley sat alone and concentrated on the coming game, on the components of his own play, and on the importance to him and his team of what would occur" (p. 85).

Bradley clearly conceived of basketball as more than recreation, or what Deshimaru calls urban sport. For Bradley, it was something that pertained to life—"an ordeal," "discipline," and "the conquest of pain" (pp. 51, 65). For coach Van Breda Kolff, basketball was merely a game (p. 51). But for Bradley the game had taken on added dimensions—some of which are quite similar to Deshimaru's descriptions of the true martial arts. Let us return to our initial list of statements. Joe Hyams would argue with the characterization of sport in (ii), (x), (xi), and (xv). He thinks that one comes to The Way by being exposed to the martial arts. One would have to be totally insensitive not to be drawn to The Way once one is exposed to it. Hyams would disagree with (iii) and (iv), too. He would say that in defeat there is victory (pp. 139ff.) and that spirit (*shin*) comes after technique (*waza*) and body (*tai*). Bradley's testimony casts doubt on (v), (vii), (viii), (ix), and in a way, (xv). Given my above analysis, I would suggest that there are more affinities than differences between the Asian and the Western (non-Sartrean) conceptions of sport.[33] Can we speak of just one generic concept of sport?

Analogous to the forms in the martial arts are the various moves and shots in basketball. The reverse pivot, the rocker step, going back door, finger roll, layups, the jump shot, hook shot, foul shot, and so on, have the same sort of exercises, practices, rituals, and mimes that are embedded in the martial arts—the step forward and strike with shoulder, mirror trails elbow, white crane spreads wings, brush knee and push, snake creeps down, golden cock on one leg, and so forth.[34] The preparation skills and practice make these moves second nature to a participant. Each action is broken down into a sequence of six moves. In the context of tennis we have: (1) reaction, (2) preparation, (3) movement toward the ball, (4) ball-racket contact, (5) recovery, and (6) positioning for the next shot. These moves form what is called the Tennis Episode (TE).[35] This model is easily adapted to other realms of human movement.

The TE can be changed to a Martial Arts Episode (MAE). The model interpreted this way would yield the following six limited elements: (1) reaction, (2) preparation, (3) movement toward opponent, (4) opponent contact, (5) recovery, and (6) positioning for the next move or form. The MAE is essentially no different from the TE. The model can be generalized to the Sport Episode (SE). Most actions in sport can be analyzed as an instance of SE. SEs are rarely the same; they vary with each occurrence. Some are "slow," some quick. Moreover, SEs vary according to each individual's bodily characteristics and style. Such variation provides backing for the argument for intuition. Whatever "pause" there is must be one of intuition rather than thought. At first the moves are a product of thought, just as in the martial arts, but they later become a product of intuition. There is a "series" of temporal movements to be accomplished. A component theory of human action is helpful here in dissecting the movement.[36] But it should be noted that my treatment of sport here is strictly outward and measurable—there is a good deal more to the "inward" nature of it in which East and West differ. Illustrations: the relative importance of bodily to mental strength (*no* Western sport would have 80-year-old masters), and the identity of sport prowess and wisdom in the Zen tradition (in the West we dare not idealize our sport champions for any qualities except athletic). All of this may be traced metaphysically to the naturalism of the Orient and the humanism (like Sartre's) of the West. The practice of the martial arts forms reinforces the natural animal movements, and it is in this way that metaphysical naturalism is expressed on the practical level of living. But similarities of the two sport traditions are still acknowledged, even by those who are schooled in Eastern practices and philosophies.

VI

IN THE MIDDLE of *The Zen Way to the Martial Arts*, Deshimaru's argument takes on a different twist—one that complicates my previous discussion. He does acknowledge the application to sport of the kind of action he has described for the martial arts, at least once in the text:

> Sometimes one realizes that it is possible to act without consciousness or ego, spontaneously, as in the creative arts, or sports, or any other act in which body and mind are both wholly immersed. The action takes place of itself before any conscious thought; it is a pure action, essence of zazen. (p. 55)

But Deshimaru no longer has urban sport or sport as recreation in mind when he speaks of "sport." Here he aligns sport with the creative or artistic, or sport can be practiced in an artistic manner, i.e., with total immersion. Bradley was our case study above. Perhaps the conceptual similarity between the practice of sport in East and West is found in the notion of art or the artistic. An activity

137

practiced as an art makes it possible for that action to be a pure action. But are actions, even pure actions, without thought? What is meant by "thought" here?

Let us now turn to the nature of thought. Deshimaru retorts: "Professors, and especially philosophers, devote all their time to thinking; none of them ever dreams of undertaking a critique of thought itself" (p. 54). Apparently Deshimaru is unaware of Martin Heidegger's works. Deshimaru's description of zazen as "pure thought without any personal consciousness embodying it, in harmony with the consciousness of the universe" (p. 54) is close to what Heidegger called nonobjective or meditative thinking.[37] On the nature of thought, Deshimaru says that zazen "generates an attitude of mind which we call *hishiryo*: a state of thought without thinking, of consciousness beyond thought" (p. 10). "A state of thought beyond thought" sounds contradictory only if we ignore a distinction between meditative and calculative thought—a distinction Heidegger had drawn in the West, most notably in *Discourse on Thinking*.[38] The noncontradictory expansion of *hishiryo* is: a state of meditative thought beyond calculative thought. Deshimaru clearly means meditative thought by "thought":

> One of the things Zen means is the effort of practicing meditation, zazen. It is the effort to reach *the realm of thought* without discrimination, consciousness beyond all categories, embracing and transcending every conceivable expression in language. This dimension can be attained through the practice of zazen and of Bushido [the way of the samurai]. (p. 12; my italics)

And "In zazen you must not dwell upon any single thought, your *thought* must abide *nowhere*" (p. 51; my italics). "Nowhere" refers to no object or no object of individualization. (Heidegger's nonobjective thinking is close to this characterization.)

For "calculative thought," Deshimaru foresees: "In the practice of Budo there can be no conscious thought. There is no time for thinking, not even an instant" (p. 17). Again, time is moment. Also, "It is your mind, your consciousness, that must not panic or calculate—just adjust completely to whatever is happening" (p. 36). At this point we begin wondering whether or not Deshimaru has built sport into a straw man. Do not the last two prescriptions apply to sport as well as to artistic sport? What he says about concentration surely works in sport, and indeed always has: "Concentrate all the time on your breathing, your breathing *out*, which should be slow and long and reach as far down as possible into your abdomen, your *hara*. And never take your eyes off your opponent's eyes; that way you can follow his inner movements" (p. 36). In basketball a player follows his opponent's head. McPhee remarks: "Bradley watches the man's head. If it turns too much to the right, he moves quickly to the left. If it turns too much to the left, he goes to the right" (p. 57). This becomes a perceptual matter.

In *Zen Training*, Sekida constantly draws analogies with zazen and other situations, many of which are taken from the realm of sport. For example, in discussing the effects of a faulty posture, he comments:

> Tensing the shoulders necessarily results in physical and mental disturbance. We can see this happening, incidentally, not only in zazen, but in other situations. The baseball pitcher's sudden loss of control, for example, is often attributable to the unusual straining of his shoulders due to his excitement. We must use the same care in zazen that we would in athletics or gymnastics. (p. 45)

How different is Sekida's perspective on sport from Deshimaru's! Only once does Deshimaru acknowledge pure action (without calculative thought) in sport (p. 55). When the philosophical premises are flushed out into the open where they can be examined, the bifurcation between "East" and "West" begins to break down, and we truly see the need for an overall, generic concept of sport. In the realm of sport there are attitudes and techniques for performing actions similar to those found in the true martial arts. Is it possible to come to the philosophy—the true spirit behind the martial arts—through sport and not through the practice of zazen? As we have seen, Hyams thinks so. His book is an interesting contrast to Deshimaru's text. There are many paths to Budo. Sport may lead to self-knowledge just as zazen may. Basketball did just that for Bradley. However, the Zen masters obviously mean something more sharply defined than what Bradley described. He came across things that worked for him; they were accidental and not a part of a tradition. The West is undoubtedly learning from the Eastern tradition, as the literature from this awareness movement testifies.

On behalf of Deshimaru's critique of urban sport, I must add that, for the experience of sport for *average* athletes, there is much truth in what he says. Indeed the corruption of sport is as much a concern for him as it is for us. I have dealt with the exceptional cases to show that at least a few have achieved a fairly high degree of "pure action" in the West. Bradley, Brodie, Shriver are exceptional in that they have performed countless repetitions of their skills and have the requisite concentration to carry these out in a Zenlike manner. Gallwey appreciated this unusual situation and attempted to bring their learning techniques to the public, but he promised things in the short term that only come through years of practice.

Bradley's locational sense is comparable to the state of awareness of one's environment in Zen; it is suggestive of a sixth sense (Hyams, p. 97) if you like. Instinctive action has always been the preferred action in sport. And after having reviewed Deshimaru's text, I believe that his fears of losing the true spirit behind the martial arts are unfounded. Athletes of unusual dedication and training—regardless of culture—will discover these spiritual and aesthetic values that Deshimaru associates with the true martial arts. The principle that governs them also governs sport when it is practiced as an art—as Bill Bradley played basketball. It is the practitioners that make the difference between the true and the false martial arts and the different concepts of sport. This is not to be taken as lessening the importance of what is distinctively Japanese in the martial arts; it is only to say that the West shares some of those cultural associations with its sport, even though those associations may be more an individual matter than in the East.

Does the Zen experience, as Gallwey and company claim, result in self-knowledge? Much of this depends on what self-knowledge is taken to be. Is it psychological information about ourselves? Or is the self that power which Gallwey felt in that tennis match and Sekida describes in his Zen experience? If it is the latter, then we have a sense of the term that stands for that process in which we lose ourselves (the psychological self) to become part of the perfect game or shot—the "It" that Herrigel's master talked about (pp. 76–77). Perhaps what Herrigel says about "doing it right" best describes it:

> All right is accomplished only in a state of true selflessness in which the doer cannot be present any longer as "himself." Only the spirit is present, a kind of awareness which shows no trace of egohood and for that reason ranges without limit through all distances and depths, with "eyes that hear and with ears that see." / Thus the teacher lets his pupil voyage onward through himself. . . . The important thing is that an inward movement is thereby initiated. . . . The inward work, however, consists in his turning the man he is, and the self he feels himself and perpetually finds himself to be, into the raw material of a training and shaping whose end is mastery. In it, the artist and the human being meet in something higher. The man, the art, the work—it is all one. (pp. 67–69)

Here we find Herrigel voicing substantially the same thing that Sekida did, only in less technical terms. The "end" or object of Zen practice is "Jishu-zammai" or the samādhi of self-mastery. This exalted state of "doing it right"—perfection—and its inner control are surely what "self-knowledge" means in this context. What is the nature of the self in *self*-knowledge or the samādhi of *self*-mastery? Of course it should be a selfless self (*ānatta, ānatman*). Then what is *ānatta*? One of the most prominent Zen philosophers, Shin'ichi Hisamatsu,[39] has emphatically differentiated between a particular samādhi and a total or holistic samādhi. The former is a sort of Zen technique, whereas the latter is the realization *as me* of the Formless Self, the ultimate reality or the entirety of the universe. An awareness of this oneness with the universe as a whole is found in Aikidō by its most mature and sensitive students. This is the most genuine sense of "appreciation" of which we spoke in the previous chapter.

Anything less than this exalted state does not do justice to what we have discussed here. As Sekida says of Sumo wrestlers: "Zazen is child's play compared to the feats of these athletes!" (p. 88). Tim Gallwey in that third set experienced "Jishu-zammai," and knew it.[40]

SIX

Is "Choking" an Action?

I

SEVERAL ACTIONS in sport warrant philosophical analysis because of their interesting complexity and the challenge they initiate for established theories. In addition to cheating and faking, the activity of choking (in the psychological sense) in sport is philosophically interesting. The former two notions have been subject to some analysis but choking has not.[1] All three—but especially choking—serve as examples in which the analytical philosophy of action loses some of its precision and clarity. Not that this is a vice, though. In the end these three actions may help redirect, if not settle, some of the issues in action theory today.

In a recent article entitled "Do Our Intentions Cause Our Intentional Actions?" Irving Thalberg makes the following two claims:

> I conclude that it will be very difficult for attackers of the causal theory to invent or find instances of action that are at once sustainingly produced by the agent's intention *and* deviantly produced by his nervousness. After that, they still have to show these actions are not done intentionally.[2]

It is easier than Thalberg thinks to come up with examples of action that are at once (sustainingly) produced by the agent's intention and deviantly produced by his or her nervousness. A look within the world of sport reveals a family of actions known as "chokes" that appear to satisfy these conditions. In golf a *choked putt* is an action that is at once (sustainingly) produced by the agent's intention—the golfer is intending to sink the ball—*and* deviantly produced by his or her nervousness. However, the attackers of the causal theory should not be overjoyed with such instances, because these actions may or may not be done intentionally, depending upon the circumstances. They always involve nervousness, however. I shall try to explain this equivocal situation below.

Many sports people, from recreationists to world-class athletes, are plagued by choking, or what in golf is called the "yips." Here is a recent description of the phenomenon:

> You study the putt and settle confidently over the ball. This one's in the hole [you think] . . . then suddenly it happens. / Your palms get slick and the putter develops a mind of its own. The ball appears to be far away and the cup is shrinking by the moment. Shortly before the target closes entirely, you jab the putt and send the ball skidding past the hole. / Welcome to the club. You have just had a case of the yips, golf's gift to the human nervous system. And don't feel lonely, said veteran touring pro Don January. Everybody who ever has swung a 5-iron in earnest has had them, even the top players in the $175,000 Senior Players ReUnion Pro-Am this week [early June 1985] at Bent Tree Country Club [in Dallas] and they should know better. / "It happens to everybody from time to time, and believe me it ain't no fun," said January, 54, who has won $2.1 million in his career. "It's like being trapped inside a burning house and not being able to get out." / Ben Hogan, perhaps the finest shotmaker the game ever has known, was a notable sufferer. The old master froze over putts so badly in his last few tournaments, he no longer plays before an audience.[3]

Hogan added that the difference between competitive golf and pleasure golf is like the difference between ice hockey and tennis. A bit overstated, to say the least, but his point is that competitive golf has pressure. Choking, or the yips, occurs when one can't handle the pressure.

Choking is of interest to the philosopher because its classification appears problematic. (Deviant behavior has been of interest to philosophers since the days of Empedocles.) My initial questions are twofold: is choking or yipping a (bodily) movement, an (intentional) action, or both? And is a choked putt, or a choked sport action, one act or many? To answer these questions and related ones, let me review some portions of Thalberg's article mentioned above, and his book *Perception, Emotion and Action*.[4] He has taken on the critics of the causal theory of intentional action (particularly Donald Davidson).[5] An agent causal theorist holds that an action X is intentional if and only if our intention to do X, or the appropriate amalgam or mixture of believing and wanting to do X, causes us to do X. In golf, putting would clearly be an intentional action under this definition. To perform the action *putting*, the golfer wants to sink the putt, believes he or she has made the right reading of the lay, the green, and has selected the proper club. Moreover he or she may intend to sink it, although intending is not a necessary link in the causal chain because acting intentionally has a "wider" field than does action preceded by intent. The golfer may have simply read the putt and then made the putt. Yet afterward the golfer may say that addressing the ball, gently swinging the club, and keeping the head stationary throughout the stroke are all things he or she intended, but that these things may not have been intended before acting.[6] (In the end Thalberg seems to collapse this distinction in arguing for a full-blown, "sustained" causal theory. More on this follows later in the chapter.) If there are acts that qualify as (intentional) actions (however problematic it is to come up with an adequate definition of *action*), putting is surely one of them; but are the yips or chokes putting? This "second-order" activity superimposed on putting seems to complicate things. Let me draw our attention to some of Don January's descriptive remarks.

January makes it sound like choking is something unwillful and involuntary over which the golfer has no control; after all, no golfer wants to get the yips. He says, "It's like being trapped inside a burning house and not being able to get out." And, "then suddenly it happens. Your palms get slick and the putter develops a mind of its own. . . . You jab the putt [and] . . . a case of the yips, golf's gift to the human nervous system." Such language suggests bodily movement rather than a human action that is intentional. The golfer is *overwhelmed* by a yip. Is this the correct analysis? Well, I am not sure. Let us explore some alternate routes of interpretation.

Is choking like acting nervously? Is choking a putt like an act that results wholly from nervousness? Can nervousness modify behavior in such a way that you end up not doing X intentionally even though you had the intention to do X? It would seem so, for in the yips there are deviant causal chains that interfere with the intention, and hence putting is done without some of the requisite intention(s). In other words, there is a failing to do X though the agent is still intending to do it. Indeed we have January's and Hogan's testimonies to this effect. Choking moves causally in one direction, from bodily changes to mental changes—if anything, it *subtracts* from the action. I haven't heard of people choking and ending up performing better, but I guess we can't rule that out. It is often thought that something, for example intentionality, is added to bodily movement to make it an act or action. So, if we accept this, the subtraction notion in choking makes sense.[7]

This discussion takes me to my next question: Can the yips or choking be controlled? Other athletes seem to think so. Some tennis players, like Rod Laver, think that when they feel their arm turn to iron and the court shrink when about to serve, they shake their arm and say to themselves, "This is silly, it's just a game."[8] According to some, then, mental changes can cause the nervousness or the lack of nervousness in performing some sport action.

Some behavior is not actual choking, but closely resembles it—what some golf pros and Laver call "whiskey wrists": "Your grips don't feel right and your shots are jerky. You're not necessarily choking, but you're so rattled you don't know where you are. You're rushing, you want to get it all over—yet you're not anxious to lose" (p. 276). (By this last remark, Laver is not implying that one is anxious to lose in choking. There may be episodes like that, but this condition—being anxious to lose—is by no means a salient feature of choking.) Nevertheless Laver has advice that in turn may make choking and whiskey wrists controllable: "When you've got those whiskey wrists, pause and try to think about a couple of key things. Keep your eye on the ball. Forget where your opponent is, and try to see the ball hit your racket. And bend your knees. That'll help loosen you up. Take a deep breath" (p. 276-277). With these prescriptions in mind, Laver said of his 1962 match with Roy Emerson, "There weren't going to be any nerves for me the rest of the way." And there weren't. Laver won 4-6, 8-6, 13-11, 6-4 at Forest Hills to win the Grand Slam. Laver shows that mental changes can cause bodily changes. We must have at least some theory or reading that permits causal interactionism.[9] (By such a remark, I am not implying that we must embrace dualism.) Other sport actions in the family of choking include tentative play and tight or "loose" play. An example of this last category and its remedy come from the column "Stan Smith's Tennis Class": "Freeze-up on crucial serves? Be certain to toss the ball far enough away from you to permit your normal serving motion to occur! By 'leading' with your toss into the court far enough, you'll automatically *stretch fully* in order to hit the ball . . . instead of tightening up on the shot" (*Dallas Morning News*, February 1, 1986, p. 11B). So in descending order, we have choking, whiskey wrists, tentative play, and tight or loose play. This hierarchy reflects the degree of severity of inhibition in sport acts and the lack of control—with choking the worst, tight or loose play the least severe.

If choking or whiskey wrists are somewhat controllable, then the resulting action is the product of one's desires and belief, consequently it is an action—an intentional action at that. So which is it, an action or a bodily movement? Well, it seems to be both. This is what I mean about the analysis losing precision and clarity; the phenomenon of choking doesn't seem to go neatly into one category, nor is it susceptible to only one kind of interpretation. One possible problem is the assumption that action and bodily movement are two different, unrelated concepts. As Davidson reminds us, the latter is the basis for the former (pp. 43ff).

How is the distinction drawn between bodily movement and action? On behalf of entailment theorists (that is, opponents of the analysis of human action along the lines of physical causation who hold that the relation between action and reasons for action is a logical one), Thalberg (in *Perception, Emotion and Action*, pp. 45ff) states that for the movement of your body to qualify as an action, you will have to meet a pair of conditions: (a) it must occur while you are conscious, and (b) you have to have moderate control of it at the time. Would choking qualify as an action under this criterion? Let's see. Condition (a) is surely met; if anything, there is *too much* consciousness on the part of the victim. One's beliefs about his or her general circumstances get in the way of successfully performing the sport action in question. John McEnroe, Jr., might become overly conscious of playing on Centre Court at Wimbledon and start thinking that a win there is worth over a million dollars, that he will have a place in the history of the game if he wins, and so on. And these are adequate, true beliefs about his situation.

What about condition (b)? The answer to this question may depend on what is meant by "moderate control" in the requirement. Indeed it seems that this is precisely what choking is; that is, a loss of control over the bodily movement at the time. Here we have *too little* control over our bodily mobility, and "control" in this context means that the action is "successfully executed." Davis observes that a person may initiate an act but in the process become someone who simply transmits a movement (p. 10). A situation like this could very well be a description of a choked putt, like January's description, in which case condition (b) is nullified. Since choking is a sort of paralysis of the action, (a) does not entail (b) and the denial of (b) does not entail a denial of (a). So choking slips past this argument, in that we can conceive of action in general as done by agents with some correct beliefs, and at the same time without the requisite mastery over their bodily movements. Yet because our preanalytic intuitions tell us that there are some choking cases that are controlled (to some extent) by the agent, (b) is suspect; these actions do not end up being what they should be under the restrictions of (b). With regard to the domain of sport actions, (b) would need to be modified.

From an Asian or Zen perspective, (a) may be too restrictive; (a) depends on what is meant by "conscious." In this connection, Thalberg concedes: "If you report that someone performed even a minimal 'automatic' action, we are deductively entitled to these inferences [automatic actions]" (p. 47). Hence, "conscious" is

148

sufficiently broad to cover the exercising of martial arts forms in a "nonconscious" manner. But this does not mean that an agent is totally devoid of consciousness. It has been suggested that (a) is not a requirement of a sport action. For instance, there are some American swimming coaches who try to eliminate consciousness altogether from the swimmer's events. This is a questionable practice, if not an objectionable one. Why would one want to compete if one couldn't enjoy being in the event? The particular kind of awareness associated with sporting events is one of the joys or pleasures of sport. If we eliminate it, we eliminate sport.[10] "Playing unconsciously" may be coextensive with *mushin*, which is inexactly translated as "no-mind," but the Japanese term, *mushin*, does not denote human activities that are totally devoid of consciousness. *Mushin* has an analysis similar to what I am suggesting here for "conscious."[11]

Lawrence Davis's suggestion is broad enough to capture the Eastern notion of action when he observes that agents have a special awareness of their actions that distinguishes these actions from mere bodily motions like nervous spasms (p. 2). When you move, for example, in executing a karate kick, you are aware that you are moving your body and your body is not simply moving or being moved. But this awareness may not be as special as Davis makes it out to be (see below). As Margaret Steel puts it, the performing of a sport action is *conscious* in the sense that we must be aware of what we are trying to do in order to attempt it, but what we perform is also, in a certain sense, *unconscious*.[12] We know how to execute a kick, but we do not know how we do it. Our bodies perform the actions without our minds being aware of the movements on more than a surface level. It is because sport actions are a mixture of conscious and unconscious components that we find the phenomenon of choking within its domain. Choking occurs when these two components are not synchronized.

In classical karate the context and the relation established (by the kick) with the opponent can define the act and agent as Zen action/Zen person.[13] In other words, it is the context and the relation that make the awareness special. Davis goes on to say, "This special awareness cannot itself be what must be *added* to the motion to get an action. Perhaps *the missing ingredient* is like the awareness, however, in being mental, or at least 'inner' in some sense."[14] This animated, localized state or presence (a *doing* by an agent, a *person*, for Davis) is what phenomenologists call "embodied subjectivity." So condition (*a*) is not sufficient to stand alone, but is to be viewed as a set member of a necessary joint requirement, that is, (*a*) has a partner, (*b*), that has to be operative in order for (*a*) to count.

Nonetheless the real trouble is with requirement (*b*), not (*a*). Even in the performing of a sport action that is not choked, there may not be mastery over the agent's bodily movements. In racquet sports one has to contend with an opponent who is trying to make sure that one does not have control over the stroke or shot. Since this is true of most other competitive sports as well, the conditions for action in sport need careful formulation in order to capture those acts which belong in that realm. In spite of situations like these, mastery is still thought to be characteristic of a sport action (more on this below). Of course, these requirements are imprecise and vague enough to include sport actions, but the phenomenon of choking still presents a challenge. Perhaps there is a correlation between the requirements when it comes to choking: The greater (*a*) is, the lesser (*b*) is, but the converse relation does not hold.[15] These reflections tend to substantiate Davidson's position, since the relation appears to be a causal rather than a logical one, that is, there is no entailment relation.

II

WE MIGHT ASK at this point, over and above these require-ments, What else is needed for us to have a sport action? One particular proposal is that sport actions are actions of protagonists who confront one another as they struggle to defeat each other.[16] (Here "protagonists" in the sense of "opponents" is broad enough to include nature, records, or equipment.) Bernard Jeu adds, "It is necessary to possess a definite technique and to use it with determination." This last condition implies some mastery over the move or act in question. Certain things must happen in order for a move or act to become a sport action; in sum, they are: the agent is to be conscious (with the above qualifications) of the act; the agent has some mastery over the act; the agent is a protagonist who confronts another protagonist; they struggle to defeat one another; the struggle exemplifies technique and its use in willful determination. The second requirement is a refinement of (b), and the last three are specifications on (a). Choking diminishes the second and fifth features on our list. At what point does choking nullify the conjunction of traits? It is difficult to say where to draw the line, so I have suggested a few demarcations here.

Maybe all this follows because choking is both an action and a bodily movement. Choking is, for instance, *a nervous putt*. Both components are present when a putt is choked: the nervousness and the stroke. In this case, the stroke is the intended bodily movement, and the nervousness is a mental state that is not intended and may always include some attendant bodily movement that may or may not affect the stroke. Thus, the second-order idea I introduced at the beginning of this chapter may be a good suggestion after all. But determining the status of the nervousness is immensely difficult. For instance, an athlete can experience the physiological symptoms of choking, attempt to control them, and through the ordeal give into them (that is, he or she may make a conscious decision not to fight them). Even in a situation like this, the symptoms may recede rather than remain or intensify.

One conjecture: I suspect that what has been said thus far would hold also for "concentration." Concentration and the loss of concentration, or what Australian tennis star Evonne Goolagong called "walk-abouts," may at times be actions or movements— depending on circumstances and the player's individual psychology.[17] Laver remembers that on one occasion, "My concentration burst, flooding my mind with a hundred things" (p. 292). Here again we find the language of movement, not of action; but the context of Laver's remark is clearly that of action.

Is choking significant in understanding the region of sport? I concur with McEnroe on this point:

> Choking is a part of every sport, and part of being a champion is being able to cope with it better than everyone else. But there isn't any set way of doing it; everyone finds what's best

for him. Choking at 12 feels very much the same as choking at 24. Of course, the tension that causes it gets bigger. When you are playing on Centre Court at Wimbledon in the finals, that's the ultimate tension. But choking is the same.[18]

Notice that McEnroe says that competitive tension *causes* choking. This causal explanation is at best a probable one. The following inductive argument form makes this clear:

> Most athletes who experience competitive tension choke.
> J experiences competitive tension.
>
> _____
>
> Consequently J chokes.

Now the conclusion is probably true only if both premises are true, *and* if we know J's psychological makeup. It could well be the case that J experiences competitive tension but doesn't choke. Moreover the *situation* must be relevant for this last sentence to be true. In a given situation J may or may not choke. For example, McEnroe might not have choked in the final of his first French Open but may have in the next. Or, it might be that Ivan Lendl choked in his first United States Open final but not in the second. I have choked in lesser tennis tournament events rather than in the more important ones. Even those not directly involved in a game can be affected: "After his team gave TCU its first men's SWC golf championship since the league was formed in 1926, coach Bill Woodley said, 'I played in a U.S. Amateur and a U.S. Open, but I've never been more nervous than I was Sunday. My guys were doing the playing and I was doing the choking.'"[19] Woodley used the word "choking" in the psychological sense. Why was he affected? Because as a player he was in control, but as a coach he had no control over the situation.

So choking appears to defy simple explanation or classification. Is the most we can say about it that choking is an inhibition of a sport action or performance? What that inhibition is cannot be nailed down, but is at best selected from a set of conditions that must be further specified and individualized: (1) who J is, (2) J's situation (including his or her perception of it), and (3) his or her methods for handling it. This is about as abstract and general as the analysis of choking can become.

Disambiguation of statements containing "choking" involves the following two avenues of interpretation: In tennis, when your doubles partner says "I choked on that serve," you generally interpret (generously) this statement as a remark about bodily movement. But if a partner says "you choked on that serve" (based on behavior only, not implied mental states), you probably would think he or she is ascribing responsibility for the action and, consequently, that the serve was an intentional action rather than merely a bodily movement (for example, that it was avoidable). A better serve could have been selected and should have been. So, disambiguation requires the context of conversation (in the Gricean sense) and not just additional statements or deductive inferences.[20]

Thus far the cases of choking I have discussed have been limited to individuals. But what about teams? In ordinary sport language, it is not uncommon to hear a remark like "The Dallas Cowboys choked in the NFL playoffs." Does such a use reflect the same conception we analyzed above or is it used metaphorically? Obviously the same conception is involved in such usage if we think of the team distributively rather than collectively. When someone says "The Cowboys choked," that individual usually means the receivers dropped the ball, the quarterback overthrew or underthrew the ball, linemen missed their blocks, and so on. So "choked" here refers to the *miscues*, but not to the attitudinal and physiological symptoms that occur in performing a given sport action. The team use is an extended sense of the individual use.

Do we have one action or many when a golfer chokes at putting? It is not odd to say "He chokes when he putts," suggesting by the two verbs that he performs two actions. But this sounds too Lockean—grammatically simple and unnecessary—for an adequate analysis of the action. Maybe there are not two actions present, but one action (putting) and one series of movements (that is, jabbing), and these together make up the act of choking. Don January's description appears to suggest this interpretation. We have a situation in which movement (jabbing) interferes with the action. How would we analyze this situation along the lines of the act individuation problem?

We first have the "unifiers," like Davidson (pp. 43ff.), who argue that one act generally takes place but that it has several different act descriptions. For example, let us look again at January's description of the yips. Davidson would probably maintain that one action took place in a given putt. However, an indefinite number of act descriptions can be given: "You jab at the putt," "Your palms get slick and the putter develops a mind of its own," "The ball appears to be far away and the cup is shrinking by the moment," and so on. Choking would be one act description of a given episode. In other words, there would be no ontological status given to choking over and above the action performed—the putt.

But the "multipliers," such as Alvin Goldman (ch. 2), would maintain that each nonsynonymous act description given above individuates an ontologically distinct act-token. The unity of action, apparently obliterated by this proliferation of act-tokens, is addressed by Goldman's concept of level-generation. As Goldman says, "Their [the unifiers'] single *action* corresponds to the set of all acts on a single *act-tree*" (p. 37). In the above example, each of the unifiers' act descriptions would designate an ontologically distinct act-token in an act-tree. Since the above act descriptions are not synonymous, Goldman would analyze them as numerically distinct act-tokens. This view of act predicates appears attractive when we examine Laver's remarks and foresee the controllability of choking.

Analyzing choking as a second-order episode of behavior roughly corresponds to Goldman's level-generation structure. "He chokes when he putts" becomes "He chokes *by* jabbing at the ball with his putter," where "jabbing at the ball with his putter" is synonymous with "putting." That is, when these two act predicates are synonymous, then "choking" is an additional act description of what happened. (Here we have what amounts to a semantic identity rule for "choking" in uncontrolled contexts or situations. Obviously the rule does not apply in controlled incidences.)

This point also parallels Davidson's analysis because we have a definite subclass of events that are actions; jabbing belongs to a class of events that are actions (putting), which we cannot do with

154

intentional actions (p. 45) if by this we mean that the jabbing is sustained or undertaken by an intention. In this respect, choking is like a mistake, such as miscalculating a sum or misspelling a word, in that neither of these is an intentional flubbing. So when I choke a putt by jabbing at the ball with my putter, I have not performed two numerically distinct actions. The jabbing didn't cause the choking; rather, the jabbing is an event-related description which is an action. Since choking can be conceptually related to several event-related descriptions (like jabbing), we can follow Hans Lenk's suggestion that actions such as choking are not ontological entities on a par with the events that make them up, but are interpretational constructs (p. 483). The action *choking* is semantics-impregnated in that the accompanying movements or events involve a judgment or an interpretation to make them identifiable as such. In terms of sport actions, this means that the interpretational constructs are the context for these actions: rules, norms, traditions, practices, values, frames of reference, and reference groups. This applies to choking as it does to any other sport action, except that the phenomenon involves physiological symptoms that can impair the action. Since these are controllable, they are identifiable and interpretable. Consequently choking needs to be analyzed on a semantic level and not just on an ontological level.[21]

Choking, like fakes or feints, is a representation of an action. If I choke in hitting a forehand in tennis, then I hit not the forehand I originally intended but a (usually poor) representation of it. Unlike in a fake, though, I do end up hitting a forehand; in a fake I end up with a different action from the one initially represented. In choking the type of action remains roughly the same, but not so in fakes; hence, the representation is different. Furthermore, when an athlete chokes, he or she is not *mimicking* the intended action. Rather, the action is just his or her actual nervous athletic performance. So choking is not imitating an action. A Platonic reading is out.

However, if what I have said above is correct, then the phenomenon of choking (and its related actions) are examples that may help substantiate *in some ways* Thalberg's version of the agent causal theory. He prescribes a tighter hookup:

what I call "ongoing," "continuous," or "sustained" causation. If someone's behavior is to count as intentional Xing, I believe her or his intention must continuously regulate the Xing. He probably does not *dwell* upon his intention frequently or at all while he is engaged in Xing. But it remains operative in the sense that if there are impediments to his Xing, he takes measures to circumvent them and resume Xing—unless of course his plans change. (p. 257)

We have seen what Laver's "measures" are. So choking at Xing can still be Xing intentionally *if* the agent is successfully carrying out the measures to sustain Xing throughout the course of the action. In other words, when there are no measures or the measures have not taken effect, we have a bodily Xing. This second alternative may provide counterevidence to Thalberg's second conclusion, which claims that these actions are not done intentionally. There may be impediments to an athlete Xing that he or she is in the process of dealing with. At that point, what is Xing—action or bodily movement? We may have acts that straddle the distinction. It is possible that the movements (the physical symptoms of choking) triumph over the intentions, yet the amalgam is an action because of the present intention. For example a player like Laver may effectively serve in spite of the physical symptoms of choking. In other words, Laver is able to carry on at the game of tennis even though there is an enormous amount of pressure while he is experiencing a high degree of nervousness or competitive tension.

It is remarkably difficult to say why Laver's measures work for him, yet the same type of measures fail to work for Hogan or January. If the measures are not effective or if they are absent, then choking at Xing is merely or mostly a bodily movement rather than an episode we would want to call an intentional action (under Thalberg's description). These would be extreme cases, indeed. We can well imagine a television sports commentator remarking, "Hogan stood *frozen* over the putt, and the poor fellow just jabbed at the ball, missing the hole by several feet." Hogan's act is no doubt a putt, but it doesn't belong under Thalberg's concept of an intentional action. However, Hogan's act would belong under

Davidson's concept, and this inclusion I think helps substantiate his thesis (see note 5). Also, Lenk's recommendation is further substantiated by the following observations about these incidences. No matter how bad Hogan's stroke and his stance become, his act—even his misses—count as a *putt* because of the context (rules) of the game of golf. In nongame situations we would probably want to change the name of the act because the agent no longer does X, but attempts to do X, fails to do X, and ends up doing Y. In games, however, failure still counts, and this is an important feature of play or sport.[22] No matter how miserably Hogan plays, he still putts and participates—probably much to his chagrin.

With all this in mind, the title of this chapter might have been a temporal question: When is choking an action? This implies there are conditions for choking to be an action, generally those that make champions out of talented athletes. I hope I have specified what these conditions are.[23]

SEVEN

The Knowing in Playing

I

IN A PROVOCATIVE study entitled "A Fine Forehand,"[1] Paul Ziff raises a series of epistemological questions concerning sport activities, which I shall attempt to answer here. He poses them in the following manner. Suppose a coach tells a group of players that they do not bend their knees enough when hitting the forehand. If they wish to improve their stroke, the players will attend to what they have been told. How do they do that? Since the players were told to bend their knees when they hit the ball, they do just that. That means they will move their legs and torso in such a way as to make them conform to the description supplied by their coach. And how do the players know whether or not they have done that? The coach knows by watching the players. But how do the players themselves know? Professor Ziff remarks:

> In recent years some philosophers have toyed with what they call "knowledge without observation," it supposedly being the kind of knowledge one has of one's bodily position, of the position of one's limbs and so forth. One reason why sports provide a fertile epistemological field is that one finds that often athletes (or would-be athletes) do not in fact know the position of their own limbs. Many players think they bend a great deal in stroking a ball whereas in fact they hardly bend at all. This is a particularly common illusion with respect to the service motion in tennis. . . . What I am asking is how one manages to remember positions of the body.

Any adequate treatment of these problems must account for at least two things. The first thing is the kind of knowledge involved in sport situations. Both spectator and participant are said to know things about the games that are played. The difference between the kind of knowing is not a matter of degree, but of type. And second, it must account for a player's illusion of what he or she does in a given physical activity.

The point of saying that the coach knows by looking at the player is that the coach observes what the player does—whether or not the player's actions successfully result in the given end. The coach notices whether the player has made minor adjustments in his or her footwork, grip, and so forth, plus whether the ball goes where it should. I shall label this process *the result theory*.[2] The kind of knowledge spectators have stems from observing the results of a given individual's performance. The coach or tennis instructor knows the player is hitting the stroke correctly by seeing whether or not the player is able to keep the shots in the court; that is, does the ball clear the net by several feet, land deep in the opponent's side, and so on. The coach moves on to other parts of the player's game when he or she is able to bring about the desired results.

How does this apply to the participant? How does one know (and remember) whether or not one hits the forehand correctly? By the results? Does one remember the positions of one's body by the results that one's actions produce? Or by some other means? The result theory is a plausible account of the participant's action. Persons know whether they carry out the action in question successfully only if the results of that action are obtained. Wertz's forehand, as wild as it is, is corrected and retrained by observing whether or not the results of those strokes approximate the instructor's descriptive analytical remarks. A better example of this theory may be seen in Herrigel's account of archery, in which he had a few successful shots as a result of proper breathing. From this he had thought that he understood what was meant by drawing the bow "spiritually":

So that was it: not a technical trick I had tried in vain to pick up, but liberating breath control with new and far-reaching possibilities. I say this not without misgiving, for I well know how great is the temptation to succumb to a powerful influence and, ensnared in self-delusion, to overrate the importance of an experience merely because it is so unusual. But despite all equivocation and sober reserve, *the results* obtained by the new breathing—for in time I was able to draw even the strong bow of the Master with muscles relaxed—were far too definite to be denied.[3]

However, results may be deceiving. I may be hitting the forehand better than I usually do, that is, keeping more of the balls in the court and hitting them where I want them to go. But at the same time I may be doing many things wrong, which in the long run will result in a forehand worse than I have had (if that's possible). I may be developing a hitch in my swing and facing the net on my stroke. In short the results can be misleading for the player or the observer, if results are the only guide. So the illusion is partially accounted for. But what other clues are there for our would-be athlete who desires a fine forehand?

Aside from the result theory, there is what I shall call *the feel theory*.[4] Under this account, which is a nonspectator's view, the feeling one registers when a stroke is executed properly is the athlete's guide. A person "memorizes" the particular feeling and tries to duplicate it again. This is how players know the position of their limbs and body. To repeat, it is by the distinct feeling that accompanies that particular position. I am not sure whether this feeling is as discrete as David Hume makes feelings in general out to be.[5] Hume maintains that there is a unique, measurable feeling correlating every mental state—be it thought, emotion, or whatever. Recent critics of Hume (and other traditional, modern theorists) have questioned the validity of his claim; for example, Errol Bedford comments that "Indignation and annoyance are two different emotions; but, to judge from my own case, the feelings that accompany indignation appear to differ little, if at all, from those that accompany annoyance."[6] This observation especially applies to the feeling of the same repetitive physical skill, like the execution of the forehand, where the good and the bad shots feel about

161

the same (for the overwhelming majority of tennis players, unfortunately). If conscientious players use a mirror to check whether they are bending enough (Ziff's example), the rehearsal of the stroke is not for the purpose of telling them how they look, but to allow the players to capture what it felt like to bend their knees just so much.

A straightforward example of the feel theory can be seen in Timothy Gallwey's teaching technique:

> "Can you describe to me what this hitch is actually like? Can you swing in slow motion without tossing the ball up and show me how you *do* it?" But without hitting the ball, Toney [one of the women pros who played for World Team Tennis] couldn't really show me her hitch. "So how do you know that it's really there?" I asked. / "Well, I've seen it on video tape, and I've been told by a lot of coaches that it's there." / "Yes, but maybe it's gone away. Can you *feel* it now?" / "I don't know. But I do know that my serve hasn't been getting any better." Toney served a few balls and there was a little less hitch. "Hey, that feels better. I think it's gone." / "I can still see it. Why don't you try to feel what shape and form this hitch has and exactly when it happens instead of simply deducing whether it's there by the results?" . . . / "When you saw it, the hitch, just as it was, when you actually *felt* it happening, the learning began. Awareness of the difference was what gave you control. Therefore, when anything seems to be going wrong with your game, why not try increasing your awareness of how it is before slaving so hard on changing it?"[7]

And a statement that describes the overhead for beginners and intermediates by Gladys Heldman, a well-known teaching professional, makes an explicit appeal to this theory:

> A player who has no confidence in his overhead can develop "feel" for the moving target by first grooving himself on set-ups—short, easily reachable balls that are lobbed to him while he is at net. The lobs should be short enough so that instead of having to leap or move back, he can hit the ball in front of

him with a partially downward motion. He learns to judge how long the extended arm-racket line is, and this teaches him the feeling of the height of the ball at the time he should hit it.[8]

Another way to see this theory or viewpoint expressed in tennis discussions is that a player might have *lost* his feel (see, for example, note 8). Here are some comments by Stan Smith, attempting to explain his slump which started in 1974:

> "I'm afraid I got a bit conservative in my thinking, and therefore a little slow and sluggish on the court. I guess I started trying not to lose instead of going out to win. I've got to change that around and start feeling again that I can make the good shot. . . . It's feeling that you can hit the shot you're going for, knowing you can make it when you need to" says Smith. / "When you're confident, you move to the ball and go for your shots instinctively, and you make them. When you're not confident, you have to think and force yourself to do things, you're slower, and you tend to go for the shot you think you can make, rather than the one that's right for the situation. That way your game becomes too predictable, and even if you hit a good shot, chances are your opponent knows it's coming and can anticipate and hit a good shot back."[9]

And George Toley, the University of Southern California coach that Smith saw again for diagnostic and remedial assistance, put it this way:

> We had to try to stimulate him [Smith] the other way. We practiced hitting the shots that were giving him trouble so that he'd build up enough confidence to use them in a match, instinctively. I had to get him to worry less about the results than the execution. First the footwork to get into position, then the right stroke. If you do that, the results will come.

In both of these statements we find the language of feeling: playing and moving instinctively, concentration on execution rather than results, and so on. It may be objected that the feeling

163

mentioned in these cases is not the one I have described under the feel theory—that these cases refer to the feeling of confidence and not to physical sensations and perceptions. But these feelings cannot be that easily separated when discussing physical activities in sport situations. The feeling of confidence that Smith lost was tied to those instinctive shots and movements that were replaced with calculative thinking about the moves, production of the shots, and the results. In other words, the feeling of confidence is not just *an emotional feeling*—what Moreland Perkins refers to as feeling$_e$ —but *a bodily feeling*, feeling$_b$, involving sensations and perceptions of a specific temporal order that belong to an individual's personal, subjective history.[10]

Practicing brings about a higher level of performance because the repetition of the feel of a given shot is refined. Golf is similar in this respect; Ben Hogan was one of the first athletes to use the term "muscle memory" to explain the feel one has (or does not have) for the clubs, the ball, and the course.[11] Likewise, John Barnaby, the former tennis coach at Harvard University, speaks of "muscle knowledge" in discussing the racket skills of tennis.[12] As Toley says, if the feel or feeling is there, the results will be there too.

This last point shows that there is a correlation between the feel theory and the result theory. And this is why practice helps players, in addition to explaining why some people have better forehands than others, that is, their feel does have some relation to the results. The great players, like Rod Laver and Chris Evert, have the two theories working harmoniously in play. Whereas with me— your hacker—they *fight* each other. The discrepancy between these two theories is one of the things that makes sport difficult to master for either the sportsperson or the philosopher.

The phenomenon of "choking" (like that of "slump") in tennis is usually described in terms of the feel theory. For instance Rod Laver expresses it in this fashion:

> There are times when you can get so choked up on serve that your elbow feels like it's in a cast. The net seems a million miles away, and the balls are unresponsive lumps. Stop. Take a few deep breaths. Take the racket in your hand and let your

164

racket hand hang out and release its death grip. Try to smile and consider how silly it is. It's only a game. If your motion has deserted you, just hold the ball up and pat it toward the service court. Forget style. Just remember that to get the first ball in—anyway—gives you a heck of a chance to win the point. The ball is on the other side now. A double fault gives you no chance.[13]

Observe in Laver's description that after discussing "choking" in terms of feeling, for instance—"your elbow feels like it's in a cast"—he turns and resorts to the result theory—"pat it [the ball] toward the service court." When there is a sudden loss of feel, there is not much else to rely on except results—the kind Laver describes.

II

THE RESULT theory poses interesting philosophical problems, but they are ones that do not concern me here. I shall concentrate on the feel theory for the remainder of the chapter, since I have been primarily concerned with participant sport and the feel theory is the more problematic of the two theories on this score. So far I have argued that the "feeling" appealed to in the feel theory is bodily feeling and not emotional feeling, like the feeling of remorse. However, there are many questions still left unanswered in addition to the task of making the notion of bodily feeling more precise. There are different sorts of bodily feelings and these have distinct conceptual marks. Which of these characterize the bodily feeling in sport? Are they adequate to explain the use of "feel" in Heldman's description of the overhead and Gallwey's discussion of Toney's service hitch? Let us see.

When we speak of a bodily feeling we can be speaking of either *a perceptual feeling* or *feeling as a sensation*. In perceptual feeling, as Alan White phrases it, "What is felt is not a feeling, but a perceptual object" (p. 110). For instance the feel of change in my pocket or of the snow beneath my bare feet is not a feeling of these experiences, but of those objects themselves—the change or the snow. What about the player who can develop "feel" for a moving

165

target by first grooving himself or herself on set-ups? Does Held-man's use of scare quotes around the word "feel" suggest a percep-tual feeling? A case can be made for this interpretation, in that hitting an overhead involves feeling the racket and ball throughout the stroke, plus feeling the distance the player is from the net, the ball, and the racket, and the position of himself or herself. So the first feelings cited are those White labels as perceptual. However, the latter are feelings as sensations and have no object as perceptual feelings do. But there is no perceivable criterion for the feeling of hitting an overhead as there is for feeling the difference between a half dollar and a quarter in your pocket.[14] What the routine of hitting set-ups does is give the player a somewhat artifi-cial situation where he or she has the opportunity to experience a feeling—hitting an overhead—and not to experience an object. This particular kind of feeling is not localized by a specific object, but it is still "localized" in some sense by a whole set of objects—there is a matrix of physical geometry, which encompasses the court and the players. And the "feel" is the tacit recognition of the spatial relationships that exist among these objects. For exam-ple when the overhead is performed correctly, there is the feel of racket, ball, oneself, the court, and so forth. There is the feeling of all these together in a special relationship. Once one has that complex feeling, one then has the feel for hitting overheads.

There is, though, a similarity between perceptual feelings and feelings as sensations. They are both an exercise of a skill and of ability, in that people come to know these things by the use of their appendages and from cues. But the fact remains that in perceptual feeling my attention is solely on the object and is governed by it while I am having the feeling. When I have the feel of the overhead I do not feel "overheady," just as when I feel a coin I do not feel "coiny." This is because there is not just one object involved. If there were just one object and a corresponding feeling, I would probably feel "overheady." To learn how to hit an overhead is to become aware (by feeling with one's fingers, hand, arm, and position of one's body on the court) of the objects one has to deal with—the ball, the racket, the net, and so on. But there is not just one object, so a sport action is more like a *feeling of general condition* (White's term, pp. 116f.). An example of a feeling of general condition is a felt inclination. When I have the whole shot down, I have the feel for it. I have certain felt inclinations to do so-and-so and such-and-such, like turning sideways, moving very quickly into position under the ball, pointing at the ball, arching the back, and scissoring my legs if I jump to make contact with the ball.

Now what sort of feelings as sensations are we talking about in sport actions? They are, I shall argue, those peculiar sensations that are labeled *the sensations of position*, and the claims we typically make about them are indeed those called "knowledge without observation." However, we have not established a great deal by classifying them, because this label means different things to different people. So we need to cover those conceptual features that do not apply to sport actions, so as to make the characterization in terms of the above classification easier.

One such case comes from White, who says that "we cannot sensibly ask whether a sensation might be other than it feels, as we can ask whether the heat of a radiator might be other than it feels" (p. 110); or again, "The whole idea of *means* of my getting to know whether I have a sensation is curious. It makes no sense to ask me how I got to know whether I have a twinge, what means and methods I used, whether they were reliable or unreliable, or to ask whether I might have made a mistake and have been led by my evidence to think that I had a twinge when I had not" (p. 112).

What White says about a sensation is true, but if we talk about numerous sensations or a set of sensations that make up a given stroke, then we can talk intelligently about means, methods, and evidence. So, contrary to White, in tennis lessons one constantly hears pupils asking such questions about their stroke production. Certainly they feel things and sensations. The question is whether or not they are the right ones. If players are not quite sure of the shot, they will tell the coach things about the sensations of hitting the overhead other than how it feels. This is because the feeling of those peculiar sensations are there only *after* the acquisition of the physical skill in question. Commonly athletes do not know what it feels like until they have felt it, and they cannot judge how it is going to feel. If they try to, they may be surprised.

Related to the question of evidence is the question of author-ity. Geoffrey Vesey claims: "I am the sole authority when it comes to my own bodily sensations. This is a reason (though not, I would think, a very good one) for saying that I cannot be mistaken about the location of my bodily sensations."[15] As we have already estab-lished in the first part of this chapter, one of the characteristics of sensations is that a person can be mistaken about their position. An athlete's illusion about his or her movements must be ac-counted for in an analysis of feelings and sensations. Most philoso-phers who have contributed to the analysis of this topic have conceded that I am not the sole authority on my bodily feelings and sensations that involve position, and that I can be (and fre-quently I am) mistaken about them. David Hamlyn formulates the epistemological principle in this manner:

> In all these cases [of knowing] we may be wrong; our limbs may be otherwise disposed than we think; and our intentions may be unfulfilled. In that case we did not know after all; for, in keeping with what is true of knowledge in general, being wrong prevents it from being knowledge. This does not prevent our sometimes knowing the disposition of our limbs and what we are doing or going to do, although we have no reasons of an observational kind for saying what we know.[16]

Let me illustrate what Hamlyn means by this last remark. When players bend their knees, and know that they are bending them just so much, they do not have to look at themselves in order to know it, unless they are just learning to do that task. All that is necessary is that they feel or have the sensations that normally accompany "bending one's knees"; that is, the feelings of resist-ance, weight, and pressure in their legs and thighs. So in a case of knowing without observing, we would say of players that they know how to hit a forehand without their performing in front of us by being able to tell us what sort of sensations and feelings they have in hitting the stroke.

In sport situations, when players gain a certain level of compe-tence it is through mastery of a set of skills that were first learned by observation, for example, watching others exercise those skills and practicing the maneuvers while constantly monitoring their bodies by observing what is happening. When this process has been repeated enough (with less and less observing needed for the accomplishment of the skills), the participants perform those skills by feel. Each level of play can be viewed this way: again, see the above examples of Stan Smith and of learning the overhead.

Let us take golf as an example this time. In all of my good rounds of golf I have been in a kind of unconscious, perceptual state where all of my bodily movements were performed freely in a natural and fluid way. This I attribute mostly to athletic feel—let the eyes tell the hands what to do—which came after hours and hours of practice on developing what I consider a good golf swing. At this point I felt I should start concentrating on the art of shot-making. After many more hours of practice this feel has come to me; it feels natural to hit the golf ball and see it land in a satisfactory position. In my experiences I have learned not to be conscious of thoughts like "Keep your head down," "Stay anchored," "Pause at the top," and so on. This only creates tension and in most cases results in a bad shot. The golf swing is continuous—the eyes have to tell the muscles what to do. The trained eye is central to understanding the concept of athletic feel; it is what registers those spatial relations that make up the swing.

How does one "memorize" a particular feeling? And how is the duplication of it possible? The answer to both questions, I have suggested above, is that there are certain definite sensations one has when the forehand (or overhead or golf swing) is hit just right. They give away the position of one's limbs. But knowing the position of one's limbs is not just a matter of accounting for the sensations an individual has in those limbs. The spatial relations possible with our limbs are learned and mediated—they are not known directly or immediately or noninferentially. Sport situations make this dramatically clear. One of the philosophical morals to be drawn from this discussion thus far is that sensations and bodily position cannot be equated, as some philosophers have argued.[17]

III

IN THIS section I shall try to further support the conclusions just established, namely, that the sensations and feelings that characterize the knowing in playing within games of physical skill are learned and mediated. But how are they mediated and learned? There are two competing answers to this question.

There are those who would argue that we come to know those things in sport situations by induction and repetition. It is by trial and error that we come to do something correctly, like hitting the forehand. It is by simple enumeration or by repetition that we come to learn a given activity. I shall call this *the analytical model*. There are close affinities between this model and the result theory, for it is clearly the case that this is how we assess our performances when we attend to the results of our behavior. We make repeated attempts until we meet with success. In so doing we are guided by what we have done in the past, and frequently we form generalizations as to what to do or not to do next. Advocates of this model of learning are sometimes zealous and want to say that this is the only model needed for either theory, or even claim that only one theory, the result theory, exists and that its model of learning is the only one needed. We can imagine B. F. Skinner and his disciples opting for such a position. No matter how attractive it is from the standpoint of the principle of simplicity, it should be resisted here.

The result theory and the analytical model are no doubt employed in sport situations. However, their employment is primarily seen in relatively simple skills. The more complicated the skill, the less plausible the account. Any complicated skill, such as the overhead or service, is achieved, in the first place, by trying to duplicate the whole action, the gestalt of the overhead or serve, and not by focusing exclusively on the parts of the whole action. The analytical model necessarily focuses on parts rather than the whole. The motion or action we are trying to copy comes from our coach, instructor, or another player who has mastered the skill. Margaret Steel summarizes the difficulties with the analytical model and paves the way for an alternative one, which I shall call *the skill model*. She holds that to begin with, learning a physical skill is not an inductive process. We do not learn to play tennis by generalization from past instances. Once the player has "caught on," he knows how it feels to do it right, he knows from past experience that he is doing it right, but this is not how he learned. A player may serve incorrectly twenty times, then do it correctly. Those twenty incorrect performances do not teach him how to do it right, nor do they even teach him how to avoid doing it incorrectly. In order to perform correctly, the student must in fact perform correctly. He is not learning a belief or forming an expectation about the future (although I do not deny that these play a part, for instance in estimating the angle and velocity of a tennis return). Rather he is learning how to do something. It is in this sense that what the tennis player knows can be said to be "knowing how" rather than "knowing that." (p. 98)

As she adds later, "We are not learning a series of muscle movements, but a whole flowing action." The point is that in learning to hit the overhead correctly or to serve the American twist one must acquire a new feeling and set of sensations, with which earlier feelings and sensations have no connection. However, the next twenty correct performances do perhaps teach a player. Learning a physical skill does take a lot of reinforcement—that is, repetition—to gain the sort of mastery we are talking about here. Isn't this then a form of induction? We can imagine an athlete saying: "I have performed this way twenty-seven times and have succeeded twenty-seven times; therefore, I *know* that if I do the same a twenty-eighth time, I will succeed again."

Let me use an example from my own sport experience to illustrate this qualification of Steel's explanation. I can still remember when I first hit the American twist serve. I had worked at it all one summer as a teenager. And then one afternoon, I just happened to hit it and achieved the feel. (I hit serves the rest of the afternoon so I would not forget.) The previous balls I had hit that summer (probably numbering into the thousands) had no correlation with the one

I hit which resulted in the American twist serve. If anything, past instances work against a person, because they form habits and restrict one's learning capabilities. So when it comes to the acquisition of a new complex physical skill, such as a serve in tennis, the analytical model is inadequate in accounting for the semitechnical use of "feel" in the language of sport.

But notice in my example of learning the American twist serve that I said that I *just happened* to hit it and achieved the feel. There is an important role of luck and intuitive randomness in trying different things in the acquisition of skills. Some things we pick up by chance in sport situations, just as we do in other types of situations. If one doesn't learn (most effectively) by breaking a skill down into its component parts, then one must acquire a previously unknown (to that person) skill all at once. Since one cannot already know it, one must count on luck and randomness for one's first encounter, and then reinforce it by repetition. (This is what I did the rest of that afternoon when I finally hit the serve; the first success was almost just by accident, by the way I happened to toss the ball up which resulted in the other things coming together to make that serve originate.)

Anscombe is right about the distinction of "separately describable sensations" and those sensations that are not separately describable.[18] This latter group are those that we characteristically find in sport situations. The sorts of sensations one has in the whole action of the service motion are ones simply not available unless a person has mastered the skills that make those sensations possible. However, Anscombe is, I think, wrong when she claims that there are no clues involved in knowing those sensations. There are elements in our experience that we do treat as cues in trying to master a given skill, and athletes in particular learn to recognize these early in their careers. For example, the motion of the whole swing can be a cue as to whether or not a player has mastered a given serve. Any sensation(s) in a set of sensations that make up the "feel" of an action may be construed by the player as cues to accomplishing the action.

The player acquires a whole set of complex physical skills. This is done by paying attention to the whole action to be performed.

Then out of that performance one finds another kind of learning and knowing taking place. This learning is piecemeal, and the player will pick out elements in the action and will proceed in a trial and error fashion, resembling the process I called the analytical model, but with an eye on the whole action. In examining the second kind of learning that takes place, we find that we do not have an "either/or" situation. Both models of learning are seen operating in addition to both of the theories. Only at the initial level of learning where the basic skill is acquired do we find the feel theory and the skill model adequate to account for the knowing and learning in sport situations. (Again I refer the reader to the Gallwey passage I quoted in the first section.) We do not know in advance what this particular feeling is going to be like until we finally master the skill. Then and only then, after having mastered the skill, do we achieve the particular feeling involved in sport performance, such as the American twist serve, the overhead, a golf swing, a one-and-a-half dive, or any other complex sport action. But once we do, we rely on induction and repetition to keep and refine a complex sport action.

The difficulty, and consequently the challenge, of sport pedagogy and the teaching of physical skills generally is how to reconcile the two theories I have discussed here. Instructors go back and forth between them until the skills in question are learned. Once they are mastered, the analytical model can dominate in the teaching. Gallwey and others in the Asian philosophical tradition have made us more aware of the feel theory and the skill model, as we have seen here and in chapter 5.

In closing, I wish to say that I have just touched the surface of these two theories and models. What I have done is to demonstrate that there is not one theory and model operating in evaluating performance in sport, but at least two, which have complicated relationships to each other. And observing the distinctions drawn here makes our talk about sport more intelligible. From topics on doing and knowing, we turn to the artistic in sport—something they make possible.

PART FOUR: THE ARTISTIC

EIGHT

Representation and Expression in Sport and Art

I

THE SPORT-AS-ART analogy has continually surfaced in philosophical and literary discussions of sport. Although sport fiction has always assumed the validity of the analogy,[1] such unquestioning allegiance is worth philosophical inquiry. Appraisals of sport performances have involved aesthetic or artistic judgments since the ancient Greeks. Far more recently there was a contemporary television program entitled *Artist and Athlete: The Pursuit of Perfection*, which was an exploration of the parallels between art and athletics.[2] The program featured the Pilobolus Dance Ensemble, violinist Yehudi Menuhin, and scenes from the 1980 Winter Olympics. Yet these suggested parallels are not universally accepted or appreciated. There are some persistent critics of the analogy who have advanced interesting arguments based upon subtle analyses of important underlying concepts.

One such critic is David Best, a noted British philosopher who writes in the areas of sport philosophy and aesthetics.[3] His argument has met with acceptance in the literature, but is not without its critics.[4] I shall not repeat some of the standing criticisms here; rather, I shall be concerned with some of Best's claims concerning representation and expression in sport and art. I say "some of his claims," because Best has written an excellent book on expression in movement and the arts, much of which I am in sympathy and agreement with.[5] In addition to Best is the Soviet writer, M. J. Saraf, who argues against the sport-as-art analogy.[6] Saraf's argument hinges on the notion that representation and expression in the two activities are fundamentally different. Since Best and Saraf come to similar conclusions, I shall make a composite portrait of their positions, drawing on the writings of both (though neither writer displays the entire view). Our conception of art is far richer than just the notions of representation and expression. These two concepts are thought to be the cornerstones of art, so they are a useful place to begin a discussion of sport and art. Toward the end of this chapter I shall suggest a few other ideas that are perhaps not as abstract as the two I shall be primarily concerned with here. Philosophy of art begins with these traditional notions because the most important theories of art utilize them in one way or another. If sport is to find its way into this conversation, sport's relationship to them must be mapped out.

At the outset I want it to be clear that I do believe that sport (or at least some of it) is or can be art. Or to put the point linguistically, we can ascribe the predicate "artistic" to sport performances, and the resulting sentences will not be nonsensical; nor will this reflect any "barbarous usage." There are what I take to be some very good reasons why one should assent to this view. Moreover there are many people in the sports world who have found the analogy with art a rewarding one. A good example of this situation is the previously mentioned television program, in which the goals of pursuit and perfection for each individual are thought to coincide. After having studied Best's reasons for thinking that sport is not art, I am still not convinced of two things: first, that the stance I have taken on sport as art is "wrong-headed," and second, that Ruth Saw's classification of works of art (which includes sport) is a misconception, or based on misconceptions. Her scheme more faithfully depicts ordinary language usage than does Best's. If we follow Best, we would have to deny the extension of the terms. Such linguistic legislation is curious, if not downright odd, coming from a British philosopher, trained in the ordinary language tradition, who normally embraces non-essentialism. (Non-essentialism is the view that most of our ordinary concepts, like "art" and "sport," unlike mathematical-scientific concepts, do not have necessary and sufficient conditions.)

178

Initially I want to clarify some of Best's value judgments because they reveal a great deal about his conceptions of art and sport. At the beginning of one of his essays, Best contends not only that "*no* sport is an art form" but that "sport would somehow be endowed with *greater respectability* if it could be shown to be art." And at the conclusion of "Art and Sport" he cautions us about the "common tendency to use 'art' and its cognates in very loose, metaphorical, and barbarously degenerate senses" (p. 79). Best adds that it is "highly misleading to adduce instances of such usages in support of a case for conferring on an activity the credentials of 'art' in the normal sense." There are two items I want to quarrel with here. One is that what Best takes to be the normal sense of art is not at all normal. (I shall show this in some detail below.) The second is that Best evidently has some lofty, nineteenth-century conception of art—a view suggesting that art has requirements so sacred that nothing so sweaty, physical, and mundane as sport could possibly meet them. This general orientation toward art and sport tells us much about Best's objections. In spite of his anticipation that he would be considered as "merely old-fashioned, pedantic, and illegitimately restrictive about the use of 'art,'" he surely looks that way when we view contemporary art.

Best's view of art is of what Jacques Barzun has described as art from "the classical sector—recognized, gilt-edged, consecrated art."[7] Best reiterates "the old dogma of Art, One and Indispensable," and speaks of art as if "its disparate elements formed a homogenous substance called 'Art.'" Barzun adds the following lengthy description of contemporary art:

> Beside it [the classical conception of art] stands the whole of new art, infinitely ramified. In painting and sculpture even a short list of the names attached to schools suggests how difficult it is to ascertain what anybody means by 'twentieth-century art,' let alone by adjectives such as *new, modern, avant-garde,* or *contemporary.* The twentieth-century does begin with Cubism, followed by Futurism and Constructivism, Vorticism, Expressionism, Dada, and Surrealism. These and other -isms take us through the period between

179

wars, after which—the deluge: we have had since: Abstract Expressionism, Neo-Dada, Pop and Op art, *Tachisme*, Action Painting, Kinetic Art, New Realism, Hard Edge, Junk Art, Disposable Art, Aleatory Art, Minimal Art, and finally: Anti-Art. All along, too, under the impetus of Marcel Duchamp, we have been shown happenings or arrangements designed to startle us into recognizing how conventional or arbitrary our artistic notions actually are. A few years ago, for instance, a painter in New York exhibited works done in human excrement; another exhibited molded plastic genitalia around a coffin in which he himself lay naked. A third cut off pieces of his own flesh and photographed them. A fourth made stencils of classic works in order to reproduce them by spraying canned paint on the exposed surface. (pp. 13–14)

What Barzun has described is far afield from normalcy, if normalcy is guided by a nineteenth-century conception of art. Best would probably be more startled than most of us by some of the art from the contemporary sector that is *meant* to shock, to scare—as Barzun says, "to bruise the beholder's feelings and senses, in hopes of making him into a new person of the right kind" (p. 15). Works of the Living Theatre are good examples of this trait of contemporary art. (The Living Theatre is a kind of theatrical performance that ignores the distinction between actors and spectators or audience. Actors participate in the audience space.) I have attended sporting events and experienced a similar emotional reaction as that created by the Living Theatre.

Some people now dance fondling each other's genitalia. Is this dance or an act of obscenity? Courts of law in the United States are currently trying to decide. Having looked at "sexual dancing" or art works done in human excrement, the possibility of sport as art seems downright tame—certainly uncontroversial. Any criterion broad enough to include much of the contemporary sector of art surely is comprehensive enough to include sport, but we shall look at that claim in detail in a moment. My point here is that, when leaving the classical sector and moving into the contemporary sector of art, it is naive to think of art as "exalted" and sport as not. Those kinds of value judgments make little sense.[8]

When the contemporary sector of art is reviewed, sport appears "exalted" by comparison, except when John McEnroe, Jr., acts up at Wimbledon. McEnroe's behavior leads one to think that maybe the same thing is happening to sport that has happened to art. Perhaps we have an anti-sport movement, which is analogous to the anti-art movement from a generation earlier. Several years ago at the World Championship of Tennis Finals in Dallas, Texas, Vitas Gerulaitis stuffed a ball up his pants and wiggled it out. Such behavior has the same sort of effect as the contemporary art examples.[9] The point I am trying to make here is that whatever notions Best has of art and sport, they clearly are from the classical sector. This is evident when we look at Best's examples: Shakespeare, Indian classical dancing, violin competitions, and the like. Another case in point is in his discussion of sport as art in the *"objet trouvé"* (found object) sense. He thinks that this is an extended sense of art. This was perhaps true twenty years ago, but *objets trouvés* can no longer be called art in an extended sense. These objects and ready-makes are now commonly part of our stock of art objects and of our philosophical understanding of them.[10]

Best must think that one can easily ascertain what is meant by twentieth-century art. But if this is the case, then we face problems when we look at further elaborations of twentieth-century art, because there is a movement that combines both art and games. For instance, Harold Osborne's presidential address on contemporary art mentions *ludic art*.[11] Many artists, due to an interest in spectator participation, have turned their attention to devising educational games for children and adults alike. The educational value of games has long been recognized. But as Osborne recounts it:

> What is new is the claim that the devising and demonstration of games and toys are themselves an art form properly to be displayed at exhibitions of fine art. It is this—not the social value of what is being done—that challenges reconsideration

of traditional ideas about the nature of art itself. Is village cricket an art? Or the new 'Super Mastermind'? (p. 9)

Osborne does not answer these questions, but I hope to in this section. One of the things most interesting about ludic art is that it leads one to ask a Goodman-type question.[12] When an artist plays (rather than just devises) a game, does that make the game art? If David Boriani, Livio Castiglione, Bernard Lagneau, Claude Pasquer, Alexis Yanez, Victor Lucena, Asdrubal Colmenarez, Victor Vasarely, Bruno Munari, François Morellet, Lygia Clark, Julio Le Parc, and Karl Gerstner got together and played soccer, would this constitute art? (These individuals are leading ludic artists.) Would their conferring of the title of art on their activity indeed make it so? And if so, would it be the fact that they are already established artists that would make soccer art? Goodman allows for the possibility that something may become art by functioning as art.[13] So by implication, he would say that soccer—this particular soccer match that was played at a particular time—would be art because it *functioned* as art for those involved. In other words it was their intention at the time to create art. But this is not completely satisfactory. Let us push this line of argument further and vary the point of view.

Picture Mikhail Baryshnikov playing tennis. Most would agree that he turned ballet into something athletic. Could he make tennis—the athletic—into something artistic? Here possible answers become intriguing because we have an individual who is an artist but not in the same sense as the above ludic artists. We have changed the conventions somewhat by expanding the notion of "artist"; let's go even further. Could we remove the restrictions that prevent the individuals playing from being artists? Can a sportsman become or think of himself as *painting* the spatial area with his activities—like hitting into the infield or to the outfield, changing the configurations of the players in the ball park? Or can a pitcher visualize the arc or angle of his pitch as aesthetic and perceive this as an integral part of his ritual on the mound? In dance, the movement of the human body creates a line that is related to others "drawn" by the dancer as she performs the

182

number choreographed. We can speak of similar lines drawn in sport by the participants' movements. Indeed some participants may find it helpful to think of their movements as representing a line.

I concede that very few participants find the pursuit of artistic ends helpful, but we need only a few to see perhaps the emergence of a new paradigm in sport—one that will give rise to a new way of thinking about sport and even to new games or forms of human expression. It is quite possible that in pursuing artistic goals (like in the baseball example above) an athlete might well incur failure in his or her sport's end (defined by abstract nonartistic goals—points, runs, goals, etc.). This suggests that art may be tangentially present in these sports, but not necessarily that sport here is art. The weaker claim I shall argue for here, and later suggest some ways to develop a stronger thesis.

Goodman seems to suggest that if the player thinks that what he does contributes symbolically to a vision of—and to the making of—*a world*, then what the player does is art (p. 70). In other words, the activity functions symbolically or exemplifies something (definitions of these key terms are forthcoming). This is not to say that anything is art, and that sport clearly belongs in the class of everything, so sport is (trivially) art. When an object (in this case, a game) is taken as a symbol or a sample, it becomes an art object for a certain time. When tennis is played at Wimbledon during The Lawn Tennis Championships, the game takes on the status of a symbol, or a sample, *by which the game itself is measured.* When a truly great athlete performs—for example, Boris Becker or Stefan Edberg plays a game of tennis at Wimbledon—it can be a work of art or an art form. In writing about the matches at Wimbledon, journalists talk about them as being artistic.

As a negative instance, Neil Amdur remarked in the newspapers: "McEnroe's 7–5, 6–3, 6–2 victory over Stan Smith was less artistic."[14] Obviously Amdur is comparing this match with the other performances of the day and with the tournament's history. Here tennis isn't just daily, ordinary tennis. When it is played at Wimbledon, it becomes a spectacle—a paradigmatic sample of the game. We all confer artistry upon the occasion of the game. Given

183

this line of reasoning, we would probably answer Osborne's question "Is *village* cricket an art?" negatively, unless we could confer artistic conventions upon it, that is, unless we have the right occasion(s). Usually village cricket is not an art but under the appropriate circumstances it could be. This line of argument opens up interesting new possibilities of interpretation of the sport-as-art analogy.

Incidentally Osborne gives us a clue from years earlier when he entertained the question of whether or not chess problems are an art form.[15] He concluded that "we may accept that chess is justly considered an art-form since among other things it offers scope for the creation of intellectual objects characterized by beauty" (p. 163). The game of chess has "content" for Osborne, and if chess admits this, then other games, too, admit of it—given the fulfillment of the possibilities for the creation of an intellectual object that may be characterized by beauty—because other games too can be viewed as posing problems, in fact interesting problems. It takes intelligence and ingenuity to solve the problems, if not to the degree that chess requires them. Of the game of tennis, Billie Jean King says, "The ball never comes across the net the same way twice. It is terrifically interesting to deal with the forever new features of the problem."[16]

The problematic aspect of games is one of their appeals. There are specific guidelines for the prize of beauty in sanctioned chess tournaments. The artistry of *any* game can be measured in terms of the official guidelines: correctness, economy, difficulty, vivacity, originality, richness, and logical unity. Isn't this what we mean when we say a particular game was "a great game"? We mean that it has tacitly met guidelines like those listed for chess. Frequently sport commentators describe a player's execution in these terms. Even the climate and conditions under which a given game is played can contribute: in tennis, Wimbledon or the significance to the women's movement of the Bobby Riggs/Billie Jean King match. These matches and others like them represent and may even express the game, plus portraying important social and moral issues.

Another reason why places and times like Wimbledon are of importance is that it is at such events that we compare the present matches with those of the past, and log them in terms of their artistry, originality, exemplarity, and so forth. If we remain internal to the game or match itself, we discuss the *aesthetic* qualities of the game. But the *artistic* is not assessed solely on the basis of the visual, internal properties of the game itself.[17] We place two kinds of value on sport, just as we do art. The aesthetic value of a sporting event can be appreciated or assessed on the basis of visual perception alone, for example, by noting the lines drawn by the participants' movements. Historical context and information about other games, matches, or events need not necessarily be considered relevant to its appreciation. However, artistic appreciation does require historical context and information about the details of the game as a whole beyond just one particular game. Best's own example from art suggests this possible analogue with sport. The movements of an Indian dance can be valued either aesthetically or artistically. If one understands the precise meanings given to the gestures in Indian classical dance, then one can say that one appreciates the dance artistically; if not, then the appreciation is aesthetic.

The same valuations are made in sport. The artistic merit or value of a particular sporting event is measured by whether that given game equals its moment, that is, whether or not it has lived up to its historical antecedents—its tradition. This is an underlying reason why McEnroe's match with Smith was described as being "less than artistic." The emergence of a sporting event as art depends not only on the game itself, but also, as Aristotle, Schopenhauer, and Roman Ingarden remind us, on the presence of competent observers and on its being apprehended by them in one way rather than another. This in turn depends on various historical conditions. These sporting events are compared to the previous ones that make up that game's history. Those who view sport as art are those who genuinely know the sport in question, appreciate every little move that occurs, and respect the game's history. This line of argument should take the curiosity out of the idea of the artistic moment in sport.

But Saraf says:

A theatre without spectators is an absurdity. However, spectators are not an absolute necessity for a sport competition. In other words, despite the importance of sport fans for sport, the spectacular aspect of sport is not the principal goal of sport, it makes its appearance as an accompanying phenonomen. The sharper and more intense the situation of a fight [contest] in sport, the better the show aspect. The opposite is not possible. (p. 129)

When we speak in terms of aesthetic and artistic values in sport, I think a sport competition without spectators would be an absurdity. Obviously they are not an absolute necessity because we can imagine two lone people squaring off in a foot race to decide who is the fastest, but spectators are still necessary if sport is to be *complete,* in the Aristotelian sense (see chapter 4). Why do cultures and societies build stadiums or arenas unless the sport competitions staged there are to be viewed? Isn't it absurd to conceive of a sport competition staged in an arena without spectators? The spectacular aspect of sport may not be the principal goal of sport, but it is one of the principal goals (i.e., Aristotelian goals) of sport. And for professional sport and the major sporting events (like the Grand Slam tournaments in tennis or the World Series in baseball), the spectacular aspect is a necessary ingredient—so much so that "the artistic" emerges as a dimension of the game. Employment of Kulka's distinction in the argument helps make this point clear. Moreover, T. R. Martland's argument[18] can be used to show that the spectator, the fan, is required for sport competition to be complete. The fan, for Martland, is what distinguishes sport from art: art has no fans but sport does. He argues that one cannot make sense out of the notion of a fan in the context of art. In the next chapter I use this notion as a reason for their affinity.

However, it is important in organizing either a sport show or a theatrical production that the players and spectators be provided equally with the best possible conditions for playing or acting and for viewing. Contrary to Saraf, theater does not subordinate everything to the spectators' demands as they watch staged performances. The Festival Theatre at Stratford-on-Avon, in Ontario, Canada, for instance, was very carefully designed for presentation of Shakespearean plays with special consideration given to staging and

186

dramatic action. In addition the architects were concerned with seating capacity and spectator viewing. Obviously the organizers of sporting events have the spectator in mind just as much as the participant. This is especially true in light of the increase in fan violence, since these events are so popular among the public. Indeed sporting events, in addition to movies and television, are what the public perceive as their culture and more importantly as how they participate in it.

II

BEST would probably object to this line of argument because of my inappropriate introduction of "contingent information" into the picture. By implication he has a Parmenidean view of conceptual change, that is, no change at all. He states that "even if there were a great interest in the aesthetic aspects of purposive sports, this would be a contingent matter, and such a possibility is irrelevant to the logical character of the distinction between purposive and aesthetic sports." This is a curious pronouncement. Categories like *art* and *sport* change by the very fact that people who employ the categories apply them to different objects. People's interests are not irrelevant to the logical character of a distinction. Indeed this is how distinctions develop. If American pragmatism taught us anything, it was the lesson pertaining to conceptual change.

Let me illustrate this point with a brief, general case. The category of fine art was altered in the eighteenth century with the addition of many items made prior to that time that had originally been made or used for other purposes. For example, ceramic food bowls found in ancient burial sites came to be called "fine art" by several institutions in the art world. In other words, there were groups of people who thought differently about those objects and began speaking of them as fine art—just as we speak about van Gogh's drawings and prints as fine art. So category shifts and conceptual change are contingent matters; who does what, when, and where, and perhaps even how, does matter. If any situation becomes widespread, for example how a given linguistic community comes to think about a certain activity, then this is grounds for conceptual change because the innovator has supplied us with a sample or paradigm. (Part of my reason for tracing the contemporary sector of art above was to illustrate the phenomenon of change.) If a sufficient number of gymnasts were to begin thinking about what they are doing as art and no longer just as "sport" in the non-art sense, this would transform gymnastics. Such a change took place in figure skating with Peggy Fleming's aestheticism in the 1968 Grenoble Winter Olympics.[19] People have changed all sorts of things they do and say about the sport. I think Reid is correct when he says that the players, the gymnasts, or the skaters, are the ones who will decide: "Toller Cranston and John Curry have both believed that figure-skating, for instance, *should* be regarded as an art form. And since figure-skating can undoubtedly for some people be a form of art, they have a point. But it is a point to be considered by the organizers of sport."[20] One of the things suggested by this last remark is that the *setting* of the event is to be treated differently by the performers and also by the spectators, so that their behaviors will be appropriate to the occasion. Sometimes the performers have to "reeducate" the spectators to appreciate the institutional setting as something different from what it was before.

A vivid example of this kind of situation occurred on December 27, 1980, when Peggy Fleming performed in China. She ended the program with a Chinese Butterfly number. The sleeves of her costume had long, streaming, sheer pieces of cloth that floated as she skated, suggesting the wings of a butterfly. This was all set to traditional Chinese dance music with proper lighting. Afterward Fleming said she was concerned that the audience would react negatively to her number. The musical piece had traditional associations for the Chinese, and she was afraid of offending them by presenting the piece in a setting where those associations would not normally be made (a sports building). Fortunately the Chinese Butterfly number was well received. She further explained in a television interview that in figure skating she had combined sport and art. As Reid conjectures, "Gymnastic performances may not be 'works of art.' But they can include moments of art." This temporal emphasis corresponds nicely to what Goodman was suggesting with his question "When is an object a work of art?," as opposed to the substantive question "What is art?" Moreover, the notion of a work of art has changed recently from its traditional meaning of an object, to include events and things that have little or no stability (for example, skywriting). We have seen how sport conforms to new developments in the art world; now let us look at more traditional developments, ones that may be more acceptable to Best.

Let me cite an example in which "sport" and the arts appear together. In the late seventies there appeared in Cambridge, England, at Kettle's Yard Gallery (March 4–April 2, 1978) an exhibition entitled "'L'Esprit nouveau': Art, Architecture, Music, Sport, Film, Theatre, Dance, Modern Life,'" which was sponsored by the Arts Council of Great Britain. How could sport capture the sense of "L'Esprit nouveau" unless it is possible for sport to make some sort of statement about life?[21] "Sport" was listed along with music, art, architecture, film, and so forth; those who conceived of the exhibition thought of sport on a par with those arts for the purpose of capturing "L'Esprit nouveau." The individuals who put together the exhibition saw something that Best and Saraf apparently missed. If we look and think hard enough, I suggest that we should be able to see the conceptual connections.

III

FOR SOME individuals, then, sport has both representational and expressive content. Best claims that life-issues that make up an imaginative subject of a work of art have no analogue in sport. In other words sport has no content or subject matter. But why not? How is this "significant dissimilarity" realized? How does the discontinuity arise between the two concepts? Significant dissimilarity should not be a premise but treated as a conclusion. Why is it not possible for *the body* or *human movement* to be the object of one's attention or the imagined object in sport?[22] Jon Saari has suggested that "body-builders are sculptors who turn their bodies into living and breathing works of art, walking replicas of Greek and Renaissance sculpture."[23] Are not very good, appreciative spectators supposed to be paying attention to the body, to human movement, and is not a given performance in front of them to be judged by measures or standards of an instance (sample) of this

189

"genre"? Perhaps specific cases will help to decide these semantic and pragmatic questions.

Best is simply mistaken when he states that "the performer cannot, within its [sport's] conventions, express a view of life-issues. For example, it is difficult to imagine a gymnast who included in his routine movements which expressed an attitude to[ward] war or racial discrimination." Apparently Best has not tried to imagine hard enough, or he has been around traditional gymnasts who have not used these artistic conventions. A former student of mine, Karen Kurtz, once told me of a floor routine she performed in a gymnastic competition to the music of "The Lord's Prayer." She used the routine as her way of expressing praise both to God *and* to the abilities of the human body. The movements within the routine were mostly broad, sweeping movements. The arm movements were exaggerated and the leaps were extensive. Large movements are conventionally used to convey thanks, joy, and a general openness of the human spirit. A routine done to fast, lively music would contain shorter, jazzier movements than did the "Lord's Prayer" routine. It would be inappropriate and would fail to convey what it had set out to through the choice of music.

The movements of the human body follow a fundamental logic that is dictated by its physical dimensions and the cultural associations we make with them. Because of these dimensions and associations, the movements can be independent of the intentions of performers and spectators. Contrary to the above example, a gymnast might move in a way that expressed flirtatiousness and seductiveness. If done to "The Lord's Prayer," such movements and actions would be inappropriate. This shows semantic conventions at work in a gymnast's routine. (When actions denote one object rather than another in the world, then we have a semantic connection.)

Expression, it is generally agreed, is one of the cornerstones of art, so sport seems to win this round in the bout; it has expressive content.[24] As Saraf observes:

> The expressive aspect made its appearance in sport above all and mainly in the form of a show, which requires the

190

organization of matter in accordance with the laws of aesthetic perception. Since it is not a question here of giving lasting features to a result obtained in competitive sport (weight, speed, distance) but of an evaluation of movement itself, there arises the necessity of proper organization and the creation of a motoric program. (p. 126)

Saraf, however, thinks expression works only on a syntactic level. Obviously my argument is that it is also at work on the semantic and pragmatic levels, a point to which I shall return later.

Another cornerstone of art is representation. Does sport represent anything? Again Best says no, but I think it does. Saraf states a qualified yes, but it represents something different from art. Let us look at some diverse cases of representation in sport. In the 1976 Olympics, the gymnast Kathy Johnson performed a routine that was symbolic of an eagle. Other gymnasts have been known to visualize their routines or parts of routines by drawing the letter *D*; some raise an arm and a hand to symbolize an obscene gesture toward the judges—the meaning of which is known only to the gymnast. A letter *S* might be suggested by a tennis instructor to a right-handed pupil as a way of representing the smooth, fluid motion of the serve. However, better, more sophisticated examples come from the world of tennis. Famous matches have been included in the top ten matches in the history of tennis because they represented social and political issues. First was the Budge/von Cramm match of the 1930s in which von Cramm was identified with Nazi Germany (even though he was not a citizen) and Don Budge with the nations that would become known as the Allied Forces. Their match was a symbol or sample of the approaching global conflict. Our questions pertaining to art now become ones of historiography; Kulka's distinction (see note 17) leads us toward a historiography of sport.

In more recent times the Bobby Riggs/Billie Jean King match of 1973 at the Astrodome in Houston, Texas, was heralded as "The Battle of the Sexes." This was no laughing matter, although it did have its comical moments, and women years later wore gold necklaces with a pendant that read "6–4, 6–3, 6–3" (King's score in defeating Riggs). How could anyone deny that this tennis match expressed and represented a conception of life-issues? The Riggs/ King match symbolized women's long struggle for equality *and their triumph* in a decisive and final way. Through this victory, other women could identify with Billie Jean King. Again we can employ Goodman's sample notion to this match. Why else would this match be listed as one of the greatest ever? It surely wasn't the quality of the tennis that was important, but what it represented to the society in which it was played. Of course I do not wish to assert that the match was art, merely that some tennis matches do possess representational properties of the sort that Best denies of sport. Perhaps one of the most obvious sport incidents representing life-issues comes from track: Jesse Owens's four gold medal performances at the 1936 Olympics in Berlin. Hitler's ploy to use the Olympics to show the world the supremacy of the Aryan race failed and was used by the rest of the world as a sign of its strength and of Nazi vulnerability. America's confidence grew upon hearing of Owens's feats. Sport can, and does, express semantic meaning. These cases are especially interesting because of this semiotic dimension. If they are instances of "art," then *who* are the artists? The artists are not Owens or King; if there is an artist here, it must be everyone together (there needs to be *participation* if a given thing is to function as a sign or a symbol)—both contestants and the spectators. The art is not necessarily created by their conscious planning but by the force and circumstances of the game itself.

Best would probably dismiss these examples of representation because they are extrinsic to the conventions of sport. But some representations are expressed by means of those conventions (the gymnastics, tennis, and baseball cases), so how can they be called "extrinsic" without begging the question? As Kulka draws the distinction, more than internal properties of an object are needed to assess it as artistic. The intrinsic/extrinsic dichotomy employed by Best fails to do justice to the complexity of the notions of representation and expression found in sport.

At this point let me return to Saraf's objections to the sport-as-art analogy and the troublesome notions of representation and expression. I think I have shown above that sport does indeed possess these qualities. In other words, I have the pragmatic and semantic dimensions covered, but the syntactic remains. Unlike Best, Saraf thinks that sport has the properties of representation and expression, but that they are fundamentally different from those found in the domain of art. His claim here is backed by a questionable, essentialistic argument.[25] These properties, for Saraf, are the main components of sport spectacles—how the events are staged and structurally organized. At this juncture in his argument Saraf concedes the _spectacle_ dimension, so the conditions of interpretation begin to change. The way that something is represented or expressed at all by something else is amazingly difficult to say; however, it is worth a try.

First of all it should be noticed that when we say "X represents Y" and "X expresses Y," we generally use these verbs to denote different states of affairs. _Represents_ refers to external (objective) phenomena and _expresses_ refers to internal (subjective) phenomena of an object denoted. So these verbs cover different classes of reference. Consequently the question for aesthetics and philosophy of art is, How do they mix? (This is a problem because they are so fundamentally opposed to one another.) The notions of representation and expression are two of several that are structural elements in human aesthetic experience. They help contribute answers to the question, What is art? In appreciating a work of art or an artistic performance, we generally inquire how that piece represents life or reality. Perhaps the piece suggests things outside of or external to itself. If the external is stressed, then this view becomes what is known as _imitationism_.

Expression works in the opposite direction. The piece emphasizes human terms, conveying emotions (like anger, defiance, agony), those feelings that one has in response to a situation. If the mental and subjective features are emphasized, then we have the view known as _expressionism_. For expressionism, the task (conscious or otherwise) of the artist is to create an expressive content of feeling which is conveyed by the totality of relationships in the object. For imitationism, the task (conscious or otherwise) of the artist is to imitate reality or to mirror life in creating an object, and the product is measured by how well it accomplishes this. Of course there is more than one way to do this, and the history of the idea of representation testifies to the various ways.

Now let us ask some questions about sport with the above discussion in mind. Are athletes imitationists? Some certainly are, as I have previously shown. Representation appears to be on solid ground in sport.[26] But are athletes expressionists? There is nothing unathletic about saying that someone plays a game or a sport (in order) to be expressive when we are thinking of a contact sport like rugby or football, because the athlete might choose to express anger, violence, aggression, or whatever by playing that game. But let me give expressionism another interpretation without these connotations and minus the player's intentions.

Can athletes be expressionists in their play? Imagine Boris Becker, the 1985 Wimbledon Men's Singles Champion, being told of his grandfather's death before he played Kevin Curren in the Final. It is not inconceivable to imagine descriptions of Becker's play as sad, remorseful, and so on by journalists reporting the match.[27] Becker's play may be described as expressive without his intending it to be so. Here, as with representation, expression is causally and logically independent of intentionality (in the narrow sense). And of course this applies to spectators' reactions and intentions, too. Intention is sometimes sufficient but not a necessary condition for the application of some linguistic description.

Under what conditions, if any, does X warrant being called art? If we substitute "sport" for X, does this significantly change our inquiry? The answer is no, at least in terms of the conditions imposed by the domain of art. What are these conditions? We do not want to answer that they are artistic conditions because this would be question begging. As Ward observes, this is what is wrong with the institutional theory of art: it is circular. So what kind of conditions are present? Best suggests moral-political or "life" issues. These issues would overlap *both* the concepts of representation and of expression. Goodman includes exemplification and functionality as additional disjunctive conditions, that is, only one of these disjuncts needs to hold in order for the conditions to be satisfied. A look at the philosophy of art reveals that these two notions are immensely difficult to define, even though they are still considered to be cornerstones of our understanding of art. I will continue with Blocker's general scheme for the philosophy of art in order to place these problematic concepts in perspective.

What is representation? In the early development of the concept, to represent Y meant to depict Y. If a drawing is to represent (in this sense) a horse, then it must look like a horse and not like a pig. But this is naive realism. A more sophisticated explanation is Plato's. Here we have an entity (a "form") that doesn't *look* like a Y but is some sort of (cognitive) analogue of Y. A mathematical equation or formula can represent Y. Or with Plato, a set of dialectical ideas. In any event *what* does the representing is very different from the represented. The gulf becomes even larger in Aristotle, who saw only the depiction of a type or some sort of opposition between types as necessary for representation. In the Greek plays he saw enacted themes universal to human nature—love, betrayal, revenge, and so forth. For Aristotle the character types and the plot made the theater central to Greek culture.

Since Aristotle there has been a continuing broadening of the concept of representation to the point that almost anything represents anything else by expression, symbolization, or function, provided that it is achieved by one of these three processes. Goodman argues that a signature or a sample may be a symbol or an exemplification, and that not only representational works are symbolic but also that "an abstract painting that represents nothing and is not representational at all may express, and so symbolize, a feeling or other quality, or an emotion or idea."

So the problems of representation and expression are really ones of symbolization, which Goodman wants to treat along the lines of a label or sign; or, more narrowly, symbolization can be explained as a linguistic process. Symbols possess a field of reference and denote a set of properties. Goodman sounds very much like Aristotle when he says that those properties that make something count as a painting are those that the painting makes manifest, selects, focuses upon, exhibits, heightens in our consciousness—those properties that it does not merely possess but *exemplifies*. Consequently for Goodman, "a work of art, however free of representation and expression, is still a symbol even though what it symbolizes be not things or people or feelings but certain patterns of shape, color, texture that it shows forth." Or, as Osborne adds, the problems and their solutions constitute the patterns; it is these that make some game a work of art or an object of beauty.

Saraf would agree with this syntactic analysis. Even though we cannot answer the general question "How is it that an object expresses or represents something else?" we can see how an object or an event may be taken by a given community as a symbol or as a sample. As Roberts concludes: "Sport, then, because it is denoted by predicates [like 'speed,' 'power,' 'grade,' and so on], is the sort of thing capable of conveying exemplificational meaning."[28] So the issues here boil down to whether or not sport is a symbol. And again, symbols are (*a*) labels that possess a field of reference and (*b*) denotations of classes of properties. Sport satisfies both of these conditions, which Roberts has previously demonstrated; hence, most of the crucial questions are answered. There are still problems, but they are general ones not unique to sport. Consequently this removes the possible charge of circularity or begging the question. Conceptual clarification is immensely difficult at this level of abstraction.[29]

Where does this leave us? Not much beyond where we started with David Best, but I do think we have progressed in our understanding of these issues. I believe Best's arguments are too narrow and restrictive; I have perhaps opened up things too much. But my argument is not that anything goes in art, so sport goes. My argument is that a sporting event may be a symbol, or it may in fact function as a sample at a certain time and under certain circumstances but not at others. This is why village cricket is not usually art. The occasion is the determining factor in deciding whether or not sport is art. This occasional theory of sport is developed on what Goodman has suggested for contemporary art.

The time is crucial for an event to be treated by a linguistic community as a symbol. The King/Riggs tennis match in 1973 took place when women's liberation was evolving; any earlier or later, and it wouldn't have meant as much as it did then. For a non-sport illustration, consider African art. Many people view the objects as works of art like those in a museum. But to tribal members themselves, these same objects are not art—they are voodoo dolls or magical figures that possess extraordinary powers over the domain they are placed in or over the people who handle them. The objects have different functions in different settings. If the settings are similar, then the functions are. So what may separate the object from art and religion is that the art domain possesses objects that have Goodman's five non-unique symptoms of the aesthetic: syntactic density, semantic density, relative repleteness, exemplification, and multiple and complex reference. (The religious would possess other symptoms with maybe some overlap.)

Saraf foresees these same requirements but labels the compositional uniformity between sport and art as threefold: syntactic, semantic, and sigmatic ("pragmatic"). Like Goodman, Saraf thinks that a general theory of symbols is needed to resolve the problems of art and aesthetics, although Saraf employs only the broad distinction of the theory of signs or semiotics: syntax, semantics, and pragmatics. How each of these linguistic fields of investigation functions in the realms of sport and art is left mainly unanalyzed. Like Roberts I have followed in the footsteps of Goodman in my analysis of these realms. Saraf thinks that the uniformity between sport and art is of a syntactic character only—how the activities are arranged and put together—but denies the semantic and pragmatic character of the uniformity between sport and art. I have tried in this chapter to show that their uniformity does extend beyond the syntactic to the semantic and pragmatic realms of the world.

What remains in a discussion of this sort is a more difficult task: to subdivide or classify the different types of sport in their various relations to art, thereby helping to define *when* sport can become art. This was prompted earlier by the question: If sport can be art, who is the artist? Answering this question helps to provide one broad subdivision of sport—what we might call the self-controlled sports versus the competitively controlled sports. The cases of gymnastics and ice skating are from the former category. They offer close analogues to established arts such as dance because the artist/performer's *control over his or her medium* is not contested by the competition: In fact they are contests only in the sense that a competitive dance (drama or music) audition would be a contest. There is a broad gap between all of these arts/sports and all those other sports in which two individuals or teams struggle to control the medium against each other. In these sports it seems that the achievement of art is likely to come only when one player or team momentarily gains complete control of the medium and so is *free* to merely express himself or herself, for example, a basketball player on a breakaway floating in for the jam. One further clarification that needs to be made pertaining to the issues discussed here is that sport is a *medium*. The subject of the last chapter deals with this idea, to which we now turn.

NINE

The Textuality of Sport:
A Semiotic Analysis

I

IT HAS BEEN CLAIMED that because sport has no text, sport is not art.[1] This chapter will not concern itself with the latter claim, since it has been partially dealt with in chapter 8. Rather I wish to examine the claim that sport has no text, i.e., there is nothing there to be read or interpreted. A plausible case can be developed for the sport-as-text analogy; when we view sport as a text, we examine sport from a semiotic perspective. The theory of the text developed below is taken mainly from the semiotic tradition.

With this context in mind, what is a text? To answer this elemental question, let us look at a printed page. The page before us by itself is a work. If we wish to look at the page as a physical object and its associated properties—ink, paper, size, color, and so on—then we shall call it a work. This is a minimal understanding of a work, though, because there are items like subject matter, story, plot, theme, coherence, and rationality (in the Gricean sense) that figure into the notion of a work. I will speak of the extraphysical characters later in the chapter. Once one picks up the page and reads it (as you are now doing) then the work becomes a text. Therefore a text is something that, through the process of reading, is open to linguistic interpretation, but it is also something fundamentally *understood*.[2] Through the act of interpretation, the reader (or listener) creates another text—a secondary text. The primary text (in this case, a work) may be composed of words, deeds, actions, colors, or clay.[3] In this sense a text may be *any object* that is capable of interpretation, so long as it can be seen as embodying a code involving a sender and a receiver, that is, a vehicle for communication; but some sort of "communication" must take place for there to be a *text*.

Even more challenging is the question: When is a text *literary*? A text possesses literariness when its language not only refers to the world but is self-referential in the sense that a degree of linguistic embellishment is contained in the work and is acknowledged by the author or reader or a community. Even though a text is open to interpretation, it controls the reader by its codes and conventions. Indeed a *correct* reading of a work or a text is accomplished when the reading is within the framework of the text's codes and conventions. Logically speaking, if there are correct readings, then there must also be incorrect readings of texts because one can ignore or be ignorant of the codes and conventions. We can misread works and indeed we frequently do. One of Wittgenstein's most important insights is that we should have to account for mistakes or errors before we do truths or conformatives. A multiplicity of correct readings exist, especially for literary texts. Rarely is there only one correct reading of a text. A text only exists, that is, is imbued with meaning, when it is read or interpreted.

In games players create a *work*, according to a set of conventions and codes which in turn are *read* by an audience and by each other. Just as an act of reading involves "distancing" on the part of the reader, so, too, do athletes distance themselves from their respective "readers" and from themselves personally. Individual preoccupation is replaced with that of the game and its possibilities. This common act of distancing (though different in detail) is the link between participant and spectator and between games and language. Whenever we distance ourselves we become a part of something larger than ourselves. (I shall discuss the notion of distance in greater detail later.) Games are comprised of more than just the players who play them. In a sense the players give themselves over to the game. Language functions in a similar way with its users. When I create a text I make a work that is not a self-contained entity. (This would be impossible.) The element of interpretation is ambiguous, and there may be many texts. This phenomenon also occurs in sports where, as in literature, professionals help those who read (or in this case, watch), the "work" to interpret a text.

In sports, textual events are *mediated* by announcers, commentators, and writers. These people serve a function akin to literary critics and professors in that they make prudent judgments that seek to aid first-time or casual spectators in interpreting the event. As is true in literature, the conflict of sport interpretations is inevitable, and it creates a basis for criticism and controversy. Through such criticism a culture learns or reinforces its language, traditions, and conventions. Criticism is education. Sport as text is a vital part of this process—more than most people realize.

Sport is treated by both individuals and the media as a text. Let me begin with a commonplace illustration. Imagine a group of people seated in a cafe at 6:30 A.M. enjoying their Monday morning coffee and breakfast. As they sit at the counter, they engage in a conversation that focuses upon the weekend games and sporting events. These people are from different class structures, don't know each other, and are in a public place where they can't avoid talking to each other without their normality being thrown into serious question; so what do they talk about? This situation, like many others, *calls* for communication. Sport serves as a convenient and readily accessible vehicle for communication and operates at levels that escape the intellectual scope of most people. For example, the conversation may turn to the poor officiating of a game—where instant replay reveals mistakes or poor judgment. A critical discussion of this subject allows the local people to indulge in criticism without running the risk of offending the religious, political, or moral beliefs of their peers. (This is usually why religion, politics, or sex won't work as a text for Monday morning breakfast. The game not only removes people from their ordinary worldly concerns, it allows them to enter a realm of discussion which is virtually universal; that is, everyone can interpret the text of sport.)[4]

The elements for possible discussion are:

(1) the game's crucial play;
(2) an evaluation of a game—how well it was played or how well a particular team played;

(3) an evaluation of a controversial play—the legitimacy of the play or the umpire's call of it;

(4) what team members and their combinations contributed to the game's outcome (win or loss);

(5) injuries, misfortunes or fortunes ("luck"), and weather conditions;

(6) the line (betting), and anticipation of an upcoming game;

(7) the commentator's remarks on the game;

(8) the game's personalities and records (history).

This list is not exhaustive, but it does give us a handle on possible subject matter for expatiation. What these discussions amount to are sport's "public retelling," as Lynne Belaief calls it.[5] On the positive side, what these public retellings do in terms of value for our whole culture is to train people in the semiotic subtleties of literary study so they may themselves use our communicative media to generate the ideas we need to keep that culture alive and functioning in a time of crisis.[6] Yet this important function of sport is often overlooked or ignored because it transcends the empirical game.

In "Obsessed with Sport," Joseph Epstein offers a good explanation of why sport is a text for the American public: "In a wider sense, sport is culture. For many American men [and women] it represents a common background, a shared interest. It has a binding power that transcends social class and education."[7] For many people, then, sport-talk is the only textual and literary construction that they engage in with any degree of sophistication and success. So they are eager to talk about it, and indeed it has come to dominate American life. People who have played a game and who have worked hard to master its fundamentals are those who remember the pleasure it affords. Epstein continues:

> Different sports, different pleasures. But so keen are these pleasures—pleasures of execution, of craft completed—that, along with being unforgettable, they are also worth *recapturing* in any available way, and the most available way, when reflexes have slowed, when muscle no longer responds so readily to brain, is from the grandstand or, perhaps more

often nowadays, from the chair before the television. (p. 111; my italics)

The advent of television has both enhanced and complicated the argument for the sport-as-text analogy. More than any other single force, television has shaped sport and our consciousness of it. And in elevating games to objects of criticism and interpretation over the past several decades, the medium has attributed textuality and literariness (Scholes's term) to sport. Essential to the idea of a text is that it remain open and subject to interpretation through the eight elements listed earlier, except in extraordinary cases. A correct reading is therefore one that comes from the list. Logically we are committed to labeling a reading as incorrect if it does not conform to the list, even though it is not exhaustive. Deviation has to be earned and proven. (Television announcers routinely conform to the list, but rarely do they explore all of its elements.) This prescription becomes problematic when we find an author writing about a sport or a game where the elements he selects do not conform to the list. Roger Angell, a writer for the New Yorker, is a case in point whom I shall discuss below; we surely won't want to label this work as an incorrect reading, except as I have defined correctness above. Angell violates the conventions in expanding them, and the list grows with more possible correct readings. Before going into this interpretive process, let me briefly elaborate on television's image of sport.

The push to allow the use of instant replay by the umpires is a move to make sport less of a text, for the end result is that it diminishes its interpretive dimension. Television has generally succeeded in generating a text that lacks literariness. Only words have the power to capture literariness. Michael Novak has expressed this argument most succinctly: "Television, in trusting to the eye and renouncing the function of words except as filler, makes sports trivial. The eye is the most superficial sense. Television, the medium of the eye, cheapens us."[8] Furthermore, commentators have become more verbose—filling (and it is obvious that they are just filling in the silence) the precious seconds and minutes of the games. Silence is a luxury that network television cannot afford: it is referred to as

203

"dead air." But silence is what is needed on the part of the audience in order to interpret the game for themselves so they may create their own text. The constant commentaries have continued for so many years now that the public *relies* on the commentators to make the text for them. They are no longer able to construct a text on their own without difficulty. Those of us who wish to do so are frustrated by commentators' endless babbling, which distracts us from the game. *They* become the focus of the game—or at least part of it—instead of the visual unfolding of the game itself. As Epstein says: "I have been thoroughly Schenkeled, Mussbergered, Summeralled, Coselled, DeRogotissed and Garagiolaed." In the background are the sounds of the crowd and the game, but they are not the real sounds—they are sometimes *canned* and dubbed in for effect. The media has convinced the eye that what it sees is reality and not illusion. Because of this, I am more interested in the text building that goes on in the grandstands than the media's selective projection. Deconstruction[9] needs to be employed on the media's text to expose it for what it is.[10]

II

THE MODERN master of text construction in sport is Roger Angell, who in the early seventies began to write about the heart of baseball. In the proliferation of sport our powers of identification, enthusiasm, and attention wane; Angell provides a keen insight into this overdose of coverage:

> What *is* new, and what must at times unsettle even the most devout and unselective fan, is a curious sense of loss. In the midst of all these successive spectacles and instant replays and endless reportings and recapitulations, we seem to have forgotten what we came for. More and more, each sport resembles all sports; the flavor, the joys of place and season, the unique displays of courage and strength and style that once isolated each game and fixed it in our affections have disappeared somewhere in the noise and crush.[11]

What is this "loss"? And what did we really come for? Why are we in the grandstands? The "loss" is the set of conditions for the making of a text or textuality. And the reason why we are there, in the ballpark, is to "read" a text. How are texts made? Angell hints at some answers, so I shall begin with his "inner game" (Angell's term) or what he also calls "the interior stadium." With this term, Angell exhibits how one person (a master) goes about perceiving a game as a text. But before I get any farther in my discussion, I should further clarify the idea of a text.

Robert Scholes (see note 6) gives us a provisional working definition to guide us through the rest of the analysis. A *text* is a set of signals transmitted through some medium from a sender to a receiver in a particular code or set of codes. The receiver of such a set of signals, perceiving them as a text, proceeds to interpret them according to the code or codes that are available and appropriate. This semiotic process happens most frequently and noticeably in sport, where the senders are the players themselves and we (the audience) are the receivers who proceed to interpret what they *do* according to the appropriate codes. What are those codes? Angell, again, supplies us with suggestions on where to look.

The saving grace for baseball in the midst of the noise and crush, asserts Angell, is its pace, which distinguishes it from every other sport. Its pace affords the spectator time to perceive "the perfectly observed balance, both physical and psychological, between opposing forces . . . its clean lines can be restored in retrospect." Television distorts the lines and quickens the pace of the game by commentary and advertisements. So the game's own vividness and mysteries are only discovered after one has been to the games or by "reconsiderations and reflections about the sport itself." The latter are not summations, but "reconstructions" (again Angell's term). Let me give you one of his reconstructions, so that we can use it as our primary example throughout the rest of the chapter. The setting is the World Series in 1968:

Two days later, back in St. Louis, form shows its other face as the Tigers rack up ten runs in the third inning and win by 13–1. McLain at last has his Series win. So it is Lolich against Gibson in the finale, of course. Nothing happens. Inning after inning goes by, zeros accumulate on the scoreboard, and anxiety and silence lengthen like shadows. In the sixth, Lou Brock singles. Daring Lolich, daring the Tiger infielders' nerves, openly forcing his luck, hoping perhaps to settle these enormous tensions and difficulties with one more act of bravado, he takes an excessive lead off first, draws the throw from Lolich, breaks for second, and is erased, just barely, by Cash's throw. A bit later, Curt Flood singles, and, weirdly, he too is picked off first and caught in a rundown. Still no score, Gibson and Lolich, both exhausted, pitch on. With two out in the seventh, Cash singles for the Tigers' second hit of the day. Horton is safe on a slow bouncer that *just* gets through the left side of the infield. Jim Northrup hits the next pitch deep and high but straight at Flood, who is the best center fielder in the National League. Flood starts in and then halts, stopping so quickly that his spikes churn up a green flap of turf; he turns and races back madly, but the ball sails over his head for a triple. Disaster. Suddenly, irreversibly, it has happened. Two runs are in, Freehan doubles in another, and, two innings later, the Tigers are Champions of the World. (pp. 154–155)

There are several things to take note of in Angell's reconstruction. Looking back at the list of discussive elements, we find (1), (2), (4), and (5) present in his reconstruction; but is that all? As Angell reconstructs things, the score is a poor reflection of what actually happened that day in the park:

There seemed to be something more that remained to be *said*. It was something about the levels and demands of the sport we had seen—as if the baseball itself had somehow surpassed the players and the results. It was the baseball that won. (p. 155; my italics)

This is one of the *discoveries* (p. 148) made about the game of baseball that "televised baseball does not seem capable of transmitting" (p. 150), and one must be present to discern it. Who sitting in front of a television would possibly think that "the baseball had won"? Was it the spheroid, that particular one that was hit out to

Flood, or the game ball for a particular game of the World Series (thirty to forty balls are used in the course of a major league game)? Or is the baseball a symbol or a sign for the game of baseball itself? These questions illustrate what the deconstructionists call the problem of identity: how is "the baseball" to be interpreted? They claim there is no matching of reality with its representation or interpretation (a text). Perhaps "the baseball" referred to in this passage is all three interpretations: they form separate secondary texts of which the semiotic reading (the last interpretation) is probably the best. Why? It refers to the whole game rather than just to elements within it. Holism, I have argued throughout the course of this book, is the best interpretation to be given of sport samādhi, so it is not surprising to find it voiced in the best nonfictional writers of sport.

Also on a literal level, the Tigers won; after all, only one of two teams can win. So saying that the baseball won has got to be taken metaphorically for it to make any sense. Angell does say, "It was something about the levels and demands of the sport we had seen" that needed to be said. "The baseball" is Angell's way of saying it.

The discoveries and the "perfect" games are only present in the re-creation of them through language. When a game calls forth more than the elements on our discussive list—indeed the discovery of new elements—it has forced us to speak and to build a text. The text, like Angell's text here, reflects the true nature of the game—not the players or the results or even the summary. There is more to be said. (A summary would not have mentioned the ball—that would have been too trivial to list.) It takes great imagination to transcend the present discussive list, as Angell has done, to help capture the heart or true nature of baseball. How does Angell do it? One critic, James Memmott, has rightly suggested that Angell uses a method.[12] Interestingly enough, Memmott identifies the method with the creation of poetry, notably that of Wordsworth:

> Like Wordsworth, Angell finds emblematic images, "spots of time," which break down the distinction between the present and the past and restore the feeling that had been lost. And

like Wordsworth, Angell achieves this restoration of emotion by the paradoxical technique of getting away from the event in order that he can bring the event back. (p. 158)

Let us examine the technique before we look at the spot of time. Angell describes and illustrates the technique in the following passage:

Always, it seems, there is something more to be discovered about this game. Sit quietly in the upper stand and look at the field. Half close your eyes against the sun, so that the players recede a little, and watch the movements of baseball. The pitcher, immobile on the mound, holds the inert white ball, his little lump of physics. Now, with abrupt gestures, he gives it enormous speed and direction, converting it suddenly into a line, a moving line. The batter, wielding a plane, attempts to intercept the line and acutely alter it, but he fails; the ball, a line again, is redrawn to the pitcher, in the center of this square, the diamond. (p. 155)

Angell's technique employs what is called "psychical distance" in the literature of aesthetics and philosophy of art.[13] Nearly three-quarters of a century ago, Edward Bullough first discussed the phenomenon of psychical (henceforth, "psychic") distance. Let me briefly review Bullough's claims and critics' reviews of them, so we can compare them to Angell's use of psychic distance. One of Bullough's illustrations is a fog at sea. For many people it can be an experience of discomfort. A fog is apt to produce feelings of anxiety and impending danger. But with "the insertion of Distance" (p. 393), a fog at sea can become a source of enjoyment and impersonal pleasure. He says:

Abstract from the experience of the sea fog, for the moment, its danger and practical unpleasantness, just as every one in the enjoyment of a mountain-climb disregards its physical labor and its danger (though, it is not denied, that these may incidentally enter into the enjoyment and enhance it); direct the attention to the features "objectively" constituting the phenomenon—[for example] the veil surrounding you with an opaqueness as of transparent milk, blurring the outline of things and distorting their shapes into weird grotesqueness. . . . (p. 392; my italics)

In an act of abstraction, the fog is no longer seen as a threat to one personally and practically, but is now seen or appreciated as a veil that possesses the properties of opaqueness, the blurring of form or line and the distorting of shapes. These properties, rather than evoking a concern for one's personal well-being, are attended to "with the marveling unconcern of a mere spectator" (p. 393).[14]

In Angell's case the space of the ballpark, too, is transformed into a temporal series of geometries

appearing at the same instant on the green board below us, and, mathematicians that we are, [we] can sense their solution even before they are fully drawn. It is neat, it is pretty, it is satisfying. Scientists speak of the profoundly moving aesthetic beauty of mathematics, and perhaps the baseball field is one of the few places where the rest of us can glimpse this mystery. (p. 156)

In Angell's psychic distancing there emerges an appreciation of formal properties that might otherwise be missed if one attends to the score, the players, and the rest of the elements on the discussive list. Angell says this about form: "Form is the imposition of a regular pattern upon varying and unpredictable circumstances, but the patterns of baseball, for all the game's tautness and neatness, are never regular" (p. 151). In other words the creation of a text is accomplished by the imposition of control on raw materials. In the case above, the baseball has been perceived by Angell as "a source of enjoyment and impersonal pleasure" (to use Bullough's phrase) by the insertion of distance—the baseball is no longer the "little lump of physics," but an element in geometry that gives rise to beauty.[15]

So in typical Aristotelian fashion, "distancing" is an act of abstraction that focuses our consciousness on invisible forms and relations that we draw or immediately infer from objects or elements in our environment. The fewer specific details we have, the better. The mind needs to be free from perceptual detail. This in turn becomes a necessary but not a sufficient condition for the textuality of sport. Angell's case, and indeed an athlete's performance or play, are acts of interpretation, although very different ones at that. The sport in question becomes, or for the player *has*, a text. In other words, the athlete possesses a text and attempts to carry that out during the game.

After Bullough, the notion of distance was revived in the phenomenological literature and has recently been adapted to sport by Scott Kretchmar.[16] The summation of a player's performance becomes a text; the player, who expresses certain moves or options during the game process, is not usually consciously aware of why one option may be selected over another. However, what may have seemed right at that moment may indeed turn out to be the right move or play in that situation. Other moves are more conscious and deliberate, but they all involve players distancing themselves in the context of the game or situation at hand.

The textual elements of sport fall into four broad categories. First is the set of formal rules of a given game; these rules are literally described and explained in a rulebook. Second is the group of informal rules of the game; these are usually codes that express agreements and conventions (for example, sportsmanship). Third are the strategies of offense and defense, and last is a player's style of play. Like drama and other cultural activities, sport has a "script," and scripts precede performances. These preexisting texts regulate as well as generate performance. Performance only has a potential for meaning within these preexisting texts. (This is analogous to language, where speech has meaning on the basis of grammatical rules, etc.) All contemporary sport is ultimately *intertextual*, a text based on prior texts; it is within this concept that the notions of medium and communication become more precise.

Where does this analysis take us thus far? Let me phrase things a little differently, bringing the idea of text back into the picture with the participant in the foreground. Athletes possess a text if they "distance" themselves from their normal environment and their immediate selves and attend to those possibilities that the game offers as a means of achieving the pre-lusory goals. "Distancing" seems to be one notion both spectator and participant have in common, although they differ in that the spectator has the whole game being played before him or her from which to build a text. The participant loses himself or herself in the game and his or her *playing* becomes the text. As Gadamer says: "Play fulfills its purpose [its own seriousness] only if the player loses himself in his play."[17] Distancing is needed in order to carry out either role successfully. It is also a precondition for something to be a text. Language is a very basic way in which we distance ourselves from the world and from ourselves. Indeed language has been described as occupying that space between ourselves and the world. But our *acts* also are a way in which we distance ourselves if they follow a script. Distancing may not "inherently beg for the use of language" as Kretchmar puts it (p. 101), but in the Angell case it does. Maybe this is the difference between the player's text and the spectator's text. The spectator *reads* (or *rereads*) the participant's actions or "text." The participant *reads* (or *rereads*) the game itself in performing it; perhaps we could call it a performative act—something analogous to a Searlean speech act (see chapter 3, note 7), in that it is governed by rules, conventions, and agreements, and is "stated" or expressed.

The player's text must become the spectator's text if the hermeneutical circle is to be complete. That is, the use of language is needed to articulate what the player's acts chart, so that we may make the sort of discoveries Angell has alerted us to. The hermeneutical circle moves from the work (in an empirical sense) to a text, where a full or complete text is located in one of its correct readings. But the complete text is located by reference to the whole work—the sense of "work" that transcends the empirical to include story, plot, theme, coherence, and rationality. In this sense a work is more than a string of sentences, just as a game is more than rules. The interconnections among its sentences are established in a correct reading and this feat completes the circle. From work we move to text and from text back to the work.[18] However, the hermeneutical circle enlarges itself because the spectators, especially in a game of basketball since it is in an enclosed arena, *participate* in the sense that they have an effect on the game (players pick up on what the spectators do, and this action influences their play).

The spectators' text ("play") becomes the participants' text or play. This helps explain momentum, among other things. Here we find *communication*, *medium*, and *text* coming together in the notion of sport as symbol or sign. Sport's process, the sport experience (samādhi), and their interpretation have elements in common. Through an intertextual perspective we come to see that spectators are participants in a larger sense and that they may share the athlete's "inner life." As we have seen above, there are three senses of "text" at work in sport. *Sport* has a text that is "read" during the sport, and the *text* is the result of the player *playing* the sport.

At this point let us look at Memmott's other Wordsworthian point—*the spots of time* that break down the distinction between the present and the past and restore the feeling that had been lost. Epstein concedes that the feeling is lost, but Angell holds out for a recovery of the past:

> Baseball's time is seamless and invisible, a bubble within which players move at exactly the same pace and rhythms as all their predecessors. This is the way the game was played in our youth, and even back then—back in the country days—there must have been the same feeling that time could have stopped. (p. 156)

So the game of baseball possesses a structure for breaking down the distinction between the past and the present. What Angell means by this is that the creative imagination, pondering the game of baseball, breaks down the distinction between past and present. The age-old question of historiography is: how does one capture the past in the present? The rhythms and the pace of the game tell us how to reconstruct the text. But how do they do it? Here we need to leave Memmott and Wordsworth and substitute someone who has been rediscovered in the semiotic movement: R. G. Collingwood.[19]

III

IN the mid-thirties Collingwood revolutionized our conception of history. He thought of all history as a history of thought. History is a product of human thinking, critical thinking. Collingwood argues for this conclusion by first distinguishing an event from an action. Actions are typically those kinds of events that an agent is

212

responsible for bringing about. An agent planned some X, and the plan will typically be discussed in terms of the agent's motives, desires, and thoughts. In a somewhat misleading way, Collingwood (probably following Henri Bergson's terminology) refers to the outside and the inside of an event. When a historian investigates the outside of an event, he describes everything belonging to it in terms of bodies and their movements. In other words, historians describe what people actually did; for example, they traveled from point Y to point Z. By the inside of the event Collingwood means only those things that can be described in terms of thought. Here the historian is interested in *knowing* why those people moved to Z. History does not have mere events (events with no inside) as its subject matter (this is science's domain); rather, history investigates those events that have both an inside and an outside, and these Collingwood calls actions. He writes that the historian's "work may begin by discovering the outside of an event, but it can never end there; he must always remember that the event was an action, and that his main task is to think himself into this action, to discern the thought of its agent" (p. 213). Critics have interpreted this last clause as excessively rationalistic. By "thought" I think Collingwood would include as part of the term's extension human activities involving the affections or emotions, desires, and the rest of the "subjective" dimension of our lives.[20]

In one passage in particular in *The Idea of History*, which makes this broader meaning clear, Collingwood says that man is "the only animal whose conduct is to any great extent determined by thought instead of mere impulse and appetite" (p. 216). This is given as a reason why historians constantly restrict their field to human affairs. Continuing the same point, he remarks:

> The historian is not interested in the fact that men eat and sleep and make love and thus satisfy their natural appetites: but he is interested in the social customs which they create by their thought as a framework within which these appetites find satisfaction in ways sanctioned by convention and morality.

Now we have the reason why Collingwood conceived of history as the history of thought. This concept has an important consequence for us with Angell's spots of time, because history as the history of thought, that is, historiography, brings the past and present together in the act of thinking, or "rethinking" as Collingwood calls it:

> In a sense, these thoughts are no doubt themselves events happening in time; but since the only way in which the historian can discern them is by rethinking them for himself, there is another sense, and one very important to the historian, in which they are not in time at all. (p. 217)

Angell's discovery of the geometries at play, his discovery that the baseball had won, are thoughts that we can think for ourselves— thoughts that constitute a permanent addition to the knowledge or history of baseball. Angell's spots of time are reenactments of games played.

In speaking of the historian, Collingwood also supplies us with a description of Angell's texts or spots of time: "To the historian, the activities whose history he is studying are not spectacles to be watched, but experiences to be lived through in his own mind; they are objective, or known to him, only because they are also subjective, or activities of his own." By "lived" Collingwood means rethought—not *actually* relived. It is a reliving through rethinking. In Angell's reading or constructing of the text of baseball, he has been able to successfully capture the game's rhythms and pace, its emotions and pleasures, and they become our pleasures, for with the knowledge and experience of baseball, we do indeed *experience* (by rethinking) that game's rhythms, pace, and emotions. How? Because those elements of the game of baseball can be apprehended by historical thought at any time. We can well imagine Angell having written the above description of the historian's craft.

Collingwood explains: "The peculiarity which makes it historical is not the fact of its happening in time, but the fact of its becoming known to us by our re-thinking the same thought which created the situation we are investigating, and thus, coming to understand that situation" (p. 218). A famous example from sport history, which deals with the episode of Babe Ruth pointing before the famous "called shot" home run of the 1932 World Series, testifies to, but does not exemplify, Collingwood's explanation of rethinking: Ruth's pointing wasn't out to the outfield; rather it was "at the pitcher's mound, as he shouted 'You'll be out there tomorrow!' at a Cub hurler riding him from the dugout."[21] If the same thought or feeling is created or recreated in the reading of a text—like Angell's—then we have a *correct* reading in a stronger sense than I gave earlier because it is based on identity—the identity of thought or feeling.

One possible objection to my use of Collingwood here is that he is writing about history, and Angell is not a historian of baseball; he is an essayist who uses a poetic method. But Angell may fill Collingwood's expectations of the historian better than do some sport historians. I admit important differences between them, but in his ability to capture time, narrated time, in a text by a set of discussive elements and to convey those things that created the situation described, Angell does as well as if not better than some historians of baseball. He describes baseball's episodes as actions—as the inside of events—capturing the events' inner life.

The text of sport is a product of both the conventions of a game and literary conventions. A written text about sport is not just the latter, but exhibits things like "game time" or pace, the rhythms of the game, and its emotions. This is what makes Angell's writing so special: he has been able to embody those conventions of baseball in the text so as to *share the pleasures and movements of the game with the reader.* His narrative structure captures these, and they are identified by an attentive reader. Those pleasures are passed on, much like the pleasures a son may have when a father's collegiate team wins because he remembers his dad's rooting. I am this way when Michigan plays. Epstein gives a similar account of Notre Dame—pulling for them to lose. But the pleasures afforded from playing *are* the same from one time to another. How, we may ask? The formal structure of the game, its skills and routines delineated by the rules create a web to catch those pleasures unique to that game. Those pleasures are shared by those who play and also by those who read or reread an accomplished text. Such a text can make a casual spectator an informed one, or at least an appreciative spectator—one who can "participate." Collingwood's *enactment* process and his account of the historical imagination provide us with a suitable theory for understanding how such pleasures and affections are shared or, in a sense, the same in experience. Identity or sameness ceases to be a problem here, so deconstruction is in need of qualification. Also the gulf between the participant and spectator is not as wide as I first made it out to be in chapter 7.

To overcome Sartre's humanism (the last section of chapter 4), it is necessary to deconstruct the constructive subject by thinking of difference (Jacques Derrida's *différence*) and otherness. Here *that* difference and otherness or their presence is (in) *the game*. The self is appropriated by the game (or by nature via a game). Playing a game is essentially a self-deconstructive activity. Phenomenologically, "The player experiences the game as a reality that *surpasses* him," Gadamer says (p. 98; my italics). But games are our *last* possibility of where every story has an unequivocal interpretation: a clear beginning, middle, and end. This hope (for *true* narratives or interpretations of texts) is salvaged from deconstructive criticism. However, the hope is not final or complete: "gaming" is an endless task—the activity may be "replayed" either singly (identity) as Angell does with his inner game or historically (difference) by beginning a new game. So "thinking" or gaming is not completely unsettling and unsettled as the recent deconstruction movement suggests. Sport as an academic domain provides answers or alternatives to deconstruction.

If there is an area of history that lends itself to Collingwood's theory, it is sport history. The social customs Collingwood speaks of, surrounding man's physical activities in games and sports, are more fully rule-governed in these spheres than elsewhere. So if a case is to be made for Collingwood's idealism, it is in the realm of sport. We conclude where we began—in the history of recent sport.

NOTES

Introduction: Chasing Paradigms

1. Ludwig Wittgenstein, *Philosophical Investigations*, translated by G. E. M. Anscombe (New York: The Macmillan Co., 1958), p. 5; my italics. Further references to this work and the others cited below are made parenthetically within the text unless otherwise noted.

2. Plato, *Phaedrus*, translated by W. C. Helmbold and W. G. Rabinowitz (Indianapolis: Bobbs-Merrill Co., 1956), pp. 70-71. During Plato's time (d. 347 B.C.E.), books were scrolls, so they really would roll.

3. *Talking a Good Game* can be read by itself or as part of the literature in the field of the philosophy of sport. Two sources of further readings frequently cited in the pages that follow are the anthology *Sport Inside Out: Readings in Literature and Philosophy*, edited by David L. Vanderwerken and Spencer K. Wertz (Fort Worth: Texas Christian University Press, 1985; second printing in 1988), and the collection *Philosophic Inquiry in Sport*, edited by William J. Morgan and Klaus V. Meier (Champaign, Illinois: Human Kinetics Publishers, 1988).

4. Thomas S. Kuhn, *The Structure of Scientific Revolutions* (Second edition; Chicago: University of Chicago Press, 1970).

5. Margaret Masterman, "The Nature of a Paradigm," in *Criticism and the Growth of Knowledge*, edited by Imre Lakatos and Alan Musgrave (Cambridge: Cambridge University Press, 1970), pp. 59-89.

6. Thomas S. Kuhn, "Reflections on My Critics," in *Criticism and the Growth of Knowledge*, pp. 271-272.

7. In addition to Kuhn's classic, see Adam Smith, *Powers of Mind* (New York: Random House, 1975), ch. 1, esp. pp. 20ff., and Alan R. Drengson, "Shifting Paradigms: From the Technocratic to the Person-Planetary," *Environmental Ethics*,

III (Fall 1980), pp. 221–240, who have applied the idea of paradigms to other areas of discourse.

8. My use of only two paradigms is a radical simplifying of sport history, since it portrays the history of sport as a single interplay of these paradigms. I have felt justified in doing so, because I am deliberately presenting a new, unorthodox emphasis to some intellectual trends that might otherwise go unnoticed or un-appreciated.

9. In fact the method Kuhn developed was a conscious extension of Wittgen-stein's later philosophy, which is represented in the *Philosophical Investigations*.

10. The father of the British analytical tradition is Bertrand Russell; see, for example, "On Scientific Method in Philosophy," in *Mysticism and Logic* (Garden City, New York: Doubleday & Co., Inc., 1918), pp. 93–119; especially section II. Earlier in *The Problems of Philosophy* (New York: Oxford University Press, 1912), Russell suggested that "the essential characteristic of philosophy, which makes it a study distinct from science, is *criticism*. It examines critically the principles em-ployed in science and in daily life; it searches out any inconsistencies there may be in these principles, and it only accepts them when, as a result of critical inquiry, no reason for rejecting them has appeared" (pp. 149–150). Sport is no exception—it may be singled out for critical inquiry, and over the past several decades philoso-phers have practiced Russellian criticism and a body of critical literature has evolved. So following Russell, we may define *sport philosophy* as a reflection upon the implications of our sport experience, of the beliefs we hold about the sports world, and of the things we say about them, and an attempt to render these consist-ent—or, at least, to place them within a perspective. Since the early seventies, sport has been in need of criticism, due primarily to its excessive corruption.

11. Michael Novak, *The Joy of Sports: End Zones, Bases, Baskets, Balls, and the Consecration of the American Spirit* (New York: Basic Books, Inc., 1976), p. 121.

12. Martin Heidegger, *Being and Time*, translated by John Macquarrie and Edward Robinson (New York: Harper & Row, 1962), pp. 172, 176, 181, 322, 385. Actually, Heidegger talks about "our Being-attuned" (p. 172), and the person's or "*Dasein's* openness to the world is constituted existentially by the attunement of a state-of-mind" (p. 176).

13. H. P. Grice, "Logic and Conversation," in *The Logic of Grammar*, edited by Donald Davidson and Gilbert Harman (Belmont, California: Dickenson Pub-lishing Co., 1975), pp. 66–67. Reprinted in Robert J. Fogelin, *Understanding Argu-ments: An Introduction to Informal Logic* (third edition; New York: Harcourt Brace Jovanovich, Inc., 1987), p. 407.

14. Arthur Schopenhauer, *The Will to Live*, edited by Richard Taylor (New York: Frederick Ungar Publishing Co., 1962), p. 247. Chapter 9 takes Schopen-hauer's claim seriously.

15. Interview with Sally Wilson, *Dallas Morning News*, Sports Day, Wednes-day, September 8, 1982, p. B1. The word "zone" is probably an abbreviated version of "the twilight zone" (from the television series of the fifties), and first used by

Arthur Ashe, the black American tennis champion and articulate spokesman of the sport, in the early seventies.

16. Stanley Cavell, "Must We Mean What We Say?" in *Ordinary Language: Essays in Philosophical Method,* edited by V. C. Chappell (Englewood Cliffs, New Jersey: Prentice-Hall, Inc., 1964), p. 90.

17. This is Eugen Herrigel's expression in trying to articulate what this sort of experience is like. See his insightful little book, *Zen in the Art of Archery,* translated by R. F. C. Hull (New York: Vintage Books, 1953), p. 40. We shall return to examine these ideas in detail in the last section of chapter 4 and in chapter 5.

1. Philosophy of Sport: The Three Traditions

1. W. H. Walsh, *An Introduction to Philosophy of History* (London: Hutchinson's University Library, 1951), pp. 9f.

2. John E. Smith, "The New Need for a Recovery of Philosophy," *Proceedings and Addresses of the American Philosophical Association,* LVI (1) (September 1982), pp. 16–17.

3. I have borrowed the term "harden" from Jay Rosenberg's critical review of Nelson Goodman's *Ways of Worldmaking* in *Nous,* XVI (2) (May 1982), pp. 307–311.

4. Nelson Goodman, *Ways of Worldmaking* (Indianapolis: Hackett Publishing Co., 1978), p. 6; see also, pp. 11, 65, 102.

5. Paul Weiss, *Sport: A Philosophic Inquiry* (Carbondale: Southern Illinois University Press, 1969), p. 140. The same theme runs throughout his book *The Making of Men* (Carbondale: Southern Illinois University Press, 1967). Weiss's speculative philosophy of sport marks the beginning of a new applied area of philosophy, especially in the United States. Weiss is particularly responsible for philosophers becoming interested in sport as an area of inquiry.

6. Here is what Sidney Gendin had to say about Weiss's book in a review: "By his own admission, Weiss is a man with no background in sports. A few feeble efforts to associate with athletes in locker rooms has not made up for that deficiency. Weiss writes that existentialists who preach involvement 'tend to forget how much is gained by standing away from all involvements.' (p. 81) Never has a man so slavishly followed his own advice. The result is that Weiss writes about athletes in ways that would shock anyone but no one more so than an athlete himself." *Philosophia* (Philosophical Quarterly of Israel), IV (4) (October 1974), pp. 621–622. Lately at the age of eighty-five Weiss has become an athlete, since he has started cycling and running!

7. This psychological and sociological situation only applies under a certain conception of work. Obviously, work can provide intrinsic satisfaction and be a means of self-expression. Jonathan Glover asks us to try the following thought-experiment: "Think of being a train driver, about to be replaced by a robot control, but whose job is saved by the union. The new arrangement is that you sit operating the levers, but the robot operates an identical set. Most of the time your decisions agree with those of the robot, but where they do not, the robot's levers override yours. This work would seem intolerable, because it transparently makes no difference to the world, and is at the same time not sufficiently interesting or demanding to be done, like a sport, for its own sake." In "Work," *Virtues and Values: An Introduction to Ethics*, edited by Joshua Halberstam (Englewood Cliffs, N.J.: Prentice-Hall, 1988), p. 351. Notice that Glover's moral is that if the work performed is sufficiently interesting or demanding, and done for its own sake rather than just for earning money, then it will be a kind of sport (see p. 352 also). So sport and work are not mutually exclusive, although they can be, and unfortunately often are.

8. This term and its application to theories in general I have borrowed from Ulric Neisser, *Cognition and Reality: Principles and Implications of Cognitive Psychology* (San Francisco: W. H. Freeman & Co., 1976), pp. 2f., 7f.

9. Adapted from H. Gene Blocker, *Philosophy of Art* (New York: Charles Scribner's Sons, 1979), p. 10.

10. Paul Weiss, "Games: A Solution to the Problem of the One and the Many," *Journal of the Philosophy of Sport*, VII (Fall 1980), pp. 7–14; and "The Nature of a Team," *Journal of the Philosophy of Sport*, VIII (Fall 1981), pp. 47–54.

11. Josef Pieper, "Play: A Non-Meaningful Act," in *Sport and the Body: A Philosophical Symposium*, edited by Ellen W. Gerber (Philadelphia: Lea & Febiger, 1972), p. 214; originally published in *In Tune with the World* (München: Kosel-Verlag, 1963).

12. Discussions of these questions are: Lynne Belaief, "Meanings of the Body," *Journal of the Philosophy of Sport*, IV (Fall 1977), pp. 50–67, reprinted in *Sport Inside Out*; John O'Neill, "The Spectacle of the Body," *Journal of the Philosophy of Sport*, I (September 1974), pp. 110–122; and Drew Hyland's Platonistic study, "'And That Is the Best Part of Us': Human Being and Play," *Journal of the Philosophy of Sport*, IV (Fall 1977), pp. 36–49.

13. Shirl J. Hoffman, "The Athletae Dei: Missing the Meaning of Sport," *Journal of the Philosophy of Sport*, III (September 1976), pp. 42–51. For him, "sport is an instrument to be appropriated for defining and sharing one's theological views and for directing the attention of others to spiritual considerations" (p. 42). Hoffman's essay is a defense of this sentence and the point of view it conveys.

14. See the sections "Sport and Metaphysical Speculations" and "The Body and the Being," in *Sport and the Body: A Philosophical Symposium*, pp. 65–188, for essays that deal with these ontological questions. Many of these essays have recently been reprinted in *Philosophic Inquiry in Sport*, edited by William J. Morgan and Klaus V. Meier (Champaign, Illinois: Human Kinetics Publishers, 1988), Parts II and III.

15. For openers, see Joseph C. Mihalich, *Sports and Athletics: Philosophy in Action* (Totowa, New Jersey: Littlefield, Adams & Co., 1982), especially chs. 1 and 4; Drew Hyland, "Athletic Angst: Reflections on the Philosophical Relevance of Play," in *Sport and the Body: A Philosophical Symposium*, pp. 87–94; Jean-Paul Sartre, "Play and Sport," and "The Body," ibid., pp. 95–98, 150–151 (also reprinted in *Philosophic Inquiry in Sport*, pp. 169–173, 103–105); also see the sections mentioned in note 14. Another full-scale work is Howard S. Slusher, *Man, Sport and Existence* (Philadelphia: Lea & Febiger, 1967), but it has remained virtually ignored in the literature, especially in comparison with Weiss's book on sport.

16. Maurice Merleau-Ponty, preface to *Phenomenology of Perception* entitled "What Is Phenomenology?" (1945), translated by Colin Smith (New York: Humanities Press, 1962), p. xx.

17. Maurice Natanson's paraphrase of Husserl's project, in "The World Already There: An Approach to Phenomenology," *Philosophical Topics*, XXI (4) (1982), p. 102. Natanson continued by saying that the mission of phenomenological philosophy is "the essential reconstruction of experience." The essential reconstruction of the sport experience is the goal, the aim, of phenomenological philosophy of sport.

18. Hans Lenk, "Prolegomena toward an Analytic Philosophy of Sport," *International Journal of Physical Education*, XIX (1) (1982), pp. 15–18, reprinted in *Sport Inside Out*.

19. See note 18 above, and Ernst Schubert, *Wertungsprobleme im Sportbewerb* (Vienna: Österreichischer Bundesverlag, 1980), which is about evaluation problems in sport competition and is an analytical study of the formal structures of competition. Lenk has recommended some alternative schemes himself in his writings.

20. J. O. Urmson, "What Makes a Situation Aesthetic?" *Proceedings of the Aristotelian Society*, XXXI (1957), pp. 75–92; see p. 84.

21. Robert Fogelin, "Sport: The Diversity of the Concept," in *Sport and the Body: A Philosophical Symposium*, pp. 58–61.

22. Johan Huizinga, *Homo Ludens: A Study of the Play-Element in Culture* (Boston: Beacon Press, 1950), pp. 8ff.; this famous characterization is reprinted in *Philosophic Inquiry in Sport*, pp. 3–6.

23. Bernard Suits, *The Grasshopper: Games, Life and Utopia* (Toronto: University of Toronto Press, 1978). A second edition is in preparation in which Suits attempts to answer his critics; see the next note.

24. Suits's definition is: "To play a game is to attempt to achieve a specific state of affairs (prelusory goal), using only means permitted by rules (lusory means), where the rules prohibit use of more efficient means (constitutive rules), and where the rules are accepted just because they make possible such activity (lusory attitude)" (p. 41). For some discussion of the definition, see Frank McBride, "A Critique of Mr. Suits's Definition of Game Playing," *Journal of the Philosophy of Sport*, VI (Fall 1979), pp. 69–78; reprinted in *Philosophic Inquiry in Sport*, pp. 49–54. In a review in *The Review of Metaphysics*, XXXVI (1) (September 1983), p. 201, James King thinks that the definition still does not exclude activities like lovemaking and proceedings governed by *Robert's Rules of Order* from game-playing. (I tend to agree.) Also, W. E. Cooper, *Canadian Journal of Philosophy*, XXI (2) (June 1982), pp. 409–415, and Alex

Michalos, *Teaching Philosophy*, IV (1) (January 1981), pp. 91–92, both feel that Suits's own project of assimilating Utopia to playing is incoherent, and are skeptical of the project. Aside from the Utopia part, Suits's definition moderately succeeds, and I am sure that others will advance refinements against the present objections. In any event, for the concerns of the philosophy of sport, Suits's proposed definition is adequate for setting up stipulations for discussion of some of the key conceptions in sport-talk and have helped to bring about greater clarity.

25. See Lenk, "Prolegomena," and his *Social Philosophy of Athletics: A Pluralistic and Practice-Oriented Philosophical Analysis of Top Level Amateur Sport* (Champaign, Illinois: Stipes Publishing Co., 1979), and "Action Theoretical Implications in Understanding Sport Actions," *International Journal of Physical Education*, XVI (1) (1979), pp. 23–30, reprinted in *Sport Inside Out*. This sort of criticism was made of Weiss's book by Joseph S. Ullian, *Journal of Philosophy*, LXX (1973), pp. 299–301; and by Anthony Quinton, "Locker Room Metaphysics," *New York Review of Books*, XIII (August 21, 1969), pp. 21–23; also by Gendin in the review cited in note 6 above.

26. Lenk, "Prolegomena," in *Sport Inside Out*, p. 475.

27. Paul G. Kuntz, "Aesthetics Applies to Sports as Well as to the Arts," *Journal of the Philosophy of Sport*, I (September 1974), pp. 6–35, esp. pp. 9ff., reprinted in *Sport Inside Out*, pp. 494ff. Richard Galvin and I have tried to extend the field work Kuntz initiated; see *Sport Inside Out*, pp. 510–526.

28. Immanuel Kant, *Critique of Pure Reason*, "Transcendental Logic," Introduction, translated by Norman Kemp Smith (New York: St. Martin's Press, 1963), p. 93.

29. Hans Lenk, "Notes Regarding the Relationship between the Philosophy and the Sociology of Sport," *International Review for the Sociology of Sport*, XXI (1) (1986), p. 83.

30. I am fully aware of Donald Davidson's criticism of conceptual schemes and the recent movement in analytic philosophy called "postanalytic philosophy"; again, my use of that analytical concept stems from a pragmatism that underlies my work: it is a helpful and useful way to think of "the analytic of concepts" or grid that we impose upon our unreflected experience. If anything, I conceive of my work as compatible and complimentary to this most recent movement. The two principal books to date are *Post-Analytic Philosophy*, edited by John Rajchman and Cornel West (New York: Columbia University Press, 1985), see pp. 129–143 for Davidson's essay; and Hao Wang, *Beyond Analytic Philosophy: Doing Justice to What We Know* (Cambridge: MIT Press, 1986). One main feature of postanalytic philosophy is to "de-disciplinize" itself, with an emphasis upon the questioning of basic assumptions in various fields and an attempt to create new ones. Sport philosophy clearly exhibits this feature, and with my pragmatic orientation, my book demonstrates that "postanalytic philosophy," with its interest more on historical analysis rather than logical analysis, can also be crystallized in the realm of sport and the field of physical education.

2. The Nature of Sport: Three Conceptions

1. H. Graves, "A Philosophy of Sport," *The Contemporary Review,* LXX (December 1900), pp. 877–893, reprinted in *Sport and the Body: A Philosophical Symposium,* pp. 6–15. Page references to Graves's essay are to the anthology.

2. Roger Caillois, *Man, Play, and Games,* translated by Meyer Barash (New York: The Free Press, 1961), pp. 45, 137, inter alia; reprinted in *Philosophic Inquiry in Sport,* pp. 7–15.

3. Bernard Suits, *The Grasshopper: Games, Life and Utopia,* p. 143, and his "What is a Game?" reprinted in Gerber's anthology, *Sport and the Body: A Philosophical Symposium,* pp. 19–20.

4. Kenneth Schmitz, "Sport and Play: Suspension of the Ordinary," in *Sport and the Body: A Philosophical Symposium,* pp. 25–32; on the distinction between amateur and professional, see pp. 31f.; also reprinted in *Philosophic Inquiry in Sport,* pp. 29–38.

5. These ideas first found expression in R. Scott Kretchmar's essay "From Test to Contest: An Analysis of Two Kinds of Counterpoint in Sport," *Journal of the Philosophy of Sport,* II (1975), pp. 23–30; reprinted in *Philosophic Inquiry in Sport,* pp. 223–229.

6. Harold VanderZwaag, *Toward a Philosophy of Sport* (Reading, Massachusetts: Addison-Wesley Publishing Co., 1972), pp. 205–206. See also his "Amateurism," in *The Modern Olympics,* edited by Peter Graham (Cornwall, New York: Leisure Press, 1976), ch. 4.

7. Robert Paul Churchill, *Becoming Logical: An Introduction to Logic* (New York: St. Martin's Press, 1986), p. 114.

8. Arthur Ashe, "Quotable," *Fort Worth Star Telegram,* Saturday, March 7, 1987, p. C3.

9. J. Renford Bambourgh, "Power, Authority, and Wisdom," *Southwest Philosophy Review,* IV (1987); and "Question Time," in *Philosophy in Britain Today,* edited by S. G. Shanker (Ithaca: State University of New York Press, 1986).

10. This distinction becomes important in chapter 8 in trying to discern which sports allow for the possibility for artistic expression and which ones minimize it.

11. Charles Frankel, "Individuals, Enterprises, and Institutions," *This Is TCU* (The Magazine of Texas Christian University), XII (2) (Winter 1969), pp. 5–8.

12. Robert C. Solomon, *The Passions: The Myth and Nature of Human Emotion* (Garden City, New York: Anchor Press/Doubleday, 1976), p. 212.

13. Heywood Hale Broun, "The Vanishing Vacant Mind," *Travel and Leisure,* VIII (4) (April 1978), p. 114. The ski illustration is taken from Broun's column.

14. B. J. Diggs, "Rules and Utilitarianism," *American Philosophical Quarterly,* I (1) (January 1964), p. 40. Reprinted in *Sport and the Body: A Philosophical Symposium,* 2d ed., p. 303.

15. George Leonard, *The Ultimate Athlete: Revisioning Sports, Physical Education, and the Body* (New York: Viking Press, 1974).

16. Michael Murphy, *Golf in the Kingdom* (New York: Dell Publishing Co., 1972).

17. Viktor E. Frankl, "Sports—The Asceticism of Today," in *The Unheard Cry for Meaning: Psychotherapy and Humanism* (New York: Simon & Schuster, 1978), pp. 93–101.

18. *Readings in the Aesthetics of Sport*, edited by H. T. Whiting and D. W. Masterson (London: Lepus Books, 1974), p. 122, in which David N. Aspin says: "The point of a sport, its fascination and its pleasure, lies in the sport itself. Perhaps that is another reason why scratch golfers become bored: it would seem that the pleasure, the excitement, and the attractiveness of sporting activity necessarily lie in the struggle for mastery of its intricacies and difficulties so as to achieve its objectives. Therein lies the desideratum of the whole enterprise."

19. Joseph C. Mihalich, *Sports and Athletics: Philosophy in Action*, inter alia.

20. See, for example, Klaus V. Meier, "An Affair of Flutes: An Appreciation of Play," *Journal of the Philosophy of Sport*, VII (1980), pp. 24–45; reprinted in *Philosophic Inquiry in Sport*, pp. 189–209.

21. E. F. Zeigler, *Problems in the History and Philosophy of Physical Education and Sport* (Englewood Cliffs, New Jersey: Prentice-Hall, 1968), pp. 113–114. A more recent version of this continuum was presented at the meeting of the Philosophic Society for the Study of Sport, Trinity College, Hartford, Connecticut, October 1976. Zeigler's view is also discussed in VanderZwaag's book, pp. 36–39.

22. Jane English, "Sex Equality in Sports," *Philosophy and Public Affairs*, VII (3) (Spring 1978), p. 270: "Sports offer what I will call basic benefits to which it seems everyone has an equal right: health, the self-respect to be gained by doing one's best, the cooperation to be learned from working with teammates, and the incentive gained from having opponents, the 'character' of learning to be a good loser and a good winner, the chance to improve one's skills and learn to accept criticism—and just plain fun." This article is reprinted in *Philosophic Inquiry in Sport*, pp. 329–334.

3. The Varieties of Cheating

1. Associated Press, "Player Says Refs Cheated Hogs," *Dallas Morning News*, November 10, 1978, p. B4.

2. Will Grimsley, "Sugar Ray Rated Best Fighter," *Fort Worth Star Telegram*, March 29, 1978, p. E8.

3. Mike Rabun, "'Unsatisfactory' Duran Assessed Fine of $7,500," *Dallas Morning News*, November 27, 1980, p. B4.

4. Harless Wade, "Cheating, a Fatal Disease?" *Dallas Morning News*, June 6, 1978, p. B2.

5. There is not an adequate term to cover the wider case. I have selected "unfair play" in spite of its subjective overtones, because the sport actions the

term has to cover extend beyond "illegal actions," which stresses just those sport actions that fall within the domain of rules and penalties.

6. This remark must be qualified: it is logically possible that cheating might increase the element of chance. Imagine that a mismatched player A has an 85 percent chance of winning while player B has only a 15 percent opportunity. (No ties are possible.) Player B cheats by doing X and now has a 50 percent chance of winning. The presence of "chance" in this contest is increased dramatically precisely because someone *did* cheat. But this situation violates the condition that the contest is between equal opponents (in a specifiable minimal sense) who play to the best of their natural abilities whatever those might be—whether they are "matched" or not.

7. The distinction between constitutive and regulative rules has a long, distinguished history dating from the nineteenth-century German philosopher Immanuel Kant. The most thorough discussion in recent Anglo-American philosophy is John Searle's *Speech Acts: An Essay in the Philosophy of Language* (Cambridge: Cambridge University Press, 1969), pp. 33–37. Searle draws the distinction in this way: "Regulative rules relegate antecedently or independently existing forms of behavior; for example, many rules of etiquette regulate inter-personal relationships which exist independently of the rules. But constitutive rules do not merely regulate playing football or chess, but, as it were they create the very possibility of playing such games. The activities of playing football or chess are constituted by acting in accordance with (at least a large subset of) the appropriate rules. Regulative rules regulate a pre-existing activity, an activity whose existence is logically independent of the rules. Constitutive rules constitute (and also regulate) an activity the existence of which is logically dependent on the rules" (pp. 33–34). My use of the distinction here falls within Searle's description of these activities. But some rules in games can be singled out as primarily *regulating* forms of behavior, like "roughing" the passer or kicker in football, whereas rules designating first downs, touchdowns, and field goals are primarily *constitutive* and correspond more closely to what Searle says about those rules. Noticing these different rules and how they function in games helps me to avoid what would otherwise be an ambiguity in the notions of rule and rule breaking, but in the context of games, they are all constitutive rules—some of which we single out as "regulative." For a critique of Searle's concept of institution as a system of constitutive rules, see Gordon Reddiford's penetrating study, "Constitutions, Institutions, and Games," *Journal of the Philosophy of Sport*, XII (1985), pp. 41–51.

8. T. Ainslie, *Ainslie's Complete Hoyle* (New York: Simon & Schuster, 1975).

9. Associated Press, "Cheating Charges Surfacing at Indy," *Fort Worth Star Telegram*, May 20, 1979, p. B8.

10. Jan Progan, "Man, Nature and Sport," in *Sport and the Body: A Philosophical Symposium*, pp. 197ff. Her list of the characteristics of nature sports includes: an aesthetic experience; challenge; stress-risk; union with self, nature, and other persons; and a contrast with ordinary life.

11. *Mimicry* classifies open games in which the player acts out a role rather than following a rule. The "rules" in open games tend to be ambiguous and permit conflicting interpretations of a player's actions. *Ilinx*, or the pursuit of vertigo, is a category encompassing nature sports and more. These "games" attempt to alter one's perceptions and mental stability with seizure and shock from high speeds or activities that distort the senses momentarily. Caillois would probably want to put some video games in this category. For more detail see Caillois (pp. 23ff).

12. Some philosophers argue against the notion of self-competing. For instance, James Keating (whom I discuss in the following chapter), *Competition and Playful Activities* (Washington, D.C.: University Press of America, 1978), p. 3, legislates against the idea because he interprets "the other" in Arthur O. Lovejoy's definition of "competition" as having to be another individual, a rival competitor. See Lovejoy, "Christian Ethics and Economic Competition," *The Hibbert Journal*, IX (January 1911), p. 327. Keating states that "Lovejoy characterized competition 'as an attempt to get or to keep any valuable thing either to the exclusion of others or in greater measure than others'" (pp. 2–3). Why can't the layout of the cards in a game of solitaire or the mythical Old Man Solitaire be "the other"? In ordinary language, uses of "competing" clearly include instances where the term is meaningfully applied to oneself. Novak (pp. 154, 157) lists self-competing as one of the prevalent uses of the term in America today. This may be an extended use, but that does not make it any less intelligible. Novak gives a moving account of competition for the exceptional athlete, and it should be consulted by any who have doubts. In speaking of track and field events, Novak observes: "The athlete accumulates best times or distances. 'Competition' in such sports provides both stimulation and the pressure of producing on demand. The presence of other good athletes forces one to 'outdo' oneself, to push oneself to new accomplishments. Still, one does not quite so much defeat one's rivals as defeat one's own self. Both in training and in the meet, one's attention is ultimately upon one's own performance: one's own best time, one's own best distance, one keeps trying to extend one's achievements further. To have record setting athletes as one's peers is a spur and an incentive. One must try to better their marks, but the essence of that struggle is to exceed one's own previous limits" (p. 153).

13. The distinction between challenge- or excellence-oriented activities and dominance-oriented activities raises an interesting question regarding self-competition. Ordinarily, self-competition is categorized under the challenge- or excellence-oriented model. Could self-competition be considered an effort at self-dominance? It might be for some narcissistic individuals with perverted expectations of their self-worth.

14. Bernard Gert, *The Moral Rules: A Rational Foundation of Morality* (New York: Harper & Row, 1966), pp. 106–111, 116–120. There is a lack of analysis of cheating in modern moral philosophy. Since Gert's is the best I found, I chose to label it the standard analysis.

15. Sid Moody, "Cheating in America," *Albuquerque Journal*, April 13, 1980, pp. 1, 11.

16. Barry Tarshis, "How to Protect Yourself Against the Tennis Cheater," *Tennis*, XVI (March 1979), p. 72.

17. Gunther Lueschen, "Cheating in Sport," in *Social Problems in Athletics*, edited by D. M. Landers (Urbana: University of Illinois Press, 1976), pp. 68, 69, 75.

18. For more details on promising, see Searle's *Speech Acts*, ch. 3.

19. K. M. Pearson, "Deception, Sportsmanship, and Ethics," *Quest*, XIX (January 1973), p. 117; reprinted in *Sport Inside Out*, p. 459, and in *Philosophic Inquiry in Sport*, p. 264.

20. For a complete analysis along these lines, see Charles Fried, *Contract as Promise: A Theory of Contractual Obligation* (Cambridge, Massachusetts: Harvard University Press, 1981), esp. ch. 2.

21. David Hume, *A Treatise of Human Nature*, edited by L. A. Selby-Bigge (Oxford: The Clarendon Press, 1888), p. 490; Hume's italics.

22. Paul Weiss and Jonathan Weiss, in *Right and Wrong: A Philosophical Dialogue Between Father and Son* (New York: Basic Books, 1967), do concede that it is sometimes right to cheat: "I can well understand how someone might be in the clutches of a tyrant and have in his care the protection of a great many innocent people, making it desirable for him to cheat, to lie, to violate the ordinary code" (pp. 10ff). Could there be a situation imaginable in sport parallel to that of a tyrannical ruler? Could game conditions deteriorate to the point where it would be right for a player to cheat?

23. Sissela Bok, *Lying: Moral Choice in Public and Private Life* (New York: Pantheon Books, 1978), ch. 9.

24. Associated Press, "Drysdale Admits He Hit Hitters on Purpose," *Fort Worth Star Telegram*, October 17, 1978, p. C1. Why this case is an example of cheating will be made clear in the pages that follow.

25. Some verbs that illustrate how this connection is made are: "interpreting," "recognizing," "apprehending," "identifying," and "acknowledging."

26. Lawrence H. Davis, *Theory of Action* (Englewood Cliffs, New Jersey: Prentice-Hall, 1979), p. 61. The inserted phrase in brackets is mine.

27. Bob Clanton, "Rutherford Saw 'Cheating,'" *Fort Worth Evening Star Telegram*, May 29, 1978, p. D1.

28. For instance, Pat Truly, "A Little Basic Dishonesty," *Fort Worth Star Telegram*, April 3, 1979, p. D1, used the phrase *intentional cheating*, in addition to others having used it in sport literature.

29. Hal Bock, "Lou Guesses Right, Slams Hit That Pulls Yanks Even," *Wichita Falls Times*, October 15, 1978, p. B1.

30. Associated Press, "Dodgers Incensed at Umpire's Ruling," *Wichita Falls Times*, October 15, 1978, p. B1.

31. Jim Reeves, "Reggie in Turmoil Again," *Fort Worth Star Telegram*, October 15, 1978, p. B6.

32. This assertion is not to deny that there are elaborate strategies that are consciously designed in sport, especially baseball and football—these are practiced initially in a conscious manner until mastered and then are carried out without thinking about the particulars of the play. (The details of this process of knowledge and doing are in part III.) "Intention," as umpire Pulli uses it here, does not cover this process. He means the stricter, more narrow use of the term.

33. Dan Jenkins, "Up a Tree in Toledo," *Sports Illustrated*, L (June 25, 1979), pp. 20–23.

34. From Sports Briefly column, *Fort Worth Star Telegram*, January 13, 1990, sec. 3, p. 9.

35. What are the *permissible* limits? They are probably much less precisely defined for spectators than for play on the field. For a provisional conditional, let us try the following: If spectators disrupt the play on the field, then their rooting has transgressed permissible limits.

36. One qualification: If the officials have been consistent through a given game, or during a series, or over a season, in their interpretation and ruling of vicinity tags on double plays, then a second baseman or shortstop who knowingly takes a throw "in the vicinity of the base" has in no way "cheated."

37. It is an open question as to whether *unintentional* should be equated with *accidental*. The two terms seem not to have the same range of application. I could unintentionally perform an A and not accidentally do an A; for example, a tennis player could hit his or her opponent at the net with the ball and we would normally say that the episode was unintentional on the player's part, but we would not say that it was an accident or done accidentally. (The latter sounds odd.)

38. Peter McIntosh, *Fair Play: Ethics in Sport and Education* (London: Heinemann Educational Books, 1979), p. 183.

39. The same idea is used and worked out in some detail by David Ross in his answer to *Analysis* "Problem" No. 16, "He Loads the Gun, Not the Dice," *Analysis*, XXXVIII (June 1978), p. 115.

40. Annette C. Baier, "Act and Intent," *Journal of Philosophy*, LXVII (October 8, 1970), pp. 648–658; see p. 649.

41. Roderick Chisholm, "The Structure of Intention," *Journal of Philosophy*, LXVII (October 8, 1970), pp. 633–647, see p. 637; George Pitcher, "'Intending' and Side Effects," *Journal of Philosophy*, LXVII (October 8, 1970), pp. 659–667, see pp. 665–666; Michael Stocker, "Intentions and Act Evaluations," *Journal of Philosophy*, LXVII (September 3, 1970), pp. 589–602, see p. 594; Hector-Neri Castañeda, "Intentions and the Structure of Intending," *Journal of Philosophy*, LXVII (August 5, 1971), pp. 453–466, see p. 461; and Robert Audi, "Intending," *Journal of Philosophy*, LXX (July 19, 1973), pp. 387–402, see pp. 397–400. All agree that some agent J can perform or do some action A such that an A is neither intentional nor unintentional. My contention is weaker than theirs, for I am only claiming that for cheating, unintentional ascriptions can be and are made. A brief look at the literature on intention and action shows us that the thesis that all actions are intentional is false. (See, for example, Audi, p. 400.) A more current study of intentional and unintentional actions has been made by Michael Gorr and Terence Horgan in *Philosophical Studies*, XLI (1982), pp. 251–262, but their analysis is more narrow than mine. They make the distinction between intentional and unintentional actions in terms of belief. Of unintentional actions, they say: "To call an act described as being a certain type 'unintentional' is to indicate simply that the agent did not believe (at that time) that he was performing an act of that type" (p. 254). This analysis is too narrow to accommodate most of the cases discussed in this chapter. There are clear cases of known but unintended actions; in other words, results can be foreknown but not intended. For example, a doctor does know (and believe) that he will cause pain when he gives a shot to a patient, but does not intend to do so. Consequently, some of the earlier articles mentioned above are more helpful than the Gorr-Horgan analysis.

42. Such a view is reminiscent of John Locke's discourse on the perceptual process. See any of the numerous editions of Locke's *Essay Concerning Human Understanding* (1690), Book II.

43. Nick Powell, "The Code," *United States Lawn Tennis Association* (pamphlet) (New York: USLTA, January 30, 1967), p. 3.

44. José Ortega y Gasset, *Meditations on Hunting*, translated by Howard B. Wescott (New York: Charles Scribner's Sons, 1972), p. 110.

45. A. H. Maslow, *Toward a Psychology of Being* (Princeton, New Jersey: Van Nostrand, 1962), chs. 6 and 7.

46. See Davis, *Theory of Action*, p. 63.

47. This definition is implied by H. Graves and is seen in many of the essays in *Sport and the Body: A Philosophical Symposium* (either edition), in the section on "Sport and Value-Oriented Concerns," or Part IV of *Philosophic Inquiry in Sport*, pp. 219–287.

48. The distinction between responsible and accountable actions was suggested to me by Paul Weiss. An article that discusses this distinction in some detail is Nicholas Haines, "Responsibility and Accountability," *Philosophy*, XXX (113) (April 1955), pp. 141–163. Accountability is analyzed along the lines of liability, but also according to whether an act is explicable. By "explicable," Heines means an act that has an explanation that is either in terms of "causes of" or "reasons for" an act. "The focus of the explanation is, as a rule, the act rather than the actor" (p. 142); whereas in responsibility, the converse is true—the focus is on the agent rather than the act. Haines's example is: "If now, from my window, I see a motorist fling over the wheel so that his car crashes into another I may certainly speak of the driver as 'accountable' for his act and expect to see him approached by the police or even face trial for manslaughter" (p. 142). The analytical demarcations that Haines makes also hold for the sport examples in this part of my discussion.

49. P. H. Nowell-Smith, "Ifs and Cans," *Theoria*, XXVI (2) (1960), pp. 85–101; see pp. 100–101.

50. Bob Green, "Tip to Trevino Cost Watson 2-Shot Penalty—But He Wins," *Dallas Morning News*, April 21, 1980, p. B1; my italics.

51. Mike Jones, "Burleson Near Top—and Still Climbing," *Dallas Morning News*, May 30, 1979, p. B1. What Burleson means by "cheat" is "poach," like in the doubles game of tennis when the person at net cuts off a ball that is hit toward his or her partner.

52. A case in point is U.S. District Judge Owen's ruling (February 19, 1981) that George Harrison "subconsciously" plagiarized the melody of composer Mack's "He's So Fine" (1963), in composing the 1971 hit "My Sweet Lord." The judge concluded at the time, "I do not believe he did so deliberately." Consequently, Harrison had to pay $587,000 in damages to a music company owned by his former manager. Just imagine how much Harrison would have had to pay if he had deliberately plagiarized the melody!

53. For further discussion of cheating, see Craig K. Lehman, "Can Cheaters Play the Game?" *Journal of the Philosophy of Sport*, VIII (Fall 1981), pp. 41–46, reprinted in *Sport Inside Out*; and Oliver Leaman, "Cheating and Fair Play in Sport," in *Sport and the Humanities: A Collection of Original Essays*, edited by William J. Morgan (Bureau of Educational Research and Service; Knoxville: University of Tennessee, June 1982), pp. 25–30. Both of these essays are reprinted in *Philosophic Inquiry in Sport*, pp. 277–287.

4. The Preservation of Sport

1. Francis W. Keenan has also written on sport from an Aristotelian perspective; see his "The Athletic Contest as a 'Tragic' Form of Art," in *The Philosophy of Sport: A Collection of Original Essays*, edited by Robert G. Osterhoudt (Springfield, Illinois: Charles C. Thomas, 1973), pp. 309–326. Other perspectives are possible; for instance, a Platonistic one is developed by Drew A. Hyland in "'And That Is the Best Part of Us': Human Being and Play," *Journal of the Philosophy of Sport*, IV (1977), pp. 36–49; and he also develops a Hegelian interpretation in "Opponents, Contestants, and Competitors: The Dialectic of Sport," *Journal of the Philosophy of Sport*, XI (1984), pp. 63–70.

2. Aristotle, *Physics*, Book III, Chapter 3, in *The Basic Works of Aristotle*, edited by Richard McKeon (New York: Random House, 1941), pp. 240–241. The doctrine of the four causes is listed again in Book V, Chapter 2, in the *Metaphysics*, pp. 752–753.

3. G. B. Kerferd, "Aristotle," *The Encyclopedia of Philosophy*, edited by Paul Edwards (New York: Macmillan Publishing Co., 1967), I, 157.

4. Aristotle, *Poetics*, especially sections 4, 25, 26. Bernard Jeu was one of the first philosophers to view sport as drama: "*Competitive sport is, first of all, tragedy, the calling into question of existence, or, more specifically, the immediate presence of violence and the immanence of death*" (symbolically that is), in "What Is Sport?" *Diogenes*, LXXX (Winter 1972), p. 153. Also consult Keenan's essay mentioned in note 1, whose analysis soon followed Jeu's.

5. This article is reprinted in *Philosophic Inquiry in Sport*, pp. 241–250. For a critique of this article similar to mine, see Randolph M. Feezell's "Sportsmanship," *Journal of the Philosophy of Sport*, XIII (1986), pp. 1–13, reprinted in *Philosophic Inquiry in Sport*, pp. 251–261.

6. Paul Weiss, *Sport: A Philosophic Inquiry*, p. 57.

7. Leonard first suggested this idea in *The Ultimate Athlete*, pp. 254–255.

8. John Underwood, *The Death of an American Game: The Crisis in Football* (New York: Little, Brown & Co., 1980).

9. For a neo-Marxist's critique of American sports, see Paul Hoch, *Rip Off the Big Game: The Exploitation of Sports by the Power Elite*, introduction by Jack Scott (Anchor Books; Garden City, New York: Doubleday and Co., 1972).

10. In the 1988 Winter Olympics, we found that curling has been introduced into the Games. (Curling is like ice shuffle board, played in teams, with several curlers armed with brooms who brush the ice in front of the curling stone to cut down on the resistance as it travels over the ice to its designated place.) However, the note's point is still well taken—curling is difficult to have large audiences for. If hockey continues its violence, perhaps those ice arenas can be used for curling.

11. See, for example, John Underwood, "Student Athletics: The Sham, the Shame" (special report), *Sports Illustrated*, LII (21) (May 19, 1980), pp. 36–72; and my editorial, "Return the Meaning of 'Collegiate' to College Sports," *Fort Worth Star Telegram*, Thursday Evening, November 7, 1985, p. 29A; and the editorials in the *Dallas Morning News*, for example, "SMU Scandal: Continuing Revelations Raise Ethical Questions," Wednesday, March 4, 1987, p. 14A; Doug Harlan, "The Problem in College Athletics," *Dallas Morning News*, Saturday, March 7, 1987, p. 33A. The Southern Methodist University athletic problem is a microcosm of a national problem. The solution to the local one—now under way—will perhaps pave the way to solving the larger problem.

12. The French have admirably attempted this in the 1980 French Open by presenting the first place check for $43,000 later in private to Chris Evert. The money is secondary to the prestige of the world's premier clay court title. (Barry Lorge of the *Washington Post*, "On to Wimbledon for Chris after Win," *Sunday Fort Worth Star Telegram*, June 8, 1980, p. B1.) By contrast, the prestige that the World Championship of Tennis Finals in Dallas, Texas, had lay squarely on the money the event had associated with it.

13. Jean-Paul Sartre, *Being and Nothingness: An Essay on Phenomenological Ontology*, translated by Hazel E. Barnes (New York: Philosophical Library, 1956), especially part IV, ch. 2. This phenomenological description and analysis is reprinted in *Philosophic Inquiry in Sport*, pp. 170–173.

14. Joseph S. Catalano, *A Commentary on Jean-Paul Sartre's "Being and Nothingness"* (New York: Harper & Row, 1974), p. 220; italics removed from the last sentence.

15. Sartre elsewhere (in *The Transcendence of the Ego: An Existentialist Theory of Consciousness*, translated by Forrest Williams and Robert Kirkpatrick [New York: The Noonday Press, 1957], p. 60) describes the ego this way: "The *I* is the ego as the unity of actions. The *me* is the ego as the unity of states and of qualities. The distinction that one makes between these two aspects of one and the same reality seems to us simply functional, not to say grammatical."

16. Katsuki Sekida, *Zen Training: Methods and Philosophy* (New York: John Weatherhill & Co., 1975), ch. 8. Zen training and sport are discussed in greater detail in the next chapter.

17. Jan Progen has rightly listed this trait as one of the important characteristics of nature sports; see her "Man, Nature and Sport," in *Sport and the Body: A Philosophical Symposium*, p. 200. This trait, the feeling of union with nature, is also discussed in terms of wilderness travel by Alan R. Drengson in the context of Zen art and Rasa Yoga; see his "Wilderness Travel as an Art and as a Paradigm for Outdoor Education," *Quest*, XXXII (2) (1980), pp. 110–120, reprinted in *Sport Inside Out*.

18. Hans-Georg Gadamer, *Truth and Method* (New York: Crossroad Publishing Co., 1975), p. 93.

19. It is curious that Sartre did not entertain this possibility, because for two and a half months in 1928, he had weekly talks with the Japanese philosopher Shuzo Kuki. Recently it has been revealed by Stephen Light that Sartre was really introduced to Husserl and Heidegger by Kuki and not by Emmanuel Levinas; see Light's *Shuzo Kuki and Jean-Paul Sartre: Influence and Counter-Influence in the Early History of Existential Phenomenology* (Carbondale: Southern Illinois University Press, 1987).

5. Zen and Yoga in Sport

1. This sentence is a summary of a claim commonly made in sport. There are many sports writers who have popularized Eastern ideas of sport. Among them is W. Timothy Gallwey, who has an extensive, widely read list of books that apply Oriental philosophy (mainly Zen and Hatha Yoga) to sport. See his books *The Inner Game of Tennis* (New York: Random House, 1974), *Inner Tennis: Playing the Game* (New York: Random House, 1976), *The Inner Game of Golf* (New York: Random House, 1981), and *Inner Skiing* (New York: Bantam Books, 1985). The idea of "the perfect shot" and the mental discipline (plus exercises) leading the mind (brain?) from an ego state to an egoless one was first brought to the West's attention by the German philosopher Eugen Herrigel's *Zen in the Art of Archery* (1948). In this chapter I shall mainly speak of the Zen tradition. However, for the purposes here, "Zen" will be construed broadly enough to include Hatha Yoga, except when the latter is specifically singled out for discussion. The word "Zen" is mainly a Western term, which literally means the concentration of consciousness. The great Zen masters speak of *do* (the way). As Taisen Deshimaru recounts: "The spirit of Zen, carried from India by Bodhidharma, the semi-legendary monk of the sixth century, brought Mahayana Buddhism to China where it grew and merged with Chinese thought to become the true way." (In *The Zen Way to the Martial Arts*, translated by Nancy Amphoux [New York: E. P. Dutton, 1982], pp. 46–47.) For a brief account of Zen and sport from another insider besides Deshimaru, see T. Hirata, "The Relation of Body and Spirit in Zen-Buddhism," in *Sport in the Modern World—Chances and Problems*, edited by

Ommo Grupe and others (Heidelberg: Springer-Verlag, 1973), pp. 603–606. "Yoga" is a term in this literature which is sometimes loosely used to refer to exercises for mental and physical fitness, adapted from Indian sources. Hatha Yoga is a higher form of Hinduism and embraces the doctrine that a path to spirituality or enlightenment is through a carefully planned course of fasting, coupled with physical and mental exercises in order to concentrate the mind. Hatha Yoga is a school (a philosophical system) of Yoga—there are at least seven basic types of Yoga that are concerned with perfecting the body consciously, filling it with life force *(prāṇa)*. It is more than treating physical development as an end in itself. An ancient Indian saying testifies to this: "The mind is lord of the senses, but the breath is lord of the mind, and that depends on Nada, the Inner Voice." (In Walter B. Gibson, *The Key to Yoga* [New York: Grove Press, 1974], pp. 69ff., inter alia.) The best introductory treatment of Yoga is in *A Source Book in Indian Philosophy*, edited by Sarvepalli Radhakrishnan and Charles A. Moore (Princeton, New Jersey: Princeton University Press, 1957), ch. XIII.

2. Gallwey, *Inner Tennis: Playing the Game*, pp. 132–133. The "energy" he speaks of is *prāṇa* (life force); the "it" is the Inner Man or Nada, the Inner Voice, or the "It" of Zen.

3. See Arne Leuchs and Patricia Skalka, *Ski with Yoga: Conditioning for the Mind and Body* (Matteson, Illinois: Greatlakes Living Press, 1976), and Katsuki Sekida, *Zen Training: Methods and Philosophy*, respectively. Sekida's *Zen Training* is the best book of the lot, and I shall rely heavily on it in my critique of Gallwey.

4. See Gallwey's books (listed in note 1) and his article "This Man Can Change Your Skiing," *Ski*, January 1977, pp. 97–118; and George Leonard, *The Ultimate Athlete*.

5. Sekida, *Zen Training*, p. 95. See also notes 1 and 2.

6. Nor does it end here; David Distel of the *Los Angeles Times* has written a piece that appeared in most sports sections across the United States, which discusses vision, concentration, performance, and their interrelationships: "Centering and Visualization," *Fort Worth Star Telegram*, Saturday, August 14, 1976, sec. 4 (Sports), pp. 1–3. Obviously, Gallwey is not the only one doing this. Further application of the inner game and Eastern thought can be found in numerous books; for openers, see Dan Blackburn and Maryann Jorgenson, *Zen and the Cross Country Skier* (Pasadena, California: Ward Ritchie Press, 1976); Fred Rohe, *The Zen of Running* (New York: Random House, 1974); Donald Porter, *Inner Running* (New York: Grosset & Dunlop, 1978); Joe Hyams, *Zen in the Martial Arts* (Boston: Houghton Mifflin Co., 1979); and Deshimaru, *The Zen Way to the Martial Arts*. In a more popular vein, see Michael Murphy and Rhea A. White, *The Psychic Side of Sports* (Reading, Massachusetts: Addison-Wesley Publishing Co., 1978); Gay Hendricks and Jon Carlson, *The Centered Athlete* (Englewood Cliffs, New Jersey: Prentice-Hall, 1982); and for the two-hemispheres brain theory associated with the inner game, consult Gary Wiren and Richard Coop, *The New Gold Mind* (New York: Simon & Schuster, 1978), and Thomas E. Blakeslee, *The Right Brain: A New*

Understanding of the Unconscious Mind and Its Creative Powers (New York: PBJ Books, 1980), ch. 5 entitled "The Inner Sports Revolution," pp. 76–85. The list is almost endless. Of the works mentioned thus far, Leuchs and Skalka, *Ski with Yoga* is the most successful in applying Hatha Yoga to skiing; for example, *prāṇayama* or breathing methods and exercises. Also, Sekida dwells on the physiological basis of Zen training—comparing it at times to American football practices; see chs. 1–3, 7–8. Lately, it has been suggested by Ed Flynn, a nuclear physicist of Los Alamos, New Mexico, that "We know that people with special gifts, such as perfect (musical) pitch, exhibit brain activity different from the rest of us. That makes us wonder how many other people with unique gifts may have brain functioning that's different. Is there something special about the brain activity of a sharpshooter or a good athlete? Is it something measurable ahead of time? We think MEG [magnetoencephalography, a new field that measures the magnetic fields generated by electrical activity within the brain] can help us find out." William Hart, "New Process Studies Brain Dysfunctions," *Dallas Morning News*, October 26, 1986, p. 50A. Perhaps someday MEG researchers will measure a person's sport samādhi.

7. A few years earlier, Michael Murphy, *Golf in the Kingdom* (1972), pp. 169–171, hinted at this application, but Leonard has discussions, exercises, and all the rest. Leonard more faithfully reflects Eastern philosophy than Murphy or Gallwey, so if one wants a detailed perspective, *The Ultimate Athlete* is one of the best in this popular literature, although recently it has been criticized by Angelika Förster in "The Nature of Martial Arts and Their Change in the West," in *Mind and Body: East Meets West*, edited by Seymour Kleinman (Champaign, Illinois: Human Kinetics Publishers, 1986), p. 84, where she declares that "many Western practitioners of noncompetitive martial arts harbor the misconception that *do* totally excludes achievement or competition." She adds: "The impulse to fight can only be overcome by the martial art and fighting practice! Even the engaged Westerner may not grasp the complexity of the 'paradox,' which, in turn, leads to deep misunderstandings about the tough, more competitive disciplines (Leonard, 1975), or to self-deception or over-estimation concerning one's own degree of mastery." Again, Sekida's *Zen Training* is our best guide to date for tracing the nature of this ancient practice.

8. Adam Smith (pseudonym), "Sport Is a Western Yoga," *Psychology Today*, IX (October 1975), pp. 48–51, 74–76, reprinted in *Sport Inside Out*.

9. Simon Ramo, *Extraordinary Tennis for the Ordinary Player* (New York: Crown Publishers, 1970), pp. 13ff.

10. There is another alternative. Ted Williams claimed he could see the individual threads on a baseball. Tennis pro Jimmy Connors says he sees the path of the ball on a serve long before it crosses the net, hence his extraordinary service return. So the phenomenon of seeing the seams of the ball could be a result of gifted eyesight and not of moments of heightened perception.

11. Ellen W. Gerber, "Identity, Relation and Sport," in *Sport and the Body: A Philosophical Symposium*, p. 111.

12. Perhaps the infinitive "to involve" is a bit too strong in this sentence. *Involve* seems to apply too much action in a process that is the cessation of action. What kind of *control* is present seems to be an issue here. Drs. Harold Stein and Bernie Slatt have taken the idea of unconscious control to its extreme in *Hitting Blind: The New Visual Approach to Winning Tennis* (New York: Beaufort Books, Inc., 1981). There is always "playing within oneself," i.e., one's limitations and capacities, which is necessary for superior performance.

13. Gary Shaw, *Meat on the Hoof: The Hidden World of Texas Football* (New York: Dell Publishing Co., 1972), pp. 283–285.

14. Shurnryu Suzuki, *Zen Mind, Beginner's Mind* (New York: John Weatherhill, 1970), p. 27; my italics. There are two Suzukis: Shurnryu is of the "new school" and D. T. is of the "old school." Below I discuss the movements ("schools") in Zen. D. T. Suzuki is the one who first brought Zen to the West; see, for example, *Zen and Japanese Culture* (Bollingen Series; Princeton: Princeton University Press, 1959), originally published in 1938 in Japan.

15. For the principles of movement, the forms, and their cultural associations, see, for example, Da Liu, *T'ai Chi Ch'uan and I Ching: A Choreography of Body and Mind* (Perennial Library; New York: Harper & Row, 1972), esp. chs. II, III, and IV; and for detail, see the works by Deshimaru and Hyams mentioned in note 6.

16. Paul Weiss, *Sport: A Philosophic Inquiry*, p. 136. For convenience in the next two sections, I have used Paul Weiss's work as representative of the traditional, Western view of sport to compare and contrast with the Eastern view of sport. In later chapters I also challenge Weiss's separation of sport from art.

17. For further discussion of the ideas, see chapter 2, and especially the concept of sport as a human enterprise.

18. In Kant's system of ethics, categorical imperatives are moral injunctions, like "Thou shalt not kill," in a form so as to reflect his requirement that morality be independent of desires or what anyone would want, and hence universalizable. This is in contrast to hypothetical imperatives which have the form "if J wants X, then J must do Y." Moreover, Richard F. Galvin, "Tennis Anyone?—Problem Cases for Formal Universalization Tests," *Southwest Philosophy Review*, 11 (1985), pp. 79–85, shows that a comparative description case such as "playing tennis with a *better* player," universalized into a maxim, yields "If playing a tennis game, everyone will play with a better player," which means that there are some people who do not satisfy this description (Ivan Lendl or Steffi Graf perhaps), so these cases entail a contradiction in conception. Hence a problem with Kant's ethical theory, especially centered around sport situations.

19. Tim Gallwey's most recent efforts have been in this direction, with the assistance of Barry Green, *Inner Game of Music* (Garden City, New York: Doubleday/Anchor, 1986). It is interesting to notice that Gallwey developed his approach in sports and then moved to music. In Asia, samādhi was described and analyzed first in music before it was discussed in the context of physical movement and action (with the exception of Yoga generally).

235

20. I have relied heavily on Toshihiko Izutsu's description of samādhi in addition to Sekida's. See Izutsu, *Toward a Philosophy of Zen Buddhism* (Tehran: Imperial Iranian Academy of Philosophy, 1977), especially essay II: "Two Dimensions of Ego-Consciousness." Izutsu's book is one of the best of the new school of Zen. A good review of this work is Robert E. Carter, "*Toward a Philosophy of Zen Buddhism*: An Understanding of Zen Experience and Nishida's 'Logic of Place,'" *The Eastern Buddhist*, XIII (1) (Spring 1980), pp. 127–130.

21. Diana Morrison, *A Glossary of Sanskrit from the Spiritual Tradition of India* (Petaluma, California: Nilgiri Press, 1977), p. 36.

22. See, for example, the French philosopher Henri Bergson's *Introduction to Metaphysics* (Indianapolis: Bobbs-Merrill Publishing Co., 1949), pp. 24ff.

23. Sartre clarified this temporal dimension of consciousness, especially in *Transcendence of the Ego*, as we saw in the last section of the previous chapter.

24. Sekida describes consciousness in the following manner: "Our ordinary consciousness has been brought up and domesticated to live and behave in a world that is fenced in by the limits of time, space, and causation. These distinctions have given rise in turn to the world of opposition and discrimination in which we ordinarily find ourselves. The ordinary consciousness never dreams of the possibility of a world of other dimensions, but this ordinary attitude of mind is in fact projecting a topsy-turvy world of delusion. In absolute samādhi, time, space, and causation have fallen off, and thus our habitual way of consciousness collapses. What follows? There is a sudden realization of the world of nonopposition, when we experience the oneness of all things" (p. 121). This sequence of events happens in sport: when we suspend the ordinary, we undergo a transformation in consciousness. Sometimes these changes are like the ones described in this chapter. The world of sport shares many of these traits, and its appeal and magic for its players may lie in the fact that it does offer us this possibility—the possibility of transcendence.

25. I realize that this conditional does not cover all methods of teaching physical skills. Not all physical education instructors utilize a part/whole method, nor do all insist on one way to perform or exercise physical skills. However, a large number must practice the traditional view as I have characterized it because of the popularity of the inner game movement.

26. In baseball as it is actually played there has always been considerable idiosyncrasy, especially in batting styles and pitching deliveries, though no doubt the instructors of the game have tried to impose a rationalistic model in later years.

27. Robert Fogelin, "Sport: The Diversity of the Concept," in *Sport and the Body: A Philosophical Symposium*, p. 59.

28. Carl B. Becker, "Philosophical Perspectives on the Martial Arts in America," *Journal of the Philosophy of Sport*, IX (1982), pp. 19–29.

29 For a detailed discussion of this conception of time, see Sanat Kumar Sen, "Time in Sankhya-Yoga," *International Philosophical Quarterly*, VIII (3) (September 1968), pp. 406–426, esp. pp. 416ff.

30. The term "meditative thinking" I have borrowed from the later writings of Martin Heidegger, and it shall be discussed below in the part on the nature of thought. There is controversy here. In "Zen and Western Thought," *International Philosophical Quarterly*, XX (4) (December 1980), pp. 501–541, esp. p. 538, Masao Abe claims that "thinking" should not be applied to the Zen experience. But this may be due to his understanding of Heidegger, and a restricted use of "thinking." For a better treatment, see Peter Kreeft, "Zen in Heidegger's *Gelassenheit*," *International Philosophical Quarterly*, XI (4) (December 1971), pp. 521–545, which does assimilate "thinking" to Zen consciousness or experience.

31. This time could not have been during this conversation because learning to wait properly comes only when one is in a *purposeless* tension and Herrigel was still thinking purposefully. So the time will be when his thinking will be without purpose. Master Kenzo Awa will know when Herrigel will be ready for the new exercises.

32. John McPhee, *A Sense of Where You Are: A Profile of Bill Bradley at Princeton* (second edition; New York: Farrar, Straus and Giroux, 1978).

33. Again, see Allan Bäck and Kim Daeshik, "Towards a Western Philosophy of the Eastern Martial Arts," *Journal of the Philosophy of Sport*, VI (1979), pp. 19–28; Becker, "Philosophical Perspectives on the Martial Arts in America"; and Angelika Förster, "Neue Perspektiven für den Sport durch die Philosophie und Praxis der fernöstlichen Kampskünste," in *Topical Problems in Sport Philosophy*, edited by Hans Lenk (Cologne: Bundesinstitut für Sportwissenschaft, 1983), pp. 211–240, for the affinities-versus-differences debate.

34. See, for examples, Rolf Cahn, *Self Defense for Gentle People (K'ang Jo Fu)* (Santa Fe, New Mexico: John Muir Publications, 1974), and Da Liu, *T'ai Chi Ch'uan and I Ching: A Choreography of Body and Mind* (New York: Harper & Row, 1971).

35. See *World Tennis's* Fitness Editors, "Growing Pains," *World Tennis*, XXX (9) (February 1983), pp. 54–58. The concept of the Tennis Episode (TE) was taken from Rick Elstein and Jack Salzman, *Better Tennis Over Thirty*, forthcoming. Needless to say, this concept can apply to any age group. Its elements are not particularly limited to the over-thirty group; they just happen to be a group who can benefit the most from TE.

36. For a component theory of human action, see Irving Thalberg, *Perception, Emotion and Action* (New Haven: Yale University Press, 1977), esp. chs. 1, 4, and 5. This theory will be employed in the next chapter.

37. The connection (really just a "parallel") between Heidegger and Zen has been made before, so I shall not dwell on it here. It is well substantiated in the philosophical literature. However, there are important differences; in *On the Way to Language*, translated by Peter D. Hertz (New York: Harper & Row, 1971), pp. 1–54, there is a lengthy dialogue on language between Heidegger (the inquirer) and a Japanese friend, Kuki (whom I mentioned in chapter 4, note 19), which discusses the lack of a Japanese word for *being* and its significance to thinking (philosophical thought).

38. Martin Heidegger, *Discourse on Thinking*, a translation of *Gelassenheit* (1959) by John M. Anderson and E. Hans Freund (New York: Harper & Row, 1966).

39. Shin'ichi Hisamatsu, *Kaku no shūkyō* [*The Religion of Awakening*] (Tokyo: Shunjusha, 1980), pp. 37–39. I am indebted to Tokiyuki Nobuhara for drawing my attention to this important work.

40. For further discussion of Zen and human movement, see Roselyn E. Stone, "Of Zen and the Experience of Moving," *Quest*, XXXIII (2) (1981), pp. 96–107; and Shinobu Abe, "Zen and Sport," *Journal of the Philosophy of Sport*, XIII (1986), pp. 45–48.

6. Is "Choking" an Action?

1. See Craig K. Lehman, "Can Cheaters Play the Game?" *Journal of the Philosophy of Sport*, VIII (1981), pp. 41–46, reprinted in *Sport Inside Out* and in *Philosophic Inquiry in Sport*; chapter 4 of this book; and Terence J. Roberts, "Languages of Sport: Representation," in *Sport and the Body: A Philosophical Symposium*, second edition, edited by Ellen W. Gerber and William J. Morgan (Philadelphia: Lea & Febiger, 1979), pp. 332–339.

2. Irving Thalberg, "Do Our Intentions Cause Our Intentional Actions?" *American Philosophical Quarterly*, XXI (3) (1984), p. 259.

3. Mark McDonald, "Nerves Take Their Toll: Stakes Aren't as High, but Seniors Get Yips after All These Years," *Dallas Morning News*, June 10, 1985, p. 6B.

4. Irving Thalberg, *Perception, Emotion and Action: A Component Approach* (New Haven: Yale University Press, 1977).

5. This may sound confusing, because Davidson is a defender of a causal theory, but it is of a different sort. He is a physical causationist rather than a mental or agent causationist as Thalberg is. As Davidson says in his introduction to *Essays on Actions and Events* (Oxford: Clarendon Press, 1980), p. xi: "The theme [of this book] is the role of causal concepts in the description and explanation of human action. The thesis is that the ordinary notion of cause which enters into scientific or common-sense accounts of non-psychological affairs is essential also to the understanding of what it is to act with a reason, to have a certain intention in acting, to be an agent, to act counter to one's own best judgment, or to act freely. Cause is the cement of the universe; the concept of cause is what holds together our picture of the universe, a picture that would otherwise disintegrate into a diptych of the mental and the physical." Thalberg wants the psychological (i.e., the intentional) to play a dominant role in understanding the varieties of human acts. Davidson argues that intention is not essential to this analytic program of understanding causation in human acts. Their debate will unfold as my discussion progresses. In "Action Theory and the Social Scientific Analysis of Sport Actions" (in *Sport Inside Out*), Hans Lenk has given an excellent account of the issues and controversies in action theory within the bounds of sport and social scientific analyses of sport; I have profited from his study.

6. See Lawrence H. Davis, *Theory of Action* (Englewood Cliffs, New Jersey: Prentice-Hall, Inc., 1979), pp. 59ff.

7. The question of the addition or subtraction of an act is a variation on Wittgenstein's famous question: "Let us not forget this: when 'I raise my arm,' my arm goes up. And the problem arises: what is left over if I subtract the fact that my arm goes up from the fact that I raise my arm?" (*Philosophical Investigations*, third edition, translated by G. E. M. Anscombe (New York: The Macmillan Co., 1958), para. 621). This question, and the question "What has to be added to the physical movement to make an action?" (to which Wittgenstein responded, "Nothing"), inspired several decades of philosophers to inquire into the nature of human action. See Davis, Thalberg, Davidson, Alvin I. Goldman, *A Theory of Human Action* (Princeton: Princeton University Press, 1970), and especially Lenk for openers. Choking rekindles these Wittgensteinian questions. The subtraction question seems legitimate in reference to choking because there appears to be a loss of kinesthetic sensations in choked sport actions. My questions are: Does such a loss alter our conception of these acts? And isn't there more to my choked sport action than just the loss of kinesthetic sensations?

8. In *The Education of a Tennis Player* (New York: Simon & Schuster, 1971), with Bud Collins, Rod Laver recalls, "I had been so nervous during that 1962 match that I lost the feel of the racket completely. I actually held it wrong and hit a volley straight into the ground once. It was so comical that I laughed myself, and that helped break the tension" (p. 276). See Carlos Goffi's "Coping with Choking," *World Tennis*, XXXIII (4) (September 1985), p. 41, whose list of well-tried methods is used by players to overcome the physical symptoms of choking.

9. Causal interactionism is a doctrine usually associated with the common-sense belief that mind and body are two separate and distinct realities (this is dualism that stems from René Descartes), each causally affecting the other; bodily events can affect mental states and mental events can alter bodily states.

10. In chapter 8, I label such practices as comprising an anti-sport movement. They should be critically discussed in the literature because they pose a threat to sport.

11. See Lee Stauffer, "Mushin (Wushin) and Its Place in a Western Theory of Mind," *Southwest Philosophical Studies*, X (2) (1987), pp. 67–71.

12. Margaret Steel, "What We Know When We Know a Game," in *Sport Inside Out*, p. 82.

13. T. P. Kasulis, *Zen Action/Zen Person* (Honolulu: The University Press of Hawaii, 1981), pp. 127ff.

14. Davis, *Theory of Action*, p. 3; my italics. I have given Davis's sentences a liberal reading, especially the last one which refers to the "mental" and the "inner." I interpret these qualifications on awareness in a non-Cartesian sense, and one which I think is ultimately compatible with Eastern thought; see the previous chapter and Kasulis's *Zen Action/Zen Person*, esp. ch. 9.

15. In another "Stan Smith's Tennis Class," *Dallas Morning News*, February 11, 1986, p. 11B, we find Smith suggesting a remedy from a variation on the converse relation: "I suppose the question asked most often at clinics is 'How do you quell nervousness on critical points?!' Answer: Anything you can do to keep your body relaxed will also ease your mind. Examples: Take deep breaths between points. Bounce a ball or toss it in the air and catch it. Do some knee bends. Extend fingers of your hitting hand (don't 'clench' the racket)." There are literally thousands of instructional anecdotes like this one in newspapers, magazines, and books, along with videotape series. Most athletes—regardless of skill level—need this kind of assistance from the field of physical education.

16. Bernard Jeu, "What Is Sport?" *Diogenes*, LXXX (Winter 1972), pp. 150–163, esp. 157.

17. See Jim Loehr, "How to Whip the Walk-abouts," *World Tennis*, XXXII (8) (January 1985), p. 23.

18. John McEnroe, "Even I Choke," *World Tennis*, XXXIII (4) (September 1985), p. 40.

19. Harless Wade, "Sports Today" (column), *Dallas Morning News*, April 30, 1986, p. 2B.

20. See H. P. Grice, "Logic and Conversation," in *The Logic of Grammar*, edited by Donald Davidson and Gilbert Harman (Belmont, California: Dickenson Publishing Co., 1975), pp. 64–75; reprinted in *The Philosophy of Language*, edited by A. P. Martinich (New York: Oxford University Press, 1985), pp. 159–170.

21. I have given a semantic identity rule for governing act descriptions involving "choking" in the paragraph above. However, much is left unsaid in this admittedly rough and elemental analysis. Most of my remarks here should be interpreted as suggestions or conjectures, not as well-established conclusions. I take Lenk's recommendation to be a way out of the act individuation problem. Also, my analysis of choking is consistent with his: the player J, his or her situation, and measures for dealing with it (which belong to the inductive argument form I gave above) are all conceptualizations.

22. Bernard Suits, *The Grasshopper: Games, Life and Utopia* (Toronto: University of Toronto Press, 1978), p. 81.

23. In the next chapter, choking is placed within the context of the theory of knowledge as applied to sport; see the end of section I.

7. The Knowing in Playing

1. Paul Ziff, "A Fine Forehand," *Journal of the Philosophy of Sport*, I (September 1974), pp. 106–107, reprinted with revisions in his *Antiaesthetics* (Boston: D. Reidel Publishing Co., 1984), p. 67.

2. According to B. F. Skinner (see, for example, *About Behaviorism* [New York: Alfred A. Knopf, 1974], especially chs. 3 and 4), this process, which I label the result theory, is (or closely resembles) operant conditioning. The basic premise here is that behavior conditions behavior, that is, a person's behavior is acquired and maintained by the success of its consequences. In other words if a person engages in a type of movement or behavior that is successful or operant for him or her, then the consequences of this behavior serve as reinforcements and cause him or her to repeat that behavior on subsequent occasions. So what we have is the following sequence of events. First there are the discriminating stimuli or what the person really notices or feels. This leads to his response, which then stimulates his overt behavior, which becomes the reinforcer. This process is then repeated with each successive action. Any sport action would be analyzed or explained along these lines. But whether or not such analysis or explanation is adequate is a matter of controversy.

3. Eugen Herrigel, Zen in the Art of Archery, p. 41; my italics.

4. The counterpart to this theory in physical education and psychology is the concept of drive stimuli. The acquisition of behavior revolves around habit, that is, a habit is formed when a connection between certain cue stimuli and certain responses is formed. The individual is guided into making the correct responses in a situation by being presented with certain relevant stimuli that will elicit the desired responses. The key to the difference between other theorists and someone like Frank A. Logan in Fundamentals of Learning and Motivation (Dubuque, Iowa: W. C. Brown, 1972), inter alia, is that he hypothesizes a series of responses occurring within the individual that are related to emotion and feeling, and suggests that these internal responses themselves have drive properties that elicit the desired response.

5. See Hume's theory of the passions, "A Dissertation on the Passions," Essays and Treatises on Various Subjects (London: J. P. Mendum, n.d.), pp. 93–108; and A Treatise of Human Nature, Book II.

6. Errol Bedford, "Emotions," in Essays in Philosophical Psychology, edited by Donald F. Gustafson (New York: Doubleday & Co., 1964), p. 79. Since Hume thought that one can compare the feelings of emotional states with the bodily feelings, Bedford's point is valid. Later (see note 10) we shall distinguish the two feelings.

7. Timothy W. Gallwey, Inner Tennis: Playing the Game, pp. 96–97. Gallwey's summary is as follows: "In stroke development it is important to become more knowledgeable about the entire path of your racket on every stroke. You should become so sensitive to your racket that you come to experience it as an integral part of your body, so that whenever it leaves one of its grooved swings you will instantly be aware of it. Search your body for overtightness and pain" (p. 110). The use of the feel theory in teaching tennis is not unique to Gallwey; it has been around since the days of Bill Tilden at least. Gallwey is just a good contemporary example.

8. Gladys Heldman, "The Overhead," World Tennis, XXII (January 1975), p. 41. She adds the following pedagogical remark: "Whenever he loses the feel he should go back to the set-ups to regain his confidence, then start on lobs where he has only to move back one or two steps."

241

9. Barry Lorge, "What's Wrong with Stan Smith?" *Tennis*, XI (6) (October 1975), p. 36.

10. Moreland Perkins, "Emotion and Feeling," *Philosophical Review*, LXXV (April 1966), pp. 139–160. See also Alan R. White, *The Philosophy of Mind* (New York: Random House, 1967), ch. 5, on the different senses of "feel," which I shall discuss in the next section.

11. In some detail: "*Time* magazine reported that when Ben Hogan is playing in a tournament, he mentally rehearses each shot, just before making it. He makes the shot perfectly in his imagination—'feels' the clubhead strike the ball just as it should, 'feels' himself performing the perfect follow-through then steps up to the ball, and depends upon what he calls 'muscle memory' to carry out the shot just as he has imagined it." Maxwell Maltz, *Psycho-Cybernetics* (Englewood Cliffs, New Jersey: Prentice-Hall, 1960), p. 38. Such "imaging" is commonplace among sport psychologists and athletes today.

12. John Barnaby, *Racket Work: The Key to Tennis* (Boston: Allyn & Bacon, 1969), p. xiii inter alia.

13. Rod Laver, with Bud Collins, *The Education of a Tennis Player*, p. 116. Here is another brief example explaining another tennis ploy: "'Wrong-footing' is a favorite tactic of Kenny Rosewall, and it's a good one for the volleyer once he feels he has control of the stroke" (p. 216). Laver's use of "feel" here is more than just emotional feeling; he means also (and perhaps primarily) bodily feeling, as in the above example of "choking."

14. See Margaret Steel, "What We Know When We Know a Game," *Journal of the Philosophy of Sport*, IV (Fall 1977), p. 97, for the same point in a different context. This important article is reprinted in *Sport Inside Out*.

15. Geoffrey Vesey, "Knowledge without Observation," *Philosophical Review*, LXXII (July 1963), pp. 208–209.

16. David W. Hamlyn, *The Theory of Knowledge* (Anchor Books edition; Garden City, New York: Doubleday & Co., 1970), p. 107.

17. David Braybrooke, "Some Questions for Miss Anscombe about Intention," *Analysis*, XXII (January 1962), pp. 55–58, and G. E. M. Anscombe's *Intention* (Ithaca, New York: Cornell University Press, 1957), inter alia. Some who have questioned Anscombe's account are: Braybrooke, the above-mentioned article, pp. 49–54, and David Conway, "Sensations and Bodily Position: A Conclusive Argument?" *Philosophical Studies*, XXIV (September 1983), pp. 353–355.

18. G. E. M. Anscombe, *Intention*, pp. 14ff., and "On Sensations of Position," *Analysis*, XXII (1962), pp. 55–58.

8. Representation and Expression in Sport and Art

1. Consult *Coroebus Triumphs: The Alliance of Sport and the Arts*, edited by Susan Bandy (San Diego, California: San Diego State University Press, 1988), especially Part III, "Knowing Sport—Analysis or Experience?" edited by David L. Vanderwerken, for some criticism that makes this assumption.

2. *Artist and Athlete: The Pursuit of Perfection,* viewed on cable ARTS chan-
nel, January 12, 1984, one hour, ten minutes.

3. See David Best, "The Aesthetic in Sport," *British Journal of Aesthetics,*
XIV (3) (1974), pp. 197–213; reprinted in Best's *Philosophy and Human Movement*
(London: George Allen & Unwin, 1978), ch. 7, pp. 99–122. In "Art and Sport,"
Journal of Aesthetic Education, XIV (2) (1980), pp. 69–80, Best criticized the
suggestions I made in "Are Sports Art Forms?" *Journal of Aesthetic Education,*
XIII (1) (1979), pp. 107–109. He revised his argument and published it in "The
Aesthetic and the Artistic," *Philosophy,* LVII (221) (1982), pp. 357–372. I replied to
these in "A Response to Best on Art and Sport," *Journal of Aesthetic Education,*
XVIII (4) (1984), pp. 105–108, and "Sport and the Artistic," *Philosophy,* LX (233)
(1985), pp. 392–393, respectively. Earlier discussions of mine on this topic are:
"Toward a Sports Aesthetic," *Journal of Aesthetic Education,* XI (4) (1977), pp.
103–111; and "Beauty in Play: Aesthetics for Athletes," *Southwest Philosophical
Studies,* II (1978), pp. 77–83; plus "Aesthetics of Sport" (appendix), in *Philosophy of
Art,* by Warren E. Steinkraus (enlarged edition; Washington, D.C.: University
Press of America, 1984), pp. 213–232.

4. For a supporter of Best, see P. M. Ward, "Sport and the Institutional
Theory of Art," *Journal of Human Movement Studies,* III (1) (1977), pp. 73–81;
and for a critic, see Seymour Kleinman, "Art, Sport and Intention," *Proceedings of
the National Association for Physical Education in Higher Education* (Champaign,
Illinois: Human Kinetics, 1980), pp. 218–222, who made some similar points to
the ones I have made. Another more recent critic is Jan Boxill, "Beauty, Sport, and
Gender," *Journal of the Philosophy of Sport,* XI (1984), pp. 36–47; her sustained
attack is worth careful study, although it goes in different directions from mine.
See also C. D. Cordner, "Grace and Functionality," *British Journal of Aesthetics,*
XXIV (4) (1984), pp. 301–313, for an excellent study of these concepts in sport.

5. David Best, *Expression in Movement and the Arts* (London: Lepus Books,
1974).

6. M. J. Saraf, "Sport and Art," *International Review of Sport Sociology,* XV
(3–4) (1980), pp. 123–131.

7. Jacques Barzun, *The Use and Abuse of Art* (Princeton: Princeton University Press, 1974), p. 13.

8. This argument only applies to the designation of art as too "exalted" for
sport, but these wilder forms of contemporary art have very little positive resemblance to sport either. However, some of the art movements of the contemporary
sector do have significant resemblance to sport and I shall discuss these below.

9. Except that this ludicrous behavior is not part of the *action* of a tennis
match, which suggests that "sport" has more well-defined boundaries than "art"
does.

10. *Objets trouvés* and Duchamp's readymades have found their way into
the traditional aesthetics literature. See H. Gene Blocker's *Philosophy of Art* (New
York: Charles Scribner's Sons, 1979); James J. Fletcher, "Artifactuality Broadly

and Narrowly Speaking," *Southern Journal of Philosophy*, XX (1) (1982), pp. 41–52; P. N. Humble, "Duchamp's Readymades: Art and Anti-Art," *British Journal of Aesthetics*, XXII (1) (1982), pp. 52–64; my presidential address to the Southwestern Philosophical Society, "'Toilet Paper' (a.k.a. Artifactuality and Duchamp's *Fountain*)," *Southwest Philosophy Review*, III (1986), pp. 5–18, which is a reply to Fletcher; and Arthur C. Danto, *The Philosophical Disenfranchisement of Art* (New York: Columbia University Press, 1986), chs. I and II.

11. Harold Osborne, "Aesthetic Implications of Conceptual Art, Happenings, Etc.," *British Journal of Aesthetics*, XX (1) (1980), pp. 8–9, 20. I do not mean to imply that Osborne accepts "ludic art" as art; in fact he questions whether any of these recent movements in contemporary art could or should be called art or fine art.

12. "When Is Art?" is reprinted in Nelson Goodman's *Ways of Worldmaking* (Indianapolis: Hackett Publishing Co., 1978), ch. 4. Goodman has developed a temporal theory of art (based on functionality) that is particularly adept at handling contemporary art. I have more to say about this theory toward the end of this chapter.

13. In a note, Goodman says, "Just as what is not red may look or be red *at certain times*, so what is not art may function as or be said to be art at certain times. That an object functions as art at a given time, that it has the status of art at that time, and that it is art at that time may all be taken as saying the same thing—so long as we take none of these as ascribing to the object any stable status" (pp. 69–70).

14. Temple Pouncey described the 1982 Men's Singles final at Wimbledon between McEnroe and Connors as "not a match of artistry, classic strokes and graceful placement."

15. Harold Osborne, "Notes on the Aesthetics of Chess and the Concept of Intellectual Beauty," *British Journal of Aesthetics*, IV (2) (1964), pp. 160–163.

16. A paraphrased quote in R. Scott Kretchmar's "From Test to Contest: An Analysis of Two Kinds of Counterpoint in Sport," in *Philosophic Inquiry in Sport*, p. 227.

17. I am applying the distinction between "the aesthetic" and "the artistic" to sport as it is drawn by Tomas Kulka, "The Artistic and the Aesthetic Value of Art," *British Journal of Aesthetics*, XXI (4) (1981), pp. 336–350. Kulka's distinction is important in the last chapter, too, where I attempt a semiotic analysis of sport.

18. See T. R. Martland's article, "Not Art and Play, Mind You, nor Art and Games, but Art and Sports," *Journal of Aesthetic Education*, XIX (1985), pp. 65–71.

19. See my contribution, "Artistic Creativity in Sport," in *Sport Inside Out*, pp. 510–519.

20. L. A. Reid, "Human Movement, the Aesthetic and Art," *British Journal of Aesthetics*, XX (2) (1980), pp. 166–167.

21. Best has included "the possibility of making some sort of statement about life" as part of the definition of *art*. Both Best and I are aware that this definiens (the phrase that does the defining) is too broad: it doesn't distinguish art from documentary journalism, for example.

22. Art has accepted the idea of using the body as subject matter; for examples in painting, see Ted Castle's study of "Carolee Schneemann: The Woman Who Uses Her Body as Her Art," *Artforum*, XIX (2) (1980), pp. 64–70.

23. Jon Saari, "Review of *Pumping Iron: The Art and Sport of Body Building* by Charles Gaines with photographs by George Butler," *Journal of Popular Culture*, X (2) (1976), pp. 473–474. For an interesting discussion of body builders in an age when technological advancements make massive musculature paradoxically superfluous, see Alphonso Lingis, "Orchids and Muscles," *Journal of the Philosophy of Sport*, XIII (1986), pp. 15–28; reprinted in *Philosophic Inquiry in Sport*, pp. 125–136.

24. See Blocker's *Philosophy of Art*, ch. 3. I realize that this argument hastily generalizes from the one sport of gymnastics to the region of "sport." Up to this point, I have tried to find just one interpretation or model within this domain. I think I have done so. Now the question of truth can be addressed. The region of sport is not homogeneous: all of the sports involving direct conflict of teams or individuals have much less opportunity for expression because the control of the situation is *contested* rather than entirely in the hands of one person at a time. But even so, the Eastern martial arts place expression in a prominent position with their emphasis on natural animal symbolism in their movement forms and with the degrees of mastery (which aims at perfect control). I shall have more to say about this later in the chapter.

25. In examining Saraf's overall position, we should first of all notice that Saraf is an *essentialist* (pp. 123, 127, 129). The methodology of essentialism shapes much of Saraf's analysis of sport and art. For instance, Saraf claims that the programming of such sport champions as Peggy Fleming "goes beyond the frame of sport, ceases to be sport, due to far-reaching modification of the situation in sport, due to the above-mentioned semantic and sigmatic meanings." Essentialism harbors such ideas as sport having a frame and a sport program ceasing to be sport. Such sharp divisions between categories is easily refuted; see Best's books for some arguments against essentialism. I need not repeat these here. Since Wittgenstein, definitions of nominal kinds like "sport" have been developed along the lines of non-essentialism, which admits of borderline cases. If Fleming's program is thought of as a borderline case, then we have no image or requirement of sport *having a frame* and programs *ceasing* to be sport. We can say that sport has *evolved* to another level in such cases. Also I should point out that in semiotics or the theory of signs, the three levels of meaning—the syntactic, the semantic, and the pragmatic (what Saraf calls the sigmatic)—are interrelated, not distinct, *isolated* concepts. Saraf treats them as separate and noninteractive. Such a treatment is questionable, because what is displayed on a syntactic level has its counterparts on the semantic and pragmatic levels. (This is certainly the case here.) The elaboration of the concepts of semiotics in relation to sport is the subject of the next chapter.

26. For an altogether different study of representation in sport, see Terence J. Roberts's "Language of Sport: Representation," in *Sport and the Body: A*

Philosophical Symposium, edited by Ellen W. Gerber and William J. Morgan (second edition; Philadelphia: Lea & Febiger, 1979), pp. 332–339.

27. I concede that this is true only in the sense that *any* action he performed might then be sad, etc., and obviously this expression by itself would not make his every action a work of art.

28. Terence J. Roberts, "Languages of Sport: Exemplification and Expression," in *Sport and the Humanities: A Collection of Critical Essays,* edited by William J. Morgan (Knoxville: The Bureau of Educational Research and Service, College of Education, University of Tennessee, 1979), p. 48.

29. Again, see Roberts's study.

9. The Textuality of Sport: A Semiotic Analysis

1. Paul G. Kuntz, "Aesthetics Applies to Sports as Well as to the Arts," in *Sport Inside Out,* pp. 496, 502; Kuntz, "The Aesthetics of Sport," in *The Philosophy of Sport: A Collection of Original Essays,* edited by Robert G. Osterhoudt (Springfield, Illinois: Charles C. Thomas, 1973), p. 307; Richard Schechner, "Approaches to Theory/Criticism," *Tulane Drama Review,* X (4) (1966), p. 35; and Schechner's *Public Domain: Essays on the Theatre* (New York: Discus Books, 1969), pp. 86, 102–105.

2. A work that was "read" or "reread" but not understood at all by the reader—like someone reading a work in a language they know only how to pronounce—would not constitute that *series of acts* that would qualify as a text. The series must involve some understanding of the extraphysical characteristics of a work for the work to become a text.

3. Strictly speaking, Anthony Savile, "The Place of Intention in the Concept of Art," *Proceedings of the Aristotelian Society,* n.s., LXIX (1968-1969), pp. 101–124, reprinted in *Aesthetics,* edited by Harold Osborne (New York: Oxford University Press, 1972), pp. 158–176, is not part of the semiotic tradition, but his discussion of the conception of text is certainly compatible with it, and in several places I have found his account clearer than the European philosophers (like Jacques Derrida) who write in this tradition, so I have relied upon his analysis throughout most of mine.

4. In *Is There a Text in This Class?* (Cambridge: Harvard University Press, 1980), Stanley Fish shows that spectators of all sorts can be seen as "interpretive communities."

5. Lynne Belaief, "Meanings of the Body," in *Sport Inside Out,* p. 423.

6. Robert Scholes, *Semiotics and Interpretation* (New Haven: Yale University Press, 1982), p. 36.

7. Joseph Epstein, "Obsessed with Sport," in *Sport Inside Out,* p. 116.

8. Michael Novak, "Jocks, Hacks, Flacks, and Pricks," in *Sport Inside Out,* p. 555.

9. Deconstruction, as a literary and philosophical theory, is concerned with *reading* (or *rereading*) and with the marked limits of texts; it tries to elucidate the fabric of the text and its limit conditions, but those limits are not ontological.

In "Deconstruction: A Cautionary Tale," *Journal of Aesthetic Education*, XX (4) (Winter 1986), pp. 91–92, Joseph Margolis characterizes deconstruction as a thesis to be applied globally (like skepticism), suggesting "that proposals of *any* kind that presume to match language with reality (a reality independent of language and unencumbered linguistically)—so that the structures of the latter are correctly represented in the former, yielding truth—are forms of radical self-delusion." Deconstruction subverts our habits of handling facts. See the articles (especially Margolis's contribution) in *Hermeneutics and Deconstruction*, edited by Hugh J. Silverman and Don Ihde (Albany: State University of New York Press, 1983); and Mark C. Taylor, "Descartes, Nietzsche and the Search for the Unsayable," *The New York Times Book Review*, January 25, 1987, pp. 3, 34, and his collection *Deconstruction in Context: Literature and Philosophy* (Chicago: University of Chicago Press, 1986), for openers. Needless to say, these textual parameters for television not only need to be critically examined, they need to be shared with the society so that it will be aware of television's selective, judgmental process of presenting things. Television needs to be deconstructed because the image it projects is transmitted as the real situation rather than as an interpreted one. This rhetoric needs to be criticized. Chandler's essay cited in the next note has started this evaluation.

10. See the following critiques for further discussion along lines similar to the deconstructionists': Benjamin G. Rader, *In Its Own Image: How Television Has Transformed Sports* (New York: The Free Press, 1984), especially the last three chapters; Novak's *The Joy of Sports*, passim; and Joan Chandler, "American Televised Sport: Business as Usual," in *American Sport Culture: The Humanistic Dimensions*, edited by Wiley Lee Umphlett (Lewisburg: Bucknell University Press, 1985), pp. 83–97.

11. Roger Angell, "The Interior Stadium," in *Sport Inside Out*, p. 148. Novak says much the same thing in *The Joy of Sports*, pp. 320ff.

12. James Memmott, "Wordsworth in the Bleachers: The Baseball Essays of Roger Angell," in *Sport Inside Out*, p. 157.

13. Edward Bullough, "'Psychical Distance' as a Factor in Art and as an Aesthetic Principle," in *Philosophical Issues in Art*, edited by Patricia H. Werhane (Englewood Cliffs, New Jersey: Prentice-Hall, Inc., 1984), pp. 391–399; George Dickie, "Psychical Distance: In a Fog at Sea," in *Philosophical Issues in Art*, pp. 422–430; and Allan Casebier, "The Concept of Aesthetic Distance," in *Aesthetics: A Critical Anthology*, edited by George Dickie and R. J. Sclafani (New York: St. Martin's Press, 1977), pp. 783–799.

14. If we modify this last statement from "spectator" to "participant" or at least to include the participant, we have the insertion of distance as a remedy to *choking* in the psychological sense; see chapter 6.

15. In *The Sovereignty of the Good* (New York: Schocken Books, 1970), Iris Murdoch characterizes this experiential process in this way: "Following a hint in Plato (*Phaedrus* 250) I shall start by speaking of what is perhaps the most obvious

thing in our surroundings which is an occasion for 'unselfing', and that is what is popularly called beauty. Recent philosophers tend to avoid this term because they prefer to talk of reasons rather than of experiences. But the implication of experience with beauty seems to me to be something of great importance which should not be bypassed in favour of analysis of critical vocabularies. Beauty is the convenient and traditional name of something which art and nature share, and which gives a fairly clear sense to the idea of quality of experience and change of consciousness. I am looking out of my window in an anxious and resentful state of mind, oblivious of my surroundings, brooding perhaps on some damage done to my prestige. Then suddenly I observe a hovering Kestrel. In a moment everything is altered. The brooding self with its hurt vanity has disappeared. There is nothing now but Kestrel. [This mental state is called *outward samādhi* in Indian philosophy and *unreflected consciousness* in Sartre's humanism.] And when I return to thinking of the other matter it seems less important. And of course this is something which we may also do deliberately: give attention to nature in order to clear our minds of selfish care" (p. 84). I have maintained through this book that this "unselfing" (as Murdoch labels it) is one of the main features of the sport experience, and it also helps to explain why sport has the powerful attraction it does for people. But there is more than beauty to be found in unselfing—freedom and transcendence are there to be discovered (see chapter 5).

16. R. Scott Kretchmar, "'Distancing': An Essay on Abstract Thinking in Sport Performances," in *Sport Inside Out*, pp. 87–103.

17. Gadamer, *Truth and Method*, p. 92.

18. See Savile's essay, especially section II, on the location of the work of art itself.

19. See R. G. Collingwood, *The Idea of History* (Oxford: Oxford University Press, 1946), Part V: Epilegomena; and the first volume in Sources in the Semiotics Series, Anthony F. Russell's *Time, Logic, Philosophy, and History: A Study in the Philosophy of History Based on the Work of R. G. Collingwood*, with a foreword by Brooke Williams (New York: University Press of America, 1984), especially ch. 6.

20. See Collingwood's *The Principles of Art* (New York: Oxford University Press, 1938), ch. VIII on the relationship between thinking and feeling, in addition to *The Idea of History*, Epilegomena.

21. Tony Scherman, "Sports History: How Games Tell Us Who We Are," *The New York Times*, Monday, November 28, 1983.

SELECTED BIBLIOGRAPHY

The entries below are intended to supplement those listed in the notes for further inquiry.

Books

Almeida, Bira. *Capoeira: A Brazilian Art Form, History, Philosophy and Practice.* Berkeley, California: North Atlantic Books, 1986.

Andre, Judith, and **David N. James** (eds.). *Rethinking College Athletics.* Philadelphia: Temple University Press, 1991.

Bartell, Dick, and **Norman Macht.** *Rowdy Richard: A Firsthand Account of the National League Baseball Wars of the 1930s and the Men Who Fought Them.* Berkeley, California: North Atlantic Books, 1987.

Bayer, Claude. *Epistémologie des activités physiques et sportives.* Paris: Presses Universitaires de France, 1990.

Bowyer, J. Barton. *Cheating: Deception in War & Magic, Games & Sports, Sex & Religion, Business & Con Games, Politics & Espionage, Art & Science.* New York: St. Martin's Press, 1982.

Carse, James P. *Finite and Infinite Games: A Vision of Life as Play and Possibility.* New York: The Free Press, 1986.

Cheng, Man-ch'ing. *Lao Tzu: My Words Are Very Easy to Understand.* Translated by Tam Gibbs. Berkeley, California: North Atlantic Books, 1985.

Cheng, Man-ch'ing. *T'ai Chi Ch'uan: A Simplified Method of Calisthenics for Health and Self-Defense.* Translated by Beauson T'seng. Berkeley, California: North Atlantic Books, 1981.

Cheng-Tzu. *Cheng-Tzu's Thirteen Treatises on T'ai Chi Ch'uan.* Translated by Benjamin Pang Jeng Lo and Martin Inn. Berkeley, California: North Atlantic Books, 1987.

Cusa, Nicholas de. *The Game of Spheres (De Ludo Globi)*. Translated by Pauline Moffitt Watts. New York: Abaris Books, Inc., 1986. This metaphysical/ theological treatise of the Renaissance, which describes the universe in terms of a primitive bowling game, is perhaps the first sustained work in philosophy of sport.

The Essence of T'ai Chi Ch'uan: The Literary Tradition. Translated by Benjamin Pang Jeng Lo, Martin Inn, Susan Foe, and Robert Amacker. Berkeley, California: North Atlantic Books, 1987.

Gilbey, John F. *The Way of a Warrior*. Berkeley, California: North Atlantic Books, 1987.

Gilbey, John F. *Western Boxing and World Wrestling Story and Practice*. Berkeley, California: North Atlantic Books, 1985.

Grossinger, Richard (ed.). *The Temple of Baseball*. Berkeley, California: North Atlantic Books, 1985.

Guttmann, Allen. *Sports Spectators*. New York: Columbia University Press, 1986.

Guttmann, Allen. *A Whole New Ball Game: An Interpretation of American Sports*. Chapel Hill: University of North Carolina Press, 1988.

Haultain, Arnold. *The Mystery of Golf: A brief Account of its Origin, Antiquity & Romance; its Uniqueness; its Curiousness; & its Difficulty; its anatomical, philosophical, and moral Properties; together with diverse Concepts on other Matters to it appertaining* [1908]. Cambridge/Boston: Applewood Books, 1986.

Heckler, Richard S. (ed.). *Aikidō and the New Warrior*. Berkeley, California: North Atlantic Books, 1987.

Hyland, Drew A. *Philosophy of Sport*. New York: Paragon House, 1990.

Jenkins, Bruce. *Life after Saberhagen*. Berkeley, California: North Atlantic Books, 1987.

Jeu, Bernard. *Analyse du sport*. Paris: Presses Universitaires de France, 1986.

Kerrane, Kevin, and Richard Grossinger (eds.). *Baseball I Gave You All the Best Years of My Life*. Berkeley, California: North Atlantic Books, 1976.

Kim, Daeshik, and Allen Bäck. *Martial Meditations: Philosophy and the Essence of Martial Arts*. Akron, Ohio: The International Council on Martial Arts Education Press, 1989.

Klickstein, Bruce. *Living Aikidō: Form, Training, Essence*. Preface by George Leonard. Berkeley, California: North Atlantic Books, 1987.

Kyle, Donald G., and Gary D. Stark (eds.). *Essays on Sport History and Sport Mythology*. College Station: Texas A&M University Press, 1990.

Lenk, Hans. *Die achte Kunst: Leistungssport-Breitensport*. Zurich: Edition Interform, 1985.

Lenk, Hans, and Gunter A. Pilz. *Das Prinzip Fairness*. Zurich: Edition Interform, 1989.

Lyotard, Jean-François, and Jean-Loup Theband. *Just Gaming*. Translated by Wlad Godzich. Minneapolis: University of Minnesota Press, 1985.

250

Mandell, Richard D. *Sport: A Cultural History.* Irvington, New York: Columbia University Press, 1986.

Millman, Dan. *The Warrior Athlete: Body, Mind & Spirit.* Walpole, New Hampshire: Stillpoint Publishing, 1979.

Millman, Dan. *Way of the Peaceful Warrior: A Book That Changes Lives.* Tiburon, California: H. J. Kramer, Inc., 1984.

Mitchell, Elmer D., and **Bernard S. Mason.** *The Theory of Play.* Revised and enlarged edition. New York: The Ronald Press Co., 1948. First published in 1934.

Osterhoudt, R.G. *Philosophy of Sport: An Overview.* Champaign, Illinois: Stipes Publishing Company.

Rooney, John F. *The Recruiting Game: Toward a New System of Intercollegiate Sport.* Second edition. Lincoln, Nebraska: University of Nebraska Press, 1987.

Rudman, Daniel (ed.). *Take It to the Hoop.* Berkeley, California: North Atlantic Books, 1980.

Vanderwerken, David L. (ed.). *Sport in the Classroom: Essays on Teaching Sport-Related Courses in the Humanities.* Cranbury, New Jersey: Associated University Presses, 1990. See especially chapters five and six.

Webster-Doyle, Terrence. *Karate: The Art of Empty Self.* Berkeley, California: North Atlantic Books, 1986.

Wei-Ming, Chen. *T'ai Chi Ch'uan Ta Wen: Questions and Answers on T'ai Chi Ch'uan.* Translated by Benjamin Pang Jeng Lo and Robert Smith. Berkeley, California: North Atlantic Books, 1977.

White, Thomas I. *Right and Wrong: A Brief Guide to Understanding Ethics.* Englewood Cliffs, New Jersey: Prentice-Hall, 1988. See chapter 6, "Cheating: An Ethical Dilemma," pp. 111–127.

Articles

Abe, Shinobu. "Modern Sports and the Eastern Tradition of Physical Culture: Emphasizing Nishida's Theory of the Body." *Journal of the Philosophy of Sport,* XIV (1987), pp. 44–47.

Arnold, Peter J. "Democracy, Education, and Sport." *Journal of the Philosophy of Sport,* XVI (1989), pp. 100–110.

Arnold, Peter J. "Kinaesthetic Feelings, Physical Skills, and the Anti-Private Language Argument." *Journal of the Philosophy of Sport,* XIII (1986), pp. 29–34.

Arnold, Peter J. "Sport, the Aesthetic and Art: Further Thoughts." *British Journal of Educational Studies,* XXXVIII (2) (May 1990), pp. 160–179.

Arnold, Peter J. "Sport, Moral Education and the Development of Character." *Journal of Physical Education,* XVIII (1984), pp. 275–281.

Benardete, José. "Toward a Philosophy of Chess." *Philosophic Exchange,* XI (1979).

Best, David. "The Limits of 'Art.'" *Philosophy,* LXI (238) (October 1986), pp. 532–533.

Best, David. "Sport Is Not Art." *Journal of the Philosophy of Sport*, XII (1985), pp. 25–40.

Best, David. "Sport Is Not Art: Professor Wertz's Aunt Sally." *Journal of Aesthetic Education*, XX (2) (Summer 1986), pp. 95–98.

Bouet, Michel. "Sport Is Communication." In *Baden Baden 1981, Bulletin III, 11th Olympic Congress* (Baden Baden and Munich: Olympic Congress Publication, 1979), pp. 19–24.

Cohen, Ted. "Sports and Art: Beginning Questions." In *Language and Value*, edited by Jonathan Dancy, Julius Moraucsik, and C. C. Taylor (Stanford: Stanford University Press, 1988), pp. 258–273, 303–304.

Cordner, Christopher. "Differences between Sport and Art." *Journal of the Philosophy of Sport*, XV (1988), pp. 31–47.

Cuneo, Ernest L. "Present at the Creation: Professional Football in the Twenties." *The American Scholar*, LVI (4) (Autumn 1987), pp. 487–501.

Fairchild, David L. "Prolegomena to an Expressive Function of Sport." *Journal of the Philosophy of Sport*, XIV (1987), pp. 21–33.

Fairchild, David L. "Sport Abjection: Steroids and the Uglification of the Athlete." *Journal of the Philosophy of Sport*, XVI (1989), pp. 74–88.

Feezell, Randolph M. "On the Wrongness of Cheating and Why Cheaters Can't Play the Game." *Journal of the Philosophy of Sport*, XV (1988), pp. 57–68.

Feezell, Randolph M. "Sport, Character, and Virtue." *Philosophy Today*, XXXIII (3) (Fall 1989), pp. 204–220.

Fraleigh, Warren P. "The Sports Contest and Value Priorities." *Journal of the Philosophy of Sport*, XIII (1986), pp. 65–77.

Galvin, Richard F. "Are 'Sport Values' Real Values?" *Momentum*, XIII (2) (Autumn 1987).

Gardner, Roger. "On Performance-Enhancing Substances and the Unfair Advantage Argument." *Journal of the Philosophy of Sport*, XVI (1989), pp. 59–73.

Kövecses, Zoltán. "Toward the Semantics of Sport." *Semiotica*, XVIII (4) (1976), pp. 313–337.

Kretchmar, R. Scott. "On Beautiful Games." *Journal of the Philosophy of Sport*, XVI (1989), pp. 34–43.

Kretchmar, R. Scott. "The Strange Supremacy of Knowledge in Sport from a Moral Point of View: A Response to Fraleigh." *Journal of the Philosophy of Sport*, XIII (1986), pp. 79–88.

Lavin, Michael. "Sports and Drugs: Are the Current Bans Justified?" *Journal of the Philosophy of Sport*, XIV (1987), pp. 34–43.

Lenk, Hans. "Interpretative Action Constructs." In *Scientific Philosophy Today*, edited by J. Agassi and R. S. Cohen (Boston: D. Reidel Publishing Co., 1981), pp. 151–157.

Lenk, Hans, Elk Franke, and **Gunter Gebauer.** "Perspectives of the Philosophy of Sport." In *The Scientific View of Sport: Perspectives, Aspects, Issues*, edited by Ommo Grupe and others (New York: Springer-Verlag, 1972), pp. 31–58.

Lenk, Hans, and Gunter Gebauer. "Sport and Sports Literature from the Perspective of Methodological Interpretationism." *Aethlon: The Journal of Sport Literature*, V (2) (Spring 1988), pp. 73–86.

Lord, Catherine. "Is Chess Art?" *Philosophic Exchange*, XVI (1984–85).

Meier, Klaus V. "Performance Prestidigitation." *Journal of the Philosophy of Sport*, XVI (1989), pp. 13–33.

Meier, Klaus V. "Restless Sport." *Journal of the Philosophy of Sport*, XII (1985), pp. 64–77.

Meier, Klaus V. "Triad Trickery: Playing with Sport and Games." *Journal of the Philosophy of Sport*, XV (1988), pp. 11–30.

Morgan, William J. "The Impurity of Reason: A Reflection on the Social Critique of the Philosophy of Sport." *Journal of the Philosophy of Sport*, XV (1988), pp. 69–90.

Morgan, William J. "The Logical Incompatibility Thesis and Rules: A Reconsideration of Formalism as an Account of Games." *Journal of the Philosophy of Sport*, XIV (1987), pp. 1–20.

Murray, Thomas H. "The Bioengineered Competitor?" *National Forum*, LXIX (Fall 1989), pp. 41–42.

Racheis, James. "Chess as Art: Reflections on Richard Reti." *Philosophic Exchange*, XVI (1984–85).

Roberts, Terence J. "Sport and Representation: A Response to Wertz and Best." *Journal of the Philosophy of Sport*, XIII (1986), pp. 89–94.

Roberts, Terence J. "Sport, Art, and Particularity: The Best Equivocation." *Journal of the Philosophy of Sport*, XIII (1986), pp. 49–63.

Simpson, Alan. "Art and Games." *British Journal of Aesthetics*, XXVI (3) (Summer 1986), pp. 270–276.

Suits, Bernard. "The Trick of the Disappearing Goal." *Journal of the Philosophy of Sport*, XVI (1989), pp. 1–12.

Suits, Bernard. "Tricky Triad: Games, Play, and Sport." *Journal of the Philosophy of Sport*, XV (1988), pp. 1–9.

Thomas, Carolyn E., and Janet A. Rintala. "Injury as Alienation in Sport." *Journal of the Philosophy of Sport*, XVI (1989), pp. 44–58.

Utz, Stephen G. "The Authority of the Rules of Baseball: The Commissioner as Judge." *Journal of the Philosophy of Sport*, XVI (1989), pp. 89–99.

Wertz, S. K. "Disputed Questions on Televised Sport." In *Understanding Sport Actions*, edited by S. K. Wertz (forthcoming).

Wertz, S. K. "On *Sport Inside Out*: A Rejoinder to Feezell." *Teaching Philosophy*, XII (1) (March 1989), pp. 43–46.

Wertz, S. K. "Teaching Sport Philosophy Analytically." *Teaching Philosophy*, IX (2) (June 1986), pp. 121–146. Section III is a review of the philosophical literature.

INDEX

final cause: defined, 84; of sport, 83,
84–87
"A Fine Forehand" (Ziff), 159
Fish, Stanley, 246n.4
Fleming, Peggy, 188, 245n.25
Flood, Curt, 206–207
Flynn, Ed, 234n.6
Fogelin, Robert, 26, 28, 29, 128
football: biased officiating in, 70;
cheating in, 52–53; constitutive
rules of, 225n.7; criminal
conflict in, 90; expressive
content of, 194; inner game of,
114, 115 116, 125; orientation of
players toward time, 125; passage
of time in, 132; regulative rules
of, 53, 225n.7; reliance on
techne, 41; ritualized violence in,
80; rule-breaking in, 51, 52;
semipro, 47; strategic play in, 52,
227n.32; systemic cheating in,
77; training methods, 118–119,
120; unsportsmanlike conduct
in, 88; use of meditation in, 114;
waiting for opportunity in, 133
Forest Hills tennis tournament (1962),
147
form: in bodily movements, 117;
focusing of attention on,
209–210; imposition on
environment, 97; in sporting
events, 23, 30
formal cause, 83, 84
Förster, Angelika, 234n.7
Foyt, A. J., 66
France, Nazi occupation of, 97
Frankel, Charles, 42, 44, 45
Frankl, Viktor, 46
freedom, from ego-mind, 121, 122;
loss of, in play considered as
means to end, 121
Freehan, Bill, 206
French Open tennis tournament, 70,
152
French Open tennis tournament
(1980), 231n.12

future, the, anticipation of, in play,
124, 125–126
Futurism, 179

Gadamer, Hans-Georg, 101–102, 211,
216
Gallwey, Sally, 109
Gallwey, Timothy, 6, 123, 125, 129,
165; on changes of
consciousness, 109, 110; on
competition, 120; on discovery
of inner self, 112; experience of
inner game by, 108–109, 124,
140, 141; on self-knowledge, 120,
121; theory of inner game,
110–111; training methods of,
109, 112–113, 114, 116, 121,
126–127, 128, 140, 162, 173
Galvin, Richard F., 235n.18
games: absorption of players in, 73;
combination with art, 181–182;
exemplary, symbolic significance
of, 183–184, 184–185; forms of,
209; illegal interference with
outcome of, 52–53, 54, 69, 81;
individual, historical context of,
184–185; mastery of, 42; as realm
of unequivocal interpretation,
216; reconstructions of,
205–208, 209, 214–215;
resemblances among varieties of,
26–27, 30; as solution to social
dilemma, 23; as works, 200–201
Garagiola, Joe, 204
Gendin, Sidney, 219n.6
generosity, as quality of
sportsmanship, 87, 88
Gerber, Ellen, 114
Gerstner, Karl, 182
Gert, Bernard: on cheating as broken
promise, 58; on cheating as
example of immorality, 63, 74;
on deception in cheating, 57;
definition of cheating by, 63;
on justified cheating, 61; on
preconditions for cheating, 60,

movement *(Continued)*
of, 185; in baseball games, 208;
distinction between action and,
147–150, 239n.7; expressive
content of, 189, 190, 191;
intended, as component of
choking, 151; interference with
action, 153–154; involuntary,
choking as, 145–146, 147, 153,
156; in natural play, 113–114,
169; performance of, as art,
182–183; ritualized, 135,
136–137; rules governing, 117;
training of, 127
Munari, Bruno, 182
Munson, Thurman, 67, 68
Murdoch, Iris, 247n.15
Murphy, Michael, 46, 129
Musashi, Miyamoto, 131
muscle memory/knowledge, 164
mushin, 149
music: accompaniment of sport with,
188, 190; and states of
concentration, 124
Mussberger, Brent, 204

Natanson, Maurice, 221n.17
National Football League, 18
natural craft, profession as, 41
nature: appropriation of experience
by, 100–101, 216; competition
with, 101; connection of self
with, 101, 102; as source of
values, 102
nature sports: absence of cheating
from, 55; mastery in, 102;
possibility of cheating in, 81;
striving for excellence in, 55–56;
subjective experience of, 100–101
Navratilova, Martina, 11, 42,
114–115
Nazi party, representational use of
sport by, 191, 192
negligence, cheating as, 78–79
Neo-Dada, 180

nervousness: as cause of actions,
143–144; in choking, 143–144,
146, 151, 152, 156; control of,
146–147, 151–152, 240n.15;
modification of intent by, 146,
151
New Realism (art movement), 180
Newton, Sir Isaac, 119
New York City, experimental art in,
180
New Yorker (magazine), 203
New York Yankees, 67–68
Nicklaus, Jack, 89
Nirvāna, 115
non-essentialism, 178
Norman, Greg, 70
Northrup, Jim, 206
Notre Dame University, 215
Novak, Michael, 9, 19, 46, 70, 88; on
challenge of sport, 48; definition
of competition, 226n.12; on
enjoyment of sport, 44; on evil
in sport, 79, 80; on reform of
collegiate athletics, 94; on
spiritual value of sport, 96, 107,
121; on sports writing, 29–30;
on trivialization of sport by
television, 203
Nowell-Smith, Patrick, 78, 79

objet trouvé, 181
obscenity, delineation of art from, 180
observation: in acquisition of skills,
168–169; as basis of knowledge,
160–161
"Obsessed with Sport" (Epstein),
202–203
Oklahoma, 47
Olympics. *See* Summer Olympics;
Winter Olympics
"On the Inner Nature of Art"
(Schopenhauer), 10
Op art, 180
operant conditioning, 240n.2
opportunity, waiting for, 133–134

266

ABOUT THE AUTHOR

SPENCER KIEFER WERTZ is professor of philosophy at Texas Christian University in Fort Worth. He is a past president of the North Texas Philosophical Association, the New Mexico–West Texas Philosophical Society, the Southwestern Philosophical Society, and the Philosophic Society for the Study of Sport. He has written over seventy articles in thirty different journals and magazines. His interest in sports extends beyond the notepad— he was a champion tennis player who still continues to play, an avid jogger, and an exercise enthusiast who follows the developments in the sports world with intense, ongoing interest, looking for arguments and reasons for those developments. This is his second book. Dr. Wertz is currently working on a third book dealing with the eighteenth-century Scottish philosopher and historian David Hume.